ADVERTISING:
PRINCIPLES
AND PRACTICE

TEST ITEM FILE

Christopher Arigo • Patricia D. Taylor • John E. Weiss
Colorado State University

ADVERTISING:
PRINCIPLES
AND PRACTICE

FIFTH EDITION

WELLS

BURNETT

MORIARTY

Prentice Hall
Upper Saddle River, New Jersey 07458

Acquisitions editor: Leah Johnson
Associate editor: Anthony Palmiotto
Project editor: Joan Waxman
Manufacturer: Victor Graphics, Inc.

Printed in the United States of America

10   9   8   7   6   5   4   3   2   1

ISBN 0-13-085163-9

Prentice-Hall International (UK) Limited, *London*
Prentice-Hall of Australia Pty. Limited, *Sydney*
Prentice-Hall Canada Inc., *Toronto*
Prentice-Hall Hispanoamericana, S.A., *Mexico*
Prentice-Hall of India Private Limited, *New Delhi*
Prentice-Hall of Japan, Inc., *Tokyo*
Prentice-Hall (Singapore) Pte Ltd
Editora Prentice-Hall do Brasil, Ltda., *Rio de Janeiro*

Contents

CHAPTER 1: INTRODUCTION TO ADVERTISING

MULTIPLE CHOICE

1. Explicit objectives should drive what step(s) in a great ad campaign?
   a. Planning
   b. Execution
   c. Creation
   d. all of the above

   Answer: d Difficulty: 1 Page: 3   Key 1: R

2. Good ads work on what two levels?
   a. win awards and increase sales
   b. deliver selling message and impress the client
   c. engage the consumer's mind and deliver selling message
   d. entertain the consumer and show creativity
   e. increase sales and impress the client

   Answer: c Difficulty: 2 Page: 3   Key 1: R

3. One of the main responsibilities of an advertiser is:
   a. watching an ad for its entertainment value.
   b. learning that an ad relates to a personal need.
   c. risking change in consumer behavior.
   d. meeting its own goals and those of the consumer.
   e. all of the above

   Answer: d Difficulty: 2 Page: 4   Key 1: A

4. The central "big idea" that gets consumers' attention and sticks in their memory is associated with what dimension of great advertising?
   a. strategy
   b. selling
   c. creativity
   d. entertainment
   e. execution

   Answer: c Difficulty: 2 Page: 5   Key 1: R

5. The three dimensions of great advertising are:
   a. strategy, selling, and entertainment.
   b. creativity, selling, and planning.
   c. planning, selling, and execution.
   d. strategy, creativity, and execution.
   e. strategy, creativity, and selling.

   Answer: d Difficulty: 2 Page: 6   Key 1: R

6. You just hired a new account assistant. His/her major strength is detail work in advertising design. On what dimension of great advertising might you best put him/her to work?
   a. planning
   b. execution
   c. strategy
   d. creativity
   e. clerical

   Answer: b Difficulty: 2 Page: 6   Key 1: A

7. Paid non-personal communication from an identified sponsor using mass media to persuade or influence an audience is called:
   a. personal selling.
   b. sales promotion.
   c. marketing communication.
   d. advertising.
   e. publicity.

   Answer: d Difficulty: 1 Page: 6   Key 1: R

8. Why is the $1.2 million price tag for one Super Bowl TV commercial not considered excessively expensive?
   a. Super Bowl ads are very effective because the audience is focused on the game all day.
   b. Super Bowl advertising is very prestigious.
   c. Half of the cost is actually applied against other advertising during the year.
   d. The Super Bowl broadcast reaches over 500 million people.
   e. All advertising on television costs as much.

   Answer: d Difficulty: 2 Page: 6   Key 1: R

9. Ads delivered through interactive technology might not be considered "advertising" because:
   a. they are not paid for.
   b. they could be considered personal communication.
   c. the sponsor is not normally identified.
   d. they are strictly informational and does not seek to persuade.
   e. there is no clearly identified audience.

   Answer: b Difficulty: 2 Page: 6   Key 1: A

10. What is the most visible type of advertising?
   a. institutional
   b. brand
   c. retail
   d. public service
   e. direct-response

   Answer: b Difficulty: 2 Page: 7   Key 1: R

11. What kind of local advertising focuses on price, availability and location?
    a. national consumer
    b. business-to-business
    c. retail
    d. direct-response
    e. institutional

    Answer: c Difficulty: 2 Page: 7   Key 1: R

12. Which of the following is one of the basic types of advertising discussed in the text?
    a. brand
    b. political
    c. retail
    d. directory
    e. all of the above

    Answer: e Difficulty: 2 Page: 7   Key 1: R

13. In this type of advertising the message focuses on a product that is manufactured and distributed nationally. It concentrates on developing a distinctive brand image for that product.
    a. retail advertising
    b. direct-response advertising
    c. brand advertising
    d. business-to-business advertising
    e. institutional advertising

    Answer: c Difficulty: 2 Page: 7   Key 1: R

14. This type of advertising tries to stimulate immediate and direct sales. The consumer can respond by telephone or mail, and the product is delivered directly to the consumer by mail or other carrier.
    a. retail advertising
    b. direct-response advertising
    c. brand advertising
    d. business-to-business advertising
    e. institutional advertising

    Answer: b Difficulty: 1 Page: 7   Key 1: R

15. This type of advertising includes messages directed at other advertisers such as retailers, wholesalers and distributors, as well as industrial purchasers and professionals.
    a. institutional
    b. public service
    c. business-to-business
    d. brand
    e. retail

    Answer: c Difficulty: 2 Page: 7   Key 1: R

16. Phillip's Petroleum tells its target market about the new plastic material that Phillip's has developed that will help public roads last longer. Phillip's does not tell the target market about Phillip's gasoline. In what type of advertising is Phillip's engaged?
    a. brand
    b. institutional
    c. public service
    d. retail
    e. direct-response

    Answer: b Difficulty: 2 Page: 8   Key 1: A

17. Which of the following represents the four roles of advertising discussed in the text?
    a. marketing, business, communication, and persuasion
    b. societal, economic, communication, and marketing
    c. business, communication, societal, and political
    d. economic, informational, societal, and creative

    Answer: b Difficulty: 2 Page: 8   Key 1: R

18. The particular consumers at whom a company directs its marketing effort are called:
    a. demographics.
    b. promotional mix.
    c. marketing mix.
    d. market.
    e. target market segment.

    Answer: e Difficulty: 2 Page: 9   Key 1: R

19. The four tools available to the marketer--product, price, place, and promotion--are collectively called the:
    a. target marketing.
    b. marketing mix.
    c. advertising mix.
    d. promotional mix.
    e. all of the above

    Answer: b Difficulty: 1 Page: 9   Key 1: R

20. Which of the following represents the "marketing mix"?
    a. product, planning, place, and promotion
    b. product, price, public relations, and publicity
    c. product, price, place, and marketing communication
    d. product, promotion, planning, and price
    e. product, price, place, and public relations

    Answer: c Difficulty: 2 Page: 9   Key 1: R

21. The strategic process that a business uses to satisfy the consumers' needs and wants through goods and services is called:
    a. advertising.
    b. personal selling.
    c. marketing.
    d. promotion.
    e. economics.

    Answer: c Difficulty: 2 Page: 9   Key 1: R

22. Which of the following is a technique of marketing communication?
    a. advertising
    b. public relations
    c. personal selling
    d. sales promotion
    e. all of the above

    Answer: e Difficulty: 2 Page: 9   Key 1: R

23. When advertising teaches people to understand the advantages and disadvantages of competing computers, what role of advertising is most involved?
    a. marketing
    b. economic
    c. societal
    d. informational
    e. cultural

    Answer: b Difficulty: 2 Page: 9   Key 1: R

24. What are the two major schools of thought about the effects of advertising on the economy?
    a. market information and market strategy
    b. market power and market competition
    c. market information and market innovation
    d. market power and market information
    e. market competition and market innovation

    Answer: b Difficulty: 2 Page: 9-10   Key 1: R

25. This role of advertising mirrors fashion and design trends and contributes to our aesthetic sense.
    a. marketing
    b. communication
    c. psychological
    d. economic
    e. societal

    Answer: e Difficulty: 2 Page: 10   Key 1: R

26. Which of the following is a role of advertising?
    a. directory role
    b. marketing role
    c. reinforcement role
    d. incentive role
    e. all of the above

    Answer: b Difficulty: 2 Page: 11   Key 1: A

27. Advertising performs what basic function(s)?
    a. Provides product and brand information.
    b. Provides incentives to take action.
    c. Provides reminders.
    d. Provides reinforcement.
    e. All of the above

    Answer: e Difficulty: 2 Page: 11   Key 1: R

28. Which of the following represents the five primary players in the advertising industry?
    a. advertiser, media, FTC, advertising agency and wholesaler
    b. retailer, wholesaler, manufacturer, distributor and media
    c. advertiser, advertising agency, media, vendor and audience
    d. advertiser, manufacturer, distributor, media and ad agency
    e. advertising director, marketing director, creative director, media director and wholesale director

    Answer: c Difficulty: 3 Page: 12   Key 1: A

29. While ongoing mergers, acquisitions, and agency casualties are continually changing the rankings, what agency was the top agency worldwide in 1995?
    a. Young & Rubicam
    b. BBDO Worldwide
    c. Leo Burnett
    d. McCann-Erickson Worldwide
    e. DDB Needham

    Answer: d Difficulty: 3 Page: 12   Key 1: R

30. An _____ is an advertising function on the advertiser's staff that handles most, if not all, of the functions of an outside agency.
    a. advertising department
    b. advertising agency
    c. in-house agency
    d. promotional department
    e. institutional agency

    Answer: c Difficulty: 2 Page: 12   Key 1: R

31. What type of advertiser is most likely to have its own in-house agency?
    a. retailers
    b. manufacturers
    c. institutions
    d. individuals
    e. government

    Answer: a Difficulty: 2 Page: 13   Key 1: R

32. In the normal organizational arrangement for handling advertising in large businesses, who is directly responsible for selecting the advertising agency?
    a. public relations director
    b. marketing director
    c. brand manager
    d. advertising manager
    e. sales director

    Answer: d Difficulty: 3 Page: 13   Key 1: R

33. The most common organizational arrangement for handling advertising in a large business is:
    a. in-house agency
    b. customer service department
    c. advertising department
    d. marketing department
    e. public relations department

    Answer: c Difficulty: 2 Page: 13   Key 1: R

34. In the typical multiple-brand consumer products company, who shares the responsibility for advertising decisions with the advertising director?
    a. director of marketing
    b. brand manager
    c. advertising manager
    d. sales director
    e. public relations director

    Answer: b Difficulty: 2 Page: 13   Key 1: R

7

35. Media organizations do the following:
    a. buy space in print media.
    b. buy time in broadcast media.
    c. perform the functions of an outside ad agency.
    d. help with ad production.
    e. all of the above

    Answer: d Difficulty: 3 Page: 13   Key 1: R

36. Why might other advertising players use a vendor?
    a. to gather relevant information about their audiences.
    b. advertisers may lack expertise in a certain area.
    c. to select an ad agency.
    d. to provide media.
    e. all of the above

    Answer: b Difficulty: 3 Page: 14   Key 1: R

37. All advertising strategies start with:
    a. the consumer.
    b. the vendor.
    c. the media.
    d. the ad department.
    e. all of the above

    Answer: a Difficulty: 1 Page: 14   Key 1: R

38. The target audience denotes:
    a. the group that assists advertisers, ad agencies and media.
    b. people who deliver advertising messages consistent with the creative effort.
    c. the customer, the person who purchases the product.
    d. channels of communication that carry messages from advertiser to audience.
    e. all of the above

    Answer: c Difficulty: 1 Page: 14   Key 1: R

39. The history of advertising has been:
    a. regular and predictable.
    b. dynamic and unpredictable.
    c. static and unpredictable.
    d. consistent and predictable.
    e. all of the above

    Answer: b Difficulty: 3 Page: 14-15   Key 1: R

40. Early advertisers used what media to send messages?
    a. posters
    b. handbills
    c. classified ads
    d. all of the above
    e. none of the above

    Answer: d Difficulty: 1 Page: 16   Key 1: R

41. In the mid-1880s, what marked the beginning of the U.S. advertising industry?
    a. Inventions such as the internal combustion engine allowed businesses to mass-produce high-quality goods.
    b. The printing press.
    c. The invention of vacuum tubes for radios.
    d. The first mass-produced printed ads.
    e. All of the above

    Answer: a Difficulty: 3 Page: 16   Key 1: R

42. In terms of advertising, what does the text suggest was the major impact of the invention of moveable type by Johannes Gutenberg?
    a. reproducibility of messages
    b. increased reliability of messages
    c. increased clarity of messages
    d. move toward mass communication
    e. greater credibility of printed messages

    Answer: d Difficulty: 2 Page: 16   Key 1: R

43. What advantage did the advent of mass appeal magazines offer to advertisers?
    a. increased credibility because of their past association as a medium strictly for the wealthy and well-educated
    b. allowed for longer and more complex messages
    c. offered the first mass audience
    d. provided a cheaper medium than previously available
    e. increased dramatic appeal of ads

    Answer: b Difficulty: 2 Page: 16   Key 1: R

44. What government action paved the way for mass circulation magazines?
    a. exempted magazines from anti-trust legislation
    b. approved low postage rates for periodicals
    c. created the FTC
    d. funded interstate highway system
    e. directly subsidized magazines

    Answer: b Difficulty: 2 Page: 16   Key 1: R

45. What creative breakthrough in advertising is considered the first venture into "image" advertising?
    a. use of photographs
    b. use of newsy, "journalized" ads
    c. advertising style that resembled original art
    d. "sales" approach
    e. the Marlboro Man campaign

    Answer: c Difficulty: 2 Page: 16   Key 1: R

46. For what is Claude Hopkins known besides being perhaps the greatest copywriter of all time?
    a. creating the soft sell approach
    b. use of copy testing to improve advertising
    c. emphasizing the selling nature of advertising
    d. developing the first newspaper advertising
    e. originating the concept of brand names

    Answer: b Difficulty: 2 Page: 17   Key 1: R

47. Who wrote "Tested Advertising Methods" in 1932?
    a. Earnest Elmo Calkens
    b. Wallace Stevens
    c. John Caples
    d. Volney Palmer
    e. George Gallup

    Answer: c Difficulty: 2 Page: 17   Key 1: R

48. Albert Lasker is associated with what approach to advertising copywriting?
    a. image
    b. soft sell
    c. news
    d. reason-why
    e. inherent-drama

    Answer: d Difficulty: 2 Page: 18   Key 1: R

49. Who defined advertising as "salesmanship in print"?
    a. Claude Hopkins
    b. John Ashberry
    c. Theodore MacManus
    d. David Ogilvy
    e. Bill Bernbach

    Answer: b Difficulty: 2 Page: 18   Key 1: R

50. Your advertising strategy calls for a straight, benefit-claim-demonstration approach. Someone schooled in which of the following approaches to copywriting would fit best for your campaign?
    a. Chicago School
    b. Lasker-Hopkins
    c. Calkens-Rowell
    d. Ogilvy-Bernbach
    e. Wanamaker-Powers

    Answer: b Difficulty: 2 Page: 18   Key 1: A

51. An emphasis on image and emotion would most likely accompany:
    a. hard sell advertising.
    b. soft sell advertising.
    c. sell out advertising.
    d. television advertising.
    e. radio advertising.

    Answer: b Difficulty: 2 Page: 18   Key 1: A

52. Who developed the concept of account services?
    a. Leo Burnett
    b. J. Walter Thompson
    c. Enoch Light
    d. Stanley Resor
    e. David Ogilvy

    Answer: d Difficulty: 2 Page: 19   Key 1: R

53. Who developed the concept of the "brand name"?
    a. Stanley and Helen Resor
    b. N.W. Ayer
    c. Palmer and Associates
    d. BBDO
    e. Hopkins and Lasker

    Answer: a Difficulty: 1 Page: 19   Key 1: R

54. Television was the dominant advertising medium by the end of what decade?
    a. 1920s
    b. 1940s
    c. 1950s
    d. 1960s
    e. 1980s

    Answer: c Difficulty: 3 Page: 19   Key 1: R

55. Rosser Reeves helped advertisers cut through the clutter of products of the 1950s by proposing what advertising concept?
    a. effective advertising must entertain
    b. effective advertising must have a USP ("unique selling proposition")
    c. effective order must contribute to the development of the brand image
    d. effective advertising must include sex
    e. effective advertising must be creative

    Answer: b Difficulty: 2 Page: 20   Key 1: R

56. Who was the leader of the "Chicago School" of advertising, who believed in searching for the "inherent drama" in every product?
    a. David Ogilvy
    b. Bill Bernbach
    c. Leo Burnett
    d. Albert Lasker
    e. Claude Hopkins

    Answer: c Difficulty: 1 Page: 20   Key 1: R

57. If you needed a copywriter to write an ad with a creative approach emphasizing the dramatic value of the product, who would you hire if they happened to apply at your agency?
    a. Claude Hopkins
    b. Leo Burnett
    c. John Kennedy
    d. Albert Lasker

    Answer: b Difficulty: 2 Page: 20   Key 1: A

58. What advertising tenet(s) did David Ogilvy offer?
    a. "Big ideas are usually very complex ideas."
    b. "Never write an ad you wouldn't want your family to read."
    c. "The most important decision is how to unload your product."
    d. "Most words in copy should simply adorn the ad."
    e. all of the above

    Answer: b Difficulty: 3 Page: 21   Key 1: R

59. William Bernbach was considered to be the most innovative advertiser of all times because:
    a. he was unconcerned with mere design issues.
    b. his advertising focused on a sense of pragmatism.
    c. his advertising touched people by focusing on emotions.
    d. he believed that copy should appeal to rational thought.
    e. all of the above

    Answer: c Difficulty: 3 Page: 21   Key 1: R

60. During the 1970s and 1980s, many consumer product companies shifted budgets from media to:
    a. sales promotion
    b. TV ads
    c. radio ads
    d. long-term sales gain
    e. all of the above

    Answer: a Difficulty: 1 Page: 22   Key 1: R

61. In the early 1990s, the ad industry realized that its fate was linked to:
    a. coupons, rebates and sweepstakes
    b. the global business environment
    c. the local business environment
    d. traditional media
    e. Bill Clinton's new legislation

    Answer: b Difficulty: 2 Page: 22   Key 1: R

62. Today's advertising industry is mainly affected by:
    a. the number of ad agencies
    b. lower costs in printed media production
    c. changing technology
    d. lower costs in TV commercial production
    e. all of the above

    Answer: c Difficulty: 1 Page: 22   Key 1: R

63. Integrated Marketing Communication tools include:
    a. advertising
    b. sales promotion
    c. direct marketing
    d. personal selling
    e. all of the above

    Answer: e Difficulty: 1 Page: 22   Key 1: R

64. According to Don E. Schultz, IMC starts with:
    a. the consumer's needs and wants
    b. advertisemenst
    c. the media
    d. the advertising department
    e. all of the above

    Answer: a Difficulty: 1 Page: 22   Key 1: R

65. Outside-in advertising planning starts with:
    a. advertising messages based on what marketers believe is important
    b. a client's assumption about a solid target audience
    c. data about customer prospects to plan the advertising message
    d. none of the above
    e. all of the above

    Answer: c Difficulty: 2 Page: 22   Key 1: R

66. Although advertising has gone global:
    a. many advertisers concentrate on marketing to mass audiences.
    b. many advertisers have moved toward tighter niche markets.
    c. many marketers search for and implement media aimed at general markets.
    d. none of the above
    e. all of the above

    Answer: b Difficulty: 1 Page: 23   Key 1: R

TRUE/FALSE

67. Explicit objectives should drive the planning, creation and execution of each ad.
    a. True
    b. False

    Answer: a Difficulty: 1 Page: 3   Key 1: R

68. Defining the elements of great advertising is easy.
    a. True
    b. False

    Answer: b Difficulty: 2 Page: 3   Key 1: A

69. A good way to identify great advertising is to find out what ads consumers like the best.
    a. True
    b. False

    Answer: b Difficulty: 1 Page: 3   Key 1: A

70. The text suggests that winning advertising awards such as CLIOs, New York Art Directors, etc. is an indication of great advertising.
    a. True
    b. False

    Answer: b Difficulty: 1 Page: 3   Key 1: A

71. One can ensure that advertising will be great by using a fantasy character.
    a. True
    b. False

    Answer: b Difficulty: 1 Page: 3-5   Key 1: A

72. Advertisers and consumers have different goals for advertising.
    a. True
    b. False

    Answer: a Difficulty: 2 Page: 4   Key 1: R

73. Ultimately, advertisers want consumers to buy and keep buying their goods and services.
    a. True
    b. False

    Answer: a Difficulty: 1 Page: 4   Key 1: R

74. A good ad may feature a super-model or rock star to get the viewer's attention.
    a. True
    b. False

    Answer: a Difficulty: 1 Page: 4   Key 1: A

75. A good advertisement usually meets the six objectives of advertising.
    a. True
    b. False

    Answer: b Difficulty: 3 Page: 4   Key 1: R

76. Advertisers rarely need to understand consumers to forge a successful relationship.
    a. True
    b. False

    Answer: b Difficulty: 1 Page: 5   Key 1: R

77. An advertiser develops an ad according to very sketchy objectives.
    a. True
    b. False

    Answer: b Difficulty: 2 Page: 5   Key 1: R

78. The creative concept is a central idea that grabs attention and sticks in consumers' minds.
    a. True
    b. False

    Answer: a Difficulty: 1 Page: 5   Key 1: R

79. Three broad dimensions characterize great advertising: strategy, creativity and consumerism.
    a. True
    b. False

    Answer: b Difficulty: 3 Page: 5   Key 1: R

80. Advertisers can measure an ad's success by heightened brand awareness.
    a. True
    b. False

    Answer: a Difficulty: 2 Page: 5   Key 1: R

81. Most advertisers agree that $1.2 million dollars is much too expensive for one Super Bowl ad.
    a. True
    b. False

    Answer: b Difficulty: 2 Page: 6   Key 1: R

82. "What you say" is part of the execution dimension of great advertising.
    a. True
    b. False

    Answer: b Difficulty: 2 Page: 6   Key 1: R

83. "How you say it" comes from the strategy dimension of great advertising.
    a. True
    b. False

    Answer: b Difficulty: 2 Page: 6   Key 1: R

84. Brand advertising focuses on developing a long-term identity and image for a product.
    a. True
    b. False

    Answer: a Difficulty: 3 Page: 7   Key 1: R

85. The most visible type of advertising is national consumer advertising (also known as brand advertising).
    a. True
    b. False

    Answer: a Difficulty: 2 Page: 7   Key 1: R

86. Retail or local advertising focuses on trying to develop a distinctive image for a product.
    a. True
    b. False

    Answer: b Difficulty: 2 Page: 7   Key 1: R

87. Most critics agree that political advertising tends to focus more on issues than image.
    a. True
    b. False

    Answer: b Difficulty: 2 Page: 7   Key 1: R

88. The best known form of directory advertising is a billboard.
    a. True
    b. False

    Answer: b Difficulty: 2 Page: 7   Key 1: A

89. Direct-response advertising mostly concentrates on stimulating indirect sales.
    a. True
    b. False

    Answer: b Difficulty: 3 Page: 7   Key 1: R

90. Business-to-business advertising directs its messages at retailers, wholesalers and distributors.
    a. True
    b. False

    Answer: a Difficulty: 2 Page: 7   Key 1: R

91. Institutional advertising is designed to attract customers by emphasizing the sponsoring organization rather than the thing it sells.
    a. True
    b. False

    Answer: a Difficulty: 2 Page: 8   Key 1: A

92. Interactive advertising is delivered to individual consumers who have access to a computer and the Internet.
    a. True
    b. False

    Answer: a Difficulty: 1 Page: 8   Key 1: R

93. Marketing is the process that businesses use to satisfy consumer wants and needs through goods and services.
    a. True
    b. False

    Answer: a Difficulty: 1 Page: 9   Key 1: R

94. The particular consumers at whom a company directs its marketing efforts constitutes the target audience.
    a. True
    b. False

    Answer: a Difficulty: 1 Page: 9   Key 1: R

95. The marketing mix and the "Four P's" are two disparate concepts.
    a. True
    b. False

    Answer: b Difficulty: 1 Page: 9   Key 1: R

96. Marketing communication relies solely on traditional advertising.
    a. True
    b. False

    Answer: b Difficulty: 2 Page: 9   Key 1: R

97. Advertising rarely effects price elasticity of demand.
    a. True
    b. False

    Answer: b Difficulty: 3 Page: 10   Key 1: R

98. The main function of advertising is to provide reminders and reinforcements for consumers.
    a. True
    b. False

    Answer: b Difficulty: 2 Page: 11   Key 1: S

99. $800 billion is the industry estimate for U.S. advertising expenditures in 1998.
    a. True
    b. False

    Answer: b Difficulty: 2 Page: 12   Key 1: R

100. Most available evidence suggests advertising has the power to coerce people into decisions.
    a. True
    b. False

    Answer: b Difficulty: 1 Page: 10   Key 1: R

ESSAY

101. Discuss what makes "great" advertising. Give examples from modern and classic advertising.

    Answer:
    The notion of a "great" ad is very subjective. Ultimately, most advertisers would agree that a great add is one that helps to reach the advertiser's goals. An ad that has won awards may not necessarily be a great ad unless it also has helped to increase sales, brand awareness, etc. For example, the top ad of 1997, VW's "Sunday Afternoon, " was commended for its expressiveness, relevance, intrusiveness and its understatement. In fact, VW Golf sales did increase as a result of this ad. An older example is the *Titanic* campaign. Not only was the maiden voyage advertised as a historical event, but an informational campaign accompanied it. One could consider this campaign great because the ship filled to capacity (which, of course, later proved tragic). Great ads should satisfy the consumers' objectives by engaging them and delivering a relevant message. At the same time, ads must achieve the sponsor's objectives.
    Difficulty: 2 Page: 1-4   Key 1: S/A

102. Discuss the key points of the definition of advertising.

    Answer:
    The standard definition of advertising includes six elements. First, advertising is a paid form of communication, although some forms of advertising, such as public service announcements, use donated time and space. Second, not only is the message paid for, but the sponsor is identified. Third, most advertising tries to persuade or influence the consumer to do something, although in some cases the point of the message is simply to make consumers aware of the product or company. The message is conveyed through many different kinds of mass media reaching a large audience of potential consumers. Finally, because advertising is a form of mass communication, it is also nonpersonal. A definition of advertising, then, includes all six features.
    Difficulty: 1 Page: 6   Key 1: R/S

103. Define and discuss five types of advertising.

Answer:
Advertising is complex because so many different advertisers try to reach so many different types of audiences. One form of advertising, brand advertising or national consumer advertising, focuses on the development of a long-term, distinctive brand identity and image. White Star line developed a brand image of power, scientific wonder and unparalleled luxury for *Titanic*.

Political advertising tends to broadcast locally. Politicians use this form of advertising to get people to vote for them. Although it can be an important source of communication for voters, critics are concerned that political advertising focuses more on image than issues.

People refer to directory advertising to find out how to buy a product or service. Usually, when people consult directories, they already know what they want. The best-known form of this advertising is the Yellow Pages.

Like political advertising, retail advertising is local. It focuses on the store where consumers can purchase a variety of products or where a service is offered. The messages announce products available locally, stimulates store traffic and tries to create a distinct image for the store. Retail advertising tends to emphasize price, availability, location and hours of operation.

Public service advertising communicates a message on behalf of some good cause, such as stopping drunk driving or preventing child abuse. The ads are usually created for free by advertising professionals and the media often donate space and time.

Difficulty: 2 Page: 6-8   Key 1: R/S

104. How does the marketing role of advertising interact with the societal role of advertising?

Answer:
Marketing is the process a business uses to satisfy consumer needs and wants through goods and services. The particular consumers at whom the company directs its marketing efforts constitute the target market. The tools available to marketing include the product, its price and the means used to deliver the product, or the place, as well as promotion. Collectively, these four tools are called the marketing mix or the four Ps. However, if we look at the societal role, a question arises: do advertisers manipulate consumers, that is, do they create the need? Some critics argue that advertising has the power to dictate how people behave. They believe that even if an individual ad cannot control behavior, the cumulative effects of nonstop exposure to ads can overwhelm consumers. The evidence for these assertions are shaky, though, because so many of the factors contribute to consumer choices. Still, advertisers are not objective and often slant or omit information to their benefit in marketing communication, which includes advertising, sales promotion, public relations, etc. Advertising tends to be the most visible element, which is why it is often criticized for following trends or leading them. This debate has critics arguing that advertising has repeatedly crossed the line, influencing vulnerable groups, such as teenagers. In this way, we can see how the marketing role and the societal role of advertising often come into contact with one another.
Difficulty: 3 Page: 9-10   Key 1: R/A

105. Discuss integrated marketing communication and its implications for advertising in the 1990s.

Answer:
IMC is the practice of unifying all marketing communications tools so that they send a consistent, persuasive message to target audiences that promotes company goals. According to Don E. Schultz, IMC starts with the consumer's wants and needs. Since marketers now have the ability to gather data about customers, reflecting their wants and needs, advertising in the 1990s can shift from inside-out to outside-in advertising planning. Inside-out planning means marketers plan messages based on what they think is important. Outside-in means they start with consumer data, a significant advantage over the former approach. The implications of IMC are significant for advertising in the 1990s. First, consumer data takes the guess-work out of advertising---consumer needs and wants can be deduced from individual information. This will save advertisers time and money, both valuable commodities in the industry. Also, with increasing globalization, an integrated approach will help campaigns maintain coherence all over the world.
Difficulty: 2 Page: 22-23   Key 1: R/A

CHAPTER 2: ADVERTISING OF SOCIETY

MULTIPLE CHOICE

1. Three ethical criteria used to discuss ethics in advertising are:
   a. advocacy, reliability, and objectivity
   b. advocacy, accuracy, and acquisitiveness
   c. objectivity, reliability, and decency
   d. advocacy, assimilation, and argumentation
   e. all of the above

   Answer: b Difficulty: 3 Page: 30   Key 1: R

2. In discussing advertising ethics, which of the ethical criteria involves the fact that advertising tries to persuade the audience to do something, rather than just provide information?
   a. advocacy
   b. accuracy
   c. acquisitiveness
   d. assimilation
   e. all of the above

   Answer: a Difficulty: 2 Page: 31   Key 1: R

3. When a toy maker implies that a whole environment comes with a doll when the doll is actually sold alone, which ethical criterion is involved?
   a. decency
   b. accuracy
   c. acquisitiveness
   d. advocacy
   e. objectivity

   Answer: b Difficulty: 2 Page: 31   Key 1: A

4. When Cadillac implies that a person's measure of success is the car he can afford to buy, which ethical criteria applies?
   a. avarice
   b. accumulation
   c. assimilation
   d. advocacy
   e. acquisitiveness

   Answer: e Difficulty: 2 Page: 32   Key 1: A

5. Which ethical criterion centers on the argument that advertising symbolizes our society's preoccupation with accumulating material objects?
   a. accumulation
   b. advocacy
   c. acquisitiveness
   d. assimilation
   e. avarice

   Answer: c Difficulty: 2 Page: 32   Key 1: R

6. When critics argue that advertising promotes a society in which people believe they must have products to be happy, which criteria is involved?
   a. advocacy
   b. socialization
   c. acquisitiveness
   d. greed
   e. accuracy

   Answer: c Difficulty: 2 Page: 32   Key 1: R

7. Who, does the text suggest, must take ultimate responsibility for ethical advertising?
   a. advertising managers
   b. government
   c. individual advertising professionals
   d. advertising professional groups
   e. all of the above

   Answer: c Difficulty: 2 Page: 32   Key 1: R

8. Legally, puffery is not considered false or misleading advertising because:
   a. while the claims are false, they cannot be proven to be false.
   b. the cost of pursuing so many claims would be impossible.
   c. English Common Law allows puffery.
   d. consumers expect exaggerations and inflated claims in advertising.
   e. puffery is considered false and misleading advertising.

   Answer: d Difficulty: 2 Page: 34   Key 1: R

9. _____ is a statement in which an ad praises an item with opinions, superlatives, or exaggerations; which is stated vaguely and generally; and which states no specific fact.
   a. Padding
   b. Promotion
   c. Press agency
   d. Puffery
   e. Politicking

   Answer: d Difficulty: 2 Page: 34   Key 1: R

10. When Keebler says that its cookies are "uncommonly good," what ethical issue is involved?
    a. subliminal advertising
    b. taste
    c. advertising to children
    d. stereotyping
    e. puffery

    Answer: e Difficulty: 2 Page: 34   Key 1: A

11. Although certain ads might be in bad taste in any circumstance, what else might affect viewer reactions?
    a. Sensitivity to the product category
    b. The time the viewer receives the message
    c. Whether the person is alone or with others when viewing the ad
    d. The wrong media context
    e. All of the above

    Answer: e Difficulty: 2 Page: 35   Key 1: R

12. According to the text, current questions of taste center on which of the following issues?
    a. sexual innuendo, nudity, and violence
    b. nudity, making light of the physically challenged, and violence
    c. nudity, profanity, and exploiting the handicapped
    d. profanity, sexual innuendo, and lack of discretion about personal matters
    e. profanity, violence, and exploiting the handicapped

    Answer: a Difficulty: 2 Page: 37   Key 1: R

13. What is the best way to avoid offensive advertising messages?
    a. avoid sensitive issues
    b. be aware of current tastes
    c. pretest the ad
    d. be careful in choosing media for sensitive messages
    e. all of the above

    Answer: c Difficulty: 2 Page: 37   Key 1: R

14. Presenting a group of people in an unvarying pattern that de-emphasizes individuality is called:
    a. puffery.
    b. subliminal.
    c. stereotyping.
    d. biasing.
    e. image.

    Answer: c Difficulty: 2 Page: 37   Key 1: R

15. According to the text, what is the latest concern in the area of stereotyping women?
    a. the zealous homemaker
    b. "Supermom"
    c. obsessive housewife
    d. businesswoman
    e. "Superwoman"

    Answer: e Difficulty: 2 Page: 37   Key 1: R

16. Women want to see women portrayed:
    a. as masters of the universe.
    b. as matronly and astute.
    c. as fragile and sensual.
    d. as young and active with high goals.
    e. as mature and intelligent with varied interests and abilities.

    Answer: e Difficulty: 2 Page: 37   Key 1: R

17. What is the complaint about the stereotyping of racial and ethnic groups in advertising?
    a. underrepresented among models shown in ads
    b. shown in unflattering ways
    c. shown in the background
    d. shown as subservient
    e. all of the above

    Answer: e Difficulty: 2 Page: 38   Key 1: R

18. What is the complaint about the stereotyping of senior citizens in advertising?
    a. underrepresented among models shown in ads
    b. shown as preoccupied with household duties
    c. shown as subservient
    d. shown as full of afflictions
    e. all of the above

    Answer: d Difficulty: 2 Page: 38   Key 1: R

19. In 1977, experts estimated that the number of commercials watched annually by the average child was over:
    a. 20,000
    b. 30,000
    c. 40,000
    d. 50,000
    e. 60,000

    Answer: a Difficulty: 3 Page: 39   Key 1: R

20. Which of the following represents an inappropriate stereotyped portrayal?
    a. women as obsessive housewives
    b. senior citizens as slow, senile and full of afflictions
    c. Baby Boomers as wealthy and seekers of national possessions
    d. minorities as subservient
    e. all of the above

    Answer: e Difficulty: 2 Page: 37-39   Key 1: A

21. When groups complained to the FTC about problems in children's advertising, the FTC started proceedings to study regulation of children's advertising. What resulted from the FTC debate?
    a. The FTC formed the National Advertising Division to help deal with children's advertising.
    b. The FTC formed the Children's Advertising Commission to regulate children's advertising.
    c. The FTC proposed the Children's Television Act to Congress.
    d. The FTC turned over regulation of children's advertising to the FCC.
    e. The FTC recommendations did not result in new federal regulations until 1990.

    Answer: e Difficulty: 2 Page: 39   Key 1: R

22. Which of the following helps the advertising industry self-regulate children's advertising?
    a. Children's Advertising Review Unit
    b. Action for Children's Television
    c. Center for Science in the Public Interest
    d. Center for Assessment of Children's Advertising
    e. Federal Trade Commission

    Answer: a Difficulty: 3 Page: 40   Key 1: R

23. The Children's Television Advertising Practice Act of 1990 imposed which of the following restrictions?
    a. forbids advertisers from suggesting that more than the product itself is being offered
    b. limits the time allowed for advertising in children's television programming
    c. forbids the use of sport stars and other celebrities in children's advertising
    d. set limits on the total amount of children's advertising allowed
    e. sets up National Advertising Division to handle complaints about children's advertising

    Answer: b Difficulty: 3 Page: 40   Key 1: R

24. What ethical issue is involved with the concern for R. J. Reynolds' "Joe Camel" campaign?
    a. advertising a potentially harmful product to children
    b. use of exaggerated and inflated claims in advertising
    c. stereotyping of women in advertising
    d. use of sexual innuendo in advertising
    e. use of subliminal advertising

    Answer: a Difficulty: 2 Page: 40   Key 1: A

25. In January 1971, what action was taken by the FTC concerning cigarette advertising?
    a. banned cigarette advertising
    b. banned print cigarette advertising
    c. banned television cigarette advertising
    d. banned print and radio cigarette advertising
    e. banned TV and radio cigarette advertising

    Answer: e Difficulty: 1 Page: 40   Key 1: R

26. Opponents of banning TV and radio cigarette ads use what as the main basis of their argument?
    a. economic harm to country
    b. economic harm to workers in the tobacco industry
    c. advertisers' First Amendment rights
    d. lack of fairness
    e. corporate legal rights of tobacco producers

    Answer: c Difficulty: 1 Page: 40   Key 1: R

27. What medium could be devastated by a total ban on cigarette advertising?
    a. television
    b. radio
    c. outdoor
    d. magazines
    e. newspapers

    Answer: d Difficulty: 2 Page: 40   Key 1: R

28. Banning all tobacco advertising would:
    a. undermine freedom of expression in American society.
    b. reduce tobacco product sales.
    c. cause some magazines to go out of business.
    d. be unconstitutional.
    e. all of the above

    Answer: e Difficulty: 2 Page: 40   Key 1: R

29. A message transmitted below the threshold of normal perception so that the receiver is not consciously aware of having received it is called:
   a. supraliminal.
   b. masking.
   c. hidden.
   d. subliminal.
   e. puffery.

   Answer: d Difficulty: 1 Page: 41   Key 1: R

30. Which of the following is a practical difficulty involved with the effectiveness of subliminal advertising?
   a. what one person might not perceive consciously might be readily seen by another
   b. perceptual thresholds vary from person to person
   c. conscious messages in subliminal material may overpower subliminal messages
   d. subliminal messages are difficult to control due to factors such as distance and position
   e. all of the above

   Answer: e Difficulty: 2 Page: 41   Key 1: R

31. What part of the Bill of Rights is most concerned with freedom of expression in the United States?
   a. 1st Amendment
   b. 5th Amendment
   c. 7th Amendment
   d. 9th Amendment
   e. 4th Amendment

   Answer: a Difficulty: 1 Page: 42   Key 1: R

32. Which of the following is an U.S. Supreme Court case in which the Court did not uphold advertising's First Amendment protection?
   a. Virginia State Board of Pharmacy v. Virginia Citizens Consumer Council
   b. Valentine v. Christensen
   c. Central Hudson Gas & Electric Corp. v. Public Service Commission of New York
   d. Cincinnati v. Discovery Network

   Answer: b Difficulty: 2 Page: 43   Key 1: R

33. In what case did the Supreme Court reverse itself and rule that purely commercial advertising does have the same protection under the First Amendment as a private individual's expression?
    a. Virginia State Board of Pharmacy vs. Virginia Citizens Consumer Council
    b. New York Times vs. Sullivan
    c. Posadas de Puerto Rico Associates vs. Tourism Company of Puerto Rico
    d. Valentine vs. Christensen
    e. all of the above

    Answer: a Difficulty: 3 Page: 43   Key 1: R

34. In what case in 1942 did the Supreme Court rule that purely commercial advertising does not have the same protection under the First Amendment as a private individual's expression?
    a. Virginia State Board of Pharmacy vs. Virginia Citizens Consumer Council
    b. New York Times vs. Sullivan
    c. Posadas de Puerto Rico Associates vs. Tourism Company of Puerto Rico
    d. Central Hudson Gas & Electric Corporation vs. Public Service Commission of New York
    e. Valentine vs. Christensen

    Answer: e Difficulty: 3 Page: 43   Key 1: R

35. In the best example of current Supreme Court views about Constitutional protection of advertising, the Court ruled in which case that the state could not stop utilities from advertising?
    a. Virginia State Board of Pharmacy vs. Virginia Citizens Consumer Council
    b. New York State Board of Pharmacy vs. New York Citizens Consumer Council
    c. Valentine vs. Christensen
    d. Central Hudson Gas & Electric Corporation vs. Public Service Commission of New York
    e. Posadas de Puerto Rico Associates vs. Tourism Company of Puerto Rico

    Answer: d Difficulty: 3 Page: 43   Key 1: R

36. The Federal Trade Commission became responsible for overseeing deceptive advertising in:
    a. 1914.
    b. 1922.
    c. 1938.
    d. 1947.

    Answer: a Difficulty: 2 Page: 44   Key 1: R

37. What government agency is responsible for regulating advertising as a form of unfair competition?
    a. FCC
    b. FTC
    c. FDA
    d. DEA

    Answer: b Difficulty: 1 Page: 44   Key 1: R

38. The very existence of the FTC makes advertisers:
    a. want to avoid long legal involvement with the FTC
    b. seek to avoid even the slightest chance of deception
    c. conscious that competitors may complain to the FTC
    d. take every precaution to make sure messages are not deceptive
    e. all of the above

    Answer: e Difficulty: 2 Page: 44   Key 1: R

39. What was established during the Reagan administration years to try to regulate advertising at the state level?
    a. "RICO" suits
    b. Cease and desist orders
    c. National Association of Attorneys General
    d. National Advertising Council
    e. FDC

    Answer: c Difficulty: 3 Page: 44   Key 1: R

40. What legislative action increased the FTC's power to include the power to impose fines, to launch its own investigations without complaints from consumers and to order companies to stop questionable advertising practices?
    a. Lanham Trade-Mark Act
    b. Magnuson-Moss Warranty Act
    c. Federal Trade Commission Act
    d. Wheeler-Lea Amendment

    Answer: d Difficulty: 3 Page: 45   Key 1: R

41. The _____ regulates interstate business in adulterated or fraudulently labeled foods and drugs.
    a. Wheeler-Lea Amendment (1938)
    b. Federal Trade Commission Act (1914)
    c. Pure Food and Drug Act (1906)
    d. Lanham Act (1947)

    Answer: c Difficulty: 2 Page: 45   Key 1: R

42. The _____ provides protection for trademarks (slogans and brand names) from competitors and covers false advertising.
    a. Magnuson-Moss Warranty/FTC Improvement Act (1975)
    b. Wheeler-Lea Amendment (1938)
    c. Pure Food and Drug Act (1906)
    d. Lanham Act (1947)

    Answer: d Difficulty: 2 Page: 45   Key 1: R

43. The _____ expands FTC regulatory powers over unfair or deceptive acts or practices and allows it to require restitution for deceptively written warranties.
    a. Magnuson-Moss Warranty/FTC Improvement Act (1975)
    b. Federal Trade Commission Act (1914)
    c. Lanham Act (1947)
    d. Wheeler-Lea Amendment (1938)

    Answer: a Difficulty: 2 Page: 45   Key 1: R

44. The _____ provides the House of Representatives and the Senate jointly with veto power over FTC regulation rules.
    a. Magnuson-Moss Warranty/FTC Improvement Act (1975)
    b. Federal Trade Commission Act (1914)
    c. FTC Improvement Act (1980)
    d. Lanham Act (1947)
    e. Wheeler-Lea Amendment (1938)

    Answer: c Difficulty: 2 Page: 45   Key 1: R

45. What are the three basic elements of the FTC's current policy determining whether or not an ad is deceptive?
    a. capacity to deceive; clear influence on decision making judged from perspective of "reasonable" consumer
    b. high probability to deceive, must influence decision making and judged from normal consumer's perspective
    c. reasonable probability to deceive, high probability to influence decision making and judged from "reasonable" consumer's perspective
    d. high probability to deceive judged from "reasonable" consumer's perspective and clear influence on decision-making

    Answer: d Difficulty: 3 Page: 45   Key 1: S

46. Which of the following advertising practice has the Federal Trade Commission identified as deceptive?
    a. deceptive pricing
    b. false criticisms of competing products
    c. deceptive guarantees
    d. ambiguous statements
    e. all of the above

    Answer: e Difficulty: 2 Page: 45   Key 1: A

47. The effect of the FTC's current policy on the standard to be used to determine deception is that:
    a. the FTC has to disprove a claim's validity.
    b. the FTC can more easily prove deception.
    c. it reduces uncertainty for advertisers.
    d. the FTC cannot prove deception as easily.
    e. all of the above

    Answer: d Difficulty: 2 Page: 45   Key 1: A

48. In 1995, the FTC charged the Home Shopping Network with broadcasting deceptive claims about several vitamins and stop-smoking products. What was the problem?
    a. ambiguous statements
    b. deceptive guarantees
    c. false criticisms of competing products
    d. claims were not backed by scientific evidence

    Answer: d Difficulty: 2 Page: 45-46   Key 1: R

49. Under FTC guidelines, which of these is considered a reasonable basis for making an ad claim?
    a. having data on file to support the claim
    b. the claim is true
    c. the claim can be shown to be reasonable by a survey of target markets
    d. no one complains

    Answer: a Difficulty: 2 Page: 46   Key 1: R

50. In order for someone to endorse a product in an ad, the FTC requires that the endorser:
    a. has tried competing brands.
    b. has used the product for at least a year prior to the endorsement.
    c. has bought the product for personal use, not have been given the product.
    d. has used the product.
    e. all of the above

    Answer: d Difficulty: 2 Page: 47   Key 1: R

51. What are the most common sources of complaints concerning deceptive or unfair advertising practices?
    a. FTC monitors, public, and consumer groups
    b. competitors, public, and FTC monitors
    c. public and competitors
    d. FTC monitors and consumer groups
    e. competitors, media, and public

    Answer: b Difficulty: 2 Page: 48   Key 1: R

52. What is the first step in the regulation process after the FTC determines that an ad is deceptive?
    a. The FTC issues a cease and desist order
    b. The FTC issues consent decree
    c. The case is referred to trial before an administrative judge
    d. The FTC requests advertiser to correct ad
    e. The FTC requests advertiser to substantiate claim

    Answer: b Difficulty: 2 Page: 48   Key 1: R

53. A legal order requiring an advertiser to stop its unlawful practices is called a:
    a. stop order.
    b. corrective advertising order.
    c. consent decree.
    d. cease and desist order.
    e. deception stop order.

    Answer: d Difficulty: 2 Page: 49   Key 1: R

54. What can happen to an advertiser that refuses to sign a consent decree?
    a. nothing
    b. possible fine of $10,000 per day
    c. be sued by the Federal government in federal court
    d. people involved can be put in prison
    e. all of the above

    Answer: b Difficulty: 2 Page: 49   Key 1: R

55. Which was the landmark case involving corrective advertising?
    a. Valentine vs. Christensen
    b. Wheeler vs. Lea
    c. Warner-Lambert vs. FTC
    d. Volvo vs. Texas Attorney General
    e. Virginia State Board of Pharmacy vs. Virginia Citizen's Council

    Answer: c Difficulty: 3 Page: 49   Key 1: A

56. When does the FTC require corrective advertising?
    a. in every case of substantiated deceptive advertising
    b. if the FTC determines that irreparable harm has been done by the deceptive advertising
    c. if an administrative judge rules that specific damages have been done by deceptive advertising
    d. if consumer research shows that lasting false beliefs have been caused by the ad campaign
    e. all of the above

    Answer: d Difficulty: 2 Page: 49   Key 1: R

57. Which of the following does the FTC require in cases where consumer research determines that lasting false beliefs have resulted from an advertising campaign?
a. cease and desist order
b. stop order
c. consent decree
d. corrective advertising
e. rectification advertising

Answer: d Difficulty: 2 Page: 49   Key 1: S

58. In the 1970s, the FTC initiated a policy change for the reasonableness of claims. This change was:
a. The FTC became responsible for disproving a claim's validity.
b. Advertisers have responsibility for proving a claim's reasonableness.
c. Administrative law judges became responsible for deciding the reasonableness of a claim.
d. The National Advertising Division was given the ultimate responsibility for determining the reasonableness of a claim.

Answer: b Difficulty: 2 Page: 50   Key 1: R

59. Which one of the following agencies could take action against an advertiser or an ad agency?
a. The Food and Drug Administration
b. The Bureau of Alcohol, Tobacco and Firearms
c. The Library of Congress
d. The Federal Trade Commission
e. all of the above

Answer: e Difficulty: 2 Page: 51   Key 1: S

60. This federal agency regulates direct mail and magazine advertising and has control over the areas of obscenity, lottery and fraud.
a. The Library of Congress
b. The Internal Revenue Service
c. The Patent Office
d. The Bureau of Alcohol, Tobacco and Firearms
e. The Postal Service

Answer: e Difficulty: 2 Page: 51   Key 1: R

61. Which of the following federal agencies regulates deception in advertising and establishes labeling requirements for the liquor industry?
a. The Library of Congress
b. The Internal Revenue Service
c. The Patent Office
d. The Bureau of Alcohol, Tobacco and Firearms

Answer: d Difficulty: 2 Page: 52   Key 1: R

62. This federal agency oversees the registration of trademarks, which include both brand names and corporate or store names as well as their identifying symbols.
    a. The Library of Congress
    b. The Internal Revenue Service
    c. The Patent Office
    d. The Bureau of Alcohol, Tobacco and Firearms

    Answer: c Difficulty: 2 Page: 52   Key 1: R

63. _____ requires a balance between company profits, consumer satisfaction, and public interest.
    a. Marketing
    b. Social responsibility
    c. Corporate responsibility
    d. Societal marketing concept

    Answer: d Difficulty: 2 Page: 52   Key 1: R

64. Why have advertisers set up a variety of self-regulatory institutions?
    a. threat of legislation and costs of defending legal action
    b. ethical responsibility and fear of public criticism
    c. recognition of ineffectiveness of deceptive advertising techniques
    d. professionalism and recognition of harm of deceptive advertising practices
    e. threat of legislation and ethical responsibility

    Answer: a Difficulty: 2 Page: 52   Key 1: R

65. If a consumer feels an ad is deceptive, which of the following would NOT be one of the advertising industry's voluntary self-regulation arms available to receive the complaint?
    a. The National Advertising Review Board (NARB)
    b. The National Advertising Division (NAD)
    c. The local Better Business Bureau
    d. The American Advertising Federation

    Answer: d Difficulty: 2 Page: 53-54   Key 1: R

TRUE/FALSE

66. Advertising draws so much attention from citizens and government because it is so visible.
    a. True
    b. False

    Answer: a Difficulty: 2 Page: 29   Key 1: R

67. Advertising is not objective or neutral.
    a. True
    b. False

    Answer: a Difficulty: 1 Page: 30   Key 1: R

68. Although many laws govern advertisers, written rules and regulations do not cover many situations.
    a. True
    b. False

    Answer: a Difficulty: 1 Page: 30   Key 1: R

69. Most people are unaware that advertising tries to sell them something.
    a. True
    b. False

    Answer: b Difficulty: 2 Page: 31   Key 1: R

70. Ultimately, advertisers make the final decision about whether or not consumers buy a product.
    a. True
    b. False

    Answer: b Difficulty: 1 Page: 32   Key 1: A

71. When advertising decisions are not clearly covered by a code, rule or regulation, someone must make an ethical decision.
    a. True
    b. False

    Answer: a Difficulty: 2 Page: 32   Key 1: R

72. Various socio-political causes pay the Ad Council to develop advertising.
    a. True
    b. False

    Answer: a Difficulty: 2 Page: 33   Key 1: R

73. The federal government does not pursue claims of puffery.
    a. True
    b. False

    Answer: a Difficulty: 2 Page: 34   Key 1: R

74. When Hallmark says people buy Hallmark cards when they "want to send the very best," this is not puffery.
    a. True
    b. False

    Answer: b Difficulty: 2 Page: 34   Key 1: A

75. The same message might be considered offensive if seen on television but might not be considered offensive if read in a magazine.
    a. True
    b. False

    Answer: a Difficulty: 3 Page: 35   Key 1: A

76. Taste in advertising can be viewed objectively, with consistent agreement on what is bad taste.
    a. True
    b. False

    Answer: b Difficulty: 1 Page: 35   Key 1: R

77. Stereotyping involves presenting a group of people in an unvarying pattern that ignores individuality.
    a. True
    b. False

    Answer: a Difficulty: 2 Page: 37   Key 1: R

78. Research shows a consistent picture of gender stereotyping in advertising that has stayed fairly constant.
    a. True
    b. False

    Answer: a Difficulty: 2 Page: 37   Key 1: R

79. After years of debate over regulating children's advertising, the FTC abandoned proposed regulations and left the issue in the hands of the advertising industry.
    a. True
    b. False

    Answer: a Difficulty: 2 Page: 39   Key 1: R

80. The Food and Drug Administration is working to severely restrict tobacco advertising.
    a. True
    b. False

    Answer: a Difficulty: 2 Page: 40   Key 1: R

81. The effect on the media of a ban of tobacco advertising would be very small.
    a. True
    b. False

    Answer: b Difficulty: 2 Page: 40   Key 1: R

82. A subliminal message is transmitted in such a way that the receiver is consciously aware of receiving it.
    a. True
    b. False

    Answer: b Difficulty: 2 Page: 41   Key 1: R

83. Since the Congress adopted the First Amendment, the Supreme Court has always ruled that advertisers' have the same First Amendment rights as private citizens.
    a. True
    b. False

    Answer: b Difficulty: 2 Page: 42   Key 1: R

84. According to U.S. Supreme Court rulings, only truthful and not misleading or deceptive commercial speech is protected by the First Amendment.
    a. True
    b. False

    Answer: a Difficulty: 2 Page: 43   Key 1: R

85. Few industries have been more heavily regulated than advertising.
    a. True
    b. False

    Answer: a Difficulty: 1 Page: 42   Key 1: R

86. The FTC does not oversee advertising that targets children and the elderly.
    a. True
    b. False

    Answer: b Difficulty: 2 Page: 44   Key 1: R

87. The FTC is only a secondary governing agency over the advertising industry.
    a. True
    b. False

    Answer: b Difficulty: 2 Page: 44   Key 1: A

88. The new standard used to judge whether or not advertising is deceptive requires only that an advertisement have the capacity to deceive consumers.
    a. True
    b. False

    Answer: b Difficulty: 2 Page: 45   Key 1: R

89. The FTC's policy on ad deception makes it easier to prove that an ad is deceptive.
    a. True
    b. False

    Answer: b Difficulty: 3 Page: 45   Key 1: R

90. Data must be on file to substantiate the claims made by advertisers.
    a. True
    b. False

    Answer: a Difficulty: 2 Page: 46   Key 1: R

91. The FTC is currently working to ban competitive advertising.
    a. True
    b. False

    Answer: b Difficulty: 3 Page: 46   Key 1: A

92. If a competitive test is conducted, it should be done by an objective testing service.
    a. True
    b. False

    Answer: a Difficulty: 1 Page: 46   Key 1: R

93. The FTC says endorsement of a product by a celebrity must be based on actual use.
    a. True
    b. False

    Answer: a Difficulty: 2 Page: 47   Key 1: R

94. The FTC requires that the actual food product be used in food demonstrations in ads and prohibits the use of props.
    a. True
    b. False

    Answer: b Difficulty: 2 Page: 48   Key 1: R

95. The FTC can issue a cease and desist order when an advertiser refuses to sign a consent decree if the FTC determines substantial deception.
a. True
b. False

Answer: a Difficulty: 2 Page: 49   Key 1: R

96. The FTC requires corrective advertising when consumer research determines that an ad campaign has perpetuated lasting false beliefs.
a. True
b. False

Answer: a Difficulty: 2 Page: 49   Key 1: R

97. Advertising agencies have no liability when advertising is judged to be deceptive by the FTC.
a. True
b. False

Answer: b Difficulty: 2 Page: 50   Key 1: R

98. The National Advertising Review Board's only real power is to threaten to refer a complaint of deceptive advertising to the FTC or other federal agency.
a. True
b. False

Answer: a Difficulty: 3 Page: 53-54   Key 1: R

99. When a complaint of deceptive advertising is brought to the local Better Business Bureau, the bureau can legally order the advertiser to cease and desist if the complaint is substantiated.
a. True
b. False

Answer: b Difficulty: 3 Page: 54   Key 1: A

100. Each individual medium rarely has the choice to accept or reject a particular ad.
a. True
b. False

Answer: b Difficulty: 2 Page: 54   Key 1: R

ESSAY

101. Bogus Beer, the leading beer producer in Egomania, is about to launch a campaign that emphasizes stereotypical relationships between men and women, women as sex objects and men as insensitive and mystified by women's behavior. A central focus of the campaign is promoting beer as a means of dealing with the frustration of the conflict between the sexes. Discuss how this campaign would involve the problems of ethical concerns in advertising.

Answer:
The key ethical problem in this campaign would be stereotyping (women as sex objects and men as insensitive and mystified by women's behavior). The issue of stereotyping connects to the debate about whether advertising shapes society's values or simply mirrors them. Either way, it is critical that the advertisers for this campaign become aware of how they portray these two groups. Bogus Beer's representations of gender is inaccurate and unfair to both men and women. Research shows that gender stereotypes have unfortunately remained fairly constant over time and this campaign would simply reinforce ignorant portrayals.

Difficulty: 2 Page: 37   Key 1: A

102. Explain why puffery claims are viewed differently than other claims of deception in advertising

Answer:
Puffery claims are viewed differently than other claims in advertising because consumers expect exaggeration and inflated claims in advertising, so reasonable people would not believe these exaggerated statements ("puffs") as literal facts. For example, "Nothing outlasts an Eveready battery" is an obvious example of a puffed claim. Any reasonable person could probably list innumerable things that will outlast this brand of battery. Because puffed claims state no specific facts, there is no way to prove whether or not the claims are true. After all, puffed claims are only companies' opinions about their own products. No one could really prove or disprove the reasonableness or rationality of opinions.

Difficulty: 2 Page: 34   Key 1: S/A

103. Discuss the considerations in deciding what is and is not tasteful in advertising.

Answer:
We all have our own ideas about what constitutes good taste. These ideas vary so much that creating general guidelines for good taste in advertising is very difficult, if not impossible. One dimension concerns the product itself. Bras, laxatives, etc. provide higher levels of distaste than ads for other product categories, so viewer reactions can be influenced by sensitivity to the product category. The time the message is received and whether the person is alone or with others also affects viewer reactions. In addition, tastes change over time. For example, a 1919 *Ladies' Home Journal* ad for deodorant was extremely controversial. Now, scantily clad models are standard for many clothing line ads. Now that advertising is global, there are also cultural issues to take into account. What may be tasteful in the U.S. may be inappropriate for viewers in Iran. Of course, the best way to avoid an offensive ad is to test it first.

Difficulty: 2 Page: 34-37   Key 1: S/A

104. Discuss the actions available to the FTC for dealing with deceptive advertising practices. Include an explanation of how a claim would be determined to be deceptive.

Answer:
The FTC, whose main focus with respect to advertising is to identify and eliminate ads that deceive or mislead consumers, has several ways to deal with deceptive advertising practices. However, current FTC policy makes deception difficult to prove. If the FTC deems an ad deceptive, they would first look for scientific evidence to back the claim. Without evidence, reasonable consumers cannot make an informed decision. Then, the FTC has several courses of action to follow: consent decrees, cease and desist orders, fines, corrective advertising and consumer redress--respectively, in this order. An example of FTC action against deceptive advertising: In March 1995, the FTC charged that the Home Shopping Network was broadcasting deceptive claims about several vitamin and smoking-cessation products. In its first charge against a television shopping channel, the FTC posited that a 1993 program on HSN had made health claims about avoiding colds, curing hangovers and stopping smoking that were not backed by scientific evidence. The charges followed unsuccessful negotiations toward an out-of-court settlement. Ultimately, HSN stopped advertising these products.

Difficulty: 2 Page: 44-51   Key 1: R/A

105. What is societal marketing and how does it affect advertising?

Answer:
Although some advertisers do not act ethically, a majority of them follow a societal marketing approach. Philip Kotler defines the societal marketing concept this way:

> The organization's task is to determine the needs, wants and interest of target markets and to deliver the desired satisfactions more effectively and efficiently than its competitors in a way that preserves or enhances the consumer's and society's well-being. This requires a careful balance between company profits, consumer-want satisfaction and public interest.

This is a difficult balance to maintain, yet many advertisers follow this approach to avoid general consumer distrust. An effective system of self-regulation ensures that societal marketing is more likely to become a reality. Advertisers must ethically evaluate ads. Using ethics as a criterion, rather than laws, almost guarantees the social responsibility of an ad. Also, advertisers are engaged in prosocial messaging, producing ads that influence positive behavior, such as getting off drugs or preventing drunk driving. The key effects of such a philosophy require that advertisers self-regulate and carefully consider every ad they produce.

Difficulty: 3 Page: 52-53   Key 1: R/A

CHAPTER 3:   ADVERTISING AND THE MARKETING PROCESS

MULTIPLE CHOICE

1. Marketing's ultimate objective is:
   a. satisfy customers.
   b. make a profit for the business.
   c. find customers.
   d. retain customers.
   e. all of the above

   Answer: e Difficulty: 2 Page: 62   Key 1: R

2. Planning and executing the conception, price, promotion, and distribution of ideas, goods, and services to create exchanges that satisfy individual and organizational objectives is called:
   a. advertising.
   b. marketing.
   c. promotion.
   d. sales promotion.

   Answer: b Difficulty: 2 Page: 62   Key 1: R

3. _____ is the process whereby two or more parties give up desired resources to one another.
   a. Marketing
   b. Strategy
   c. Exchange
   d. Integration
   e. Competition

   Answer: c Difficulty: 1 Page: 62   Key 1: R

4. The analysis of the marketing environment, including the consumer, occurs in what stage of the marketing plan?
   a. strategic
   b. research
   c. implementation
   d. evaluation
   e. tactics

   Answer: b Difficulty: 2 Page: 63   Key 1: R

5. Deciding to what extent objectives were achieved occurs at what stage of the marketing plan?
   a. strategic
   b. research
   c. implementation
   d. evaluation
   e. tactics

   Answer: d Difficulty: 2 Page: 63   Key 1: R

6. The marketing mix consists of:
   a. production, promotion, publicity, performance, and pricing.
   b. product, production, pricing, promotion, and performance.
   c. performance, pricing, packaging, promotion, and distribution.
   d. product, pricing, packaging, promotion, and distribution.
   e. production, pricing, distribution, sales, and promotion.

   Answer: d Difficulty: 2 Page: 63-64   Key 1: R

7. The consumer's judgement on how close one product, service or idea comes
   to satisfying his or her needs versus a competitor's product, service or
   idea is called:
   a. adoption.
   b. product choice.
   c. decision-making.
   d. competitive advantage.
   e. purchase.

   Answer: d Difficulty: 2 Page: 63   Key 1: R

8. What are the stages of the marketing plan?
   a. research, planning, strategy, and tactics
   b. research, strategy, tactics, and evaluation
   c. research, strategy, creative, and tactics
   d. research, strategy, implementation, and evaluation
   e. research, planning, implementation, and evaluation

   Answer: d Difficulty: 2 Page: 63   Key 1: S

9. Creative decisions for advertising occur at what stage in the text's
   marketing planning process?
   a. copy strategy
   b. research
   c. evaluation
   d. implementation
   e. strategy

   Answer: d Difficulty: 2 Page: 63   Key 1: R

10. A market is:
    a. a region where goods are sold.
    b. a region where goods are bought.
    c. a particular type of buyer.
    d. all of the above
    e. none of the above

    Answer: d Difficulty: 2 Page: 64   Key 1: R

11. Which of the following is a strength of advertising?
    a. reminding customers to buy
    b. reaching a mass audience simultaneously and repeatedly
    c. informing customers about new products
    d. persuading customers to change their attitudes, beliefs, or behavior
    e. all of the above

    Answer: e Difficulty: 2 Page: 64   Key 1: R

12. Marketing to consumer markets is generally done through what means?
    a. specialized media
    b. electronic interactive media
    c. mass media
    d. interpersonal media
    e. direct media

    Answer: c Difficulty: 2 Page: 64-65   Key 1: A

13. Markets consisting of people who buy products and services for personal or household use are called:
    a. institutional.
    b. consumer.
    c. reseller.
    d. industrial.
    e. product.

    Answer: b Difficulty: 2 Page: 65   Key 1: R

14. _____ markets buy products in order to make other products, while _____ markets buy products for their own uses.
    a. Industrial, consumer
    b. Reseller, institutional
    c. Industrial, reseller
    d. Consumer, industrial
    e. Reseller, consumer

    Answer: a Difficulty: 3 Page: 65   Key 1: A

15. What are the special characteristics of advertising that other elements of the marketing mix do not possess?
    a. It is capable of reaching mass audience simultaneously and repeatedly
    b. It can inform customers about new products or changes in existing products
    c. It can remind customers to buy
    d. It can reinforce past purchases
    e. all of the above

    Answer: e Difficulty: 3 Page: 65   Key 1: S

16. Markets that include a wide variety of profit and non-profit organizations, such as hospitals and schools, that provide goods and services for the benefit of society at large are called:
    a. reseller.
    b. industrial.
    c. consumer.
    d. institutional.
    e. product.

    Answer: d Difficulty: 2 Page: 65   Key 1: R

17. Markets that consist of companies that buy products or services to use in their own businesses or to make other products are called:
    a. industrial.
    b. product.
    c. consumer.
    d. reseller.
    e. institutional.

    Answer: a Difficulty: 2 Page: 65   Key 1: R

18. Markets that include wholesalers, retailers and distributors who buy finished or semi-finished products and resell them for a profit are called?
    a. consumer.
    b. multi-channel.
    c. product.
    d. institutional.
    e. reseller.

    Answer: e Difficulty: 2 Page: 65   Key 1: R

19. What is the focus of the marketing concept?
    a. efficient production techniques
    b. productive sales force
    c. well conceived products
    d. identifying and fulfilling consumers' needs and wants
    e. all of the above

    Answer: d Difficulty: 2 Page: 67   Key 1: R

20. Before advertising can work:
    a. the product must be what the consumer wants
    b. the consumer must find the price acceptable
    c. it must be convenient for consumers to buy the product
    d. there must be people ready, able and willing to buy the product
    e. all of the above

    Answer: a Difficulty: 2 Page: 67   Key 1: A

21. _____ is taking the ideas and principles of integrated marketing communication and applying them to the marketing mix so that product, price, distribution, and promotion are in harmony and the needs of the customer are prominent.
   a. Strategic marketing
   b. Integrated marketing
   c. Marketing
   d. Competitive marketing
   e. Marketing strategy

   Answer: b Difficulty: 2 Page: 68   Key 1: R

22. What is the key to influencing customer choices?
   a. great advertising that entertains consumers
   b. good salespeople who can close sales
   c. use of sexual appeal to direct consumer attention
   d. stressing the most important need-satisfying qualities

   Answer: d Difficulty: 2 Page: 69   Key 1: R

23. What must the marketing manager do to have a practical impact on consumers?
   a. create a product with multiple need satisfying qualities
   b. offer products at an appealing price
   c. translate the product's characteristics into concrete attributes with demonstrable benefits
   d. bribe the distributors
   e. tell the consumers what they want to hear

   Answer: c Difficulty: 2 Page: 69   Key 1: R

24. Marketing begins by asking a set of questions about the product being offered. From what perspective should these questions be asked?
   a. consumer's perspective
   b. cost perspective
   c. producer's perspective
   d. society's perspective
   e. price perspective

   Answer: a Difficulty: 2 Page: 69   Key 1: A

25. Which of the following characteristics would be considered a tangible product characteristic?
   a. warranty
   b. brand name
   c. prestige
   d. image
   e. color

   Answer: e Difficulty: 1 Page: 69-70   Key 1: A

26. Which of the following is an intangible product characteristic?
    a. color
    b. taste
    c. durability
    d. warranty
    e. size

    Answer: d Difficulty: 2 Page: 69-70   Key 1: A

27. What are the stages of the product-life cycle?
    a. introduction, growth, decline, and line extension
    b. development, introduction, growth, and decline
    c. introduction, growth, maturity, and decline
    d. introduction, growth, decline, and line extension
    e. creation, introduction, growth, and maturity

    Answer: c Difficulty: 2 Page: 69   Key 1: R

28. What is the key value of branding?
    a. makes the product distinctive
    b. makes the price insignificant
    c. creates an image
    d. prevents product theft
    e. all of the above

    Answer: a Difficulty: 2 Page: 70   Key 1: R

29. The part of the brand that can be spoken, such as words, letters or numbers, is called the:
    a. brand mark
    b. brand equity
    c. trademark
    d. logo
    e. brand name

    Answer: e Difficulty: 2 Page: 71   Key 1: R

30. The part of the brand that cannot be spoken, such as a symbol, picture, design, distinctive lettering, or color combination, is called the:
    a. brand name.
    b. trademark.
    c. packaging.
    d. brand mark.
    e. brand equity.

    Answer: d Difficulty: 2 Page: 71   Key 1: R

31. The name, term, design, symbol, or any other feature that identifies the
    good, service, institution, or idea sold by a marketer is called the:
    a. brand name.
    b. logo.
    c. brand equity.
    d. brand.
    e. brand mark.

    Answer: d Difficulty: 2 Page: 71   Key 1: R

32. Hershey's is an example of a:
    a. logo.
    b. brand mark.
    c. trademark.
    d. brand name.
    e. brand image.

    Answer: d Difficulty: 2 Page: 71   Key 1: A

33. The process of creating an identity for a product through a distinctive
    name or symbol is called:
    a. image.
    b. promotion.
    c. trademark.
    d. branding.
    e. logo.

    Answer: d Difficulty: 2 Page: 71   Key 1: R

34. The reputation that the name or symbol that identifies the good,
    service, institution, or idea sold by a marketer is called the:
    a. brand equity.
    b. brand name.
    c. brand image.
    d. branding.
    e. primary demand.

    Answer: a Difficulty: 2 Page: 71   Key 1: R

35. The function of packaging is to:
    a. communicate critical information.
    b. act as a container for the product.
    c. serve as a reminder of the brand image developed in advertising.
    d. carry advertising messages.
    e. all of the above

    Answer: e Difficulty: 3 Page: 71-72   Key 1: R

36. Which of the following members of the channel of distribution is quite effective at advertising?
   a. wholesalers
   b. transporters
   c. mass media
   d. channel captains
   e. retailers

   Answer: e Difficulty: 2 Page: 72   Key 1: R

37. Individuals and institutions involved in moving products from producers to customers are the:
   a. place function of the marketing mix.
   b. channel of distribution.
   c. middlemen.
   d. teamsters.
   e. transportation system.

   Answer: b Difficulty: 2 Page: 72   Key 1: R

38. Lands' End and Spiegel are examples of:
   a. direct marketers.
   b. channel captains.
   c. institutional marketers.
   d. indirect marketers.
   e. intensive marketers.

   Answer: a Difficulty: 2 Page: 72   Key 1: A

39. When a company distributes a product without using a reseller, this is called:
   a. selective distribution.
   b. wholesaling.
   c. indirect marketing.
   d. exclusive distribution.
   e. direct marketing.

   Answer: e Difficulty: 2 Page: 72   Key 1: R

40. When a marketer distributes the product through a channel structure that includes one or more resellers, this is called:
   a. direct marketing.
   b. intensive marketing.
   c. indirect marketing.
   d. exclusive marketing.
   e. selective marketing.

   Answer: c Difficulty: 2 Page: 72   Key 1: R

41. When Proctor & Gamble tries to get consumers to contact doctors to ask for its new prescription skin cream Renova, Proctor & Gamble is using what type of distribution strategy?
a. pull strategy
b. sales promotion strategy
c. direct strategy
d. push strategy
e. market coverage strategy

Answer: a Difficulty: 2 Page: 73   Key 1: A

42. A distribution strategy in which marketing efforts are directed to the ultimate consumer so that consumer demand fuels the marketing process is called:
a. push strategy.
b. direct strategy.
c. pull strategy.
d. intensive strategy.
e. all of the above

Answer: c Difficulty: 2 Page: 73   Key 1: R

43. A distribution strategy in which marketing efforts are directed at the ultimate consumer so that consumer demand fuels the marketing process is called:
a. push strategy.
b. direct strategy.
c. pull strategy.
d. intensive strategy.

Answer: c Difficulty: 2 Page: 73   Key 1: R

44. A market coverage strategy in which only one distributor is allowed to sell the brand in a particular market is called:
a. direct distribution.
b. exclusive distribution.
c. intensive distribution.
d. selective distribution.

Answer: b Difficulty: 2 Page: 73   Key 1: R

45. A market coverage strategy that expands the number of outlets but restricts participation to those outlets that prove most profitable to the manufacturer is called:
a. profitable distribution.
b. exclusive distribution.
c. intensive distribution.
d. selective distribution.

Answer: d Difficulty: 2 Page: 73   Key 1: R

46. Placing the product in every possible outlet in order to attain total market coverage is called:
    a. channel distribution.
    b. market coverage distribution.
    c. intensive distribution.
    d. extensive distribution.
    e. indirect distribution.

    Answer: c Difficulty: 2 Page: 74   Key 1: R

47. What are the three distribution strategies discussed in the text?
    a. direct, indirect, and broad
    b. intensive, targeted, and exclusive
    c. market coverage, direct, and indirect
    d. direct, indirect, and channel
    e. intensive, selective, and exclusive

    Answer: e Difficulty: 2 Page: 74   Key 1: S

48. The maker of expensive running shoes such as New Balance would most likely be interested in what kind of distribution?
    a. intensive
    b. limited
    c. exclusive
    d. direct
    e. selective

    Answer: e Difficulty: 2 Page: 74   Key 1: A

49. An advertising message designed to deliver information about the price of the product is called:
    a. price copy.
    b. sales copy.
    c. product copy.
    d. informational copy.
    e. price lining.

    Answer: a Difficulty: 2 Page: 74   Key 1: R

50. The pricing strategy that involves the use of a single well-known price for a long period of time is called:
    a. single-price.
    b. nominal.
    c. psychological.
    d. customary.
    e. price lining.

    Answer: d Difficulty: 2 Page: 75   Key 1: R

51. When Sears, Roebuck & Company offers different types of tennis rackets on the basis of "good," "better," and "best," with prices that vary accordingly, this is called:
    a. prestige pricing.
    b. price lining.
    c. bargain pricing.
    d. tiered pricing.
    e. multiple pricing.

    Answer: b Difficulty: 2 Page: 75   Key 1: A

52. Advertising, public relations, sales promotion, and personal selling are component parts of the:
    a. marketing communication mix.
    b. advertising mix.
    c. product promotion.
    d. promotion mix.
    e. sales promotion.

    Answer: a Difficulty: 1 Page: 75   Key 1: R

53. The function of sales promotion is to:
    a. enhance the image of the marketer.
    b. generate immediate sales.
    c. develop awareness of the product.
    d. create goodwill with the consumer.
    e. inform customer about new products.

    Answer: b Difficulty: 3 Page: 75   Key 1: R

54. The element in the marketing mix that encourages consumers to purchase a product or service is called:
    a. public relations.
    b. branding.
    c. promotion.
    d. distribution.
    e. none of the above

    Answer: c Difficulty: 3 Page: 76   Key 1: R

55. Face-to-face contact between the marketer and a prospective customer that is intended to create both immediate sales and repeat sales is called:
    a. direct marketing.
    b. public relations.
    c. personal selling.
    d. marketing.
    e. sales promotion.

    Answer: c Difficulty: 1 Page: 76   Key 1: R

56. Which of the following is true about public relations?
    a. It seeks to influence attitudes about the company or product.
    b. It works with such a delay between influence and effect on sales that any relationship between public relations efforts and sales is difficult to determine.
    c. It supports the advertising campaign.
    d. It seeks to enhance the image of the marketer.
    e. all of the above

    Answer: e Difficulty: 2 Page: 76   Key 1: A

57. An extra incentive to buy now is called:
    a. personal selling.
    b. sales promotion.
    c. promotion.
    d. direct marketing.
    e. all of the above

    Answer: b Difficulty: 2 Page: 76   Key 1: R

58. Messages delivered for direct marketing products are usually called:
    a. direct advertising.
    b. point-of-sale advertising.
    c. intensive advertising.
    d. direct-response advertising.
    e. sales promotion advertising.

    Answer: d Difficulty: 2 Page: 77   Key 1: R

59. Which of the following is true about advertising compared to other forms of promotion?
    a. greater ability to reach a large number of people simultaneously
    b. contact between advertiser and audience is indirect
    c. takes longer to deliver information to the target market
    d. takes longer to create a rapport with the target market
    e. all of the above

    Answer: e Difficulty: 2 Page: 77   Key 1: S

60. A set of activities intended to improve the image of the marketer and to create goodwill is called:
    a. sales promotion.
    b. publicity.
    c. public relations.
    d. public affairs.
    e. promotion.

    Answer: c Difficulty: 2 Page: 77   Key 1: R

61. Which of the following is a characteristic of direct marketing?
    a. can occur at any location
    b. requires a database of consumer information
    c. is interactive, allowing two-way communication
    d. provides a measurable response
    e. all of the above

    Answer: e Difficulty: 2 Page: 77   Key 1: R

62. What is the fastest growing element in marketing?
    a. advertising
    b. sales promotion
    c. public relations
    d. point-of-sales/packaging
    e. direct marketing

    Answer: e Difficulty: 2 Page: 77   Key 1: R

63. The communication devices and marketing messages found at the place where the product is sold are called:
    a. direct marketing.
    b. point-of-sale/packaging.
    c. advertising.
    d. sales promotion.
    e. public relations.

    Answer: b Difficulty: 1 Page: 77   Key 1: R

64. Marketers hire agencies to plan and execute their advertising efforts because:
    a. an agency provides objective expertise.
    b. an agency provides staffing and management of all advertising activities and personnel.
    c. an agency can tell marketers when they misread consumers.
    d. an agency can draw on the collective expertise and training of its staff.
    e. all of the above

    Answer: e Difficulty: 3 Page: 79   Key 1: R

65. Which of the following is a type of ad agency?
    a. full-service agency
    b. specialized agency
    c. industry-focused agency
    d. minority agency
    e. all of the above

    Answer: e Difficulty: 1 Page: 80   Key 1: R

66. Which of the following has dramatically affected ad agencies?
    a. technological changes in media
    b. the lack of consumer information
    c. the decrease in types of available media
    d. the move towards a more mass-media based approach
    e. all of the above

    Answer: a Difficulty: 2 Page: 83   Key 1: R

TRUE/FALSE

67. It is unlikely that an ad agency could achieve its advertising goals
    without a thorough understanding of its client's marketing situation.
    a. True
    b. False

    Answer: a Difficulty: 2 Page: 61   Key 1: R

68. An exchange includes the act of trading a desired product or service for
    nothing in return.
    a. True
    b. False

    Answer: a Difficulty: 2 Page: 62   Key 1: R

69. During the research stage of the marketing plan, the planner develops
    objectives and an enduring strategy.
    a. True
    b. False

    Answer: b Difficulty: 2 Page: 63   Key 1: R

70. During the tactical stage of the marketing plan, the marketer assesses
    how well the plan achieved objectives.
    a. True
    b. False

    Answer: b Difficulty: 2 Page: 63   Key 1: R

71. Solid marketing strategy can overcome inferior advertising.
    a. True
    b. False

    Answer: b Difficulty: 1 Page: 64   Key 1: R

72. The market is a region where goods are sold and/or bought for a particular type of buyer.
    a. True
    b. False

    Answer: a Difficulty: 2 Page: 64   Key 1: R

73. College students are considered part of the institutional market.
    a. True
    b. False

    Answer: b Difficulty: 3 Page: 65   Key 1: A

74. Resellers include a wide variety of profit and non-profit organizations such as hospitals and schools.
    a. True
    b. False

    Answer: b Difficulty: 2 Page: 65   Key 1: R

75. Fred's Toyota dealership would be part of Toyota's reseller market.
    a. True
    b. False

    Answer: a Difficulty: 2 Page: 65   Key 1: A

76. Middlemen are often associated with consumer markets.
    a. True
    b. False

    Answer: b Difficulty: 3 Page: 65   Key 1: R

77. Consumers in most markets tend to be fairly uniform.
    a. True
    b. False

    Answer: b Difficulty: 2 Page: 65   Key 1: R

78. The market segments of potential consumers that a product provider selects is its target market.
    a. True
    b. False

    Answer: a Difficulty: 2 Page: 65   Key 1: A

79. Pepsi's "Pepsi Generation" campaign is an example of market aggregation strategy.
    a. True
    b. False

    Answer: a Difficulty: 2 Page: 66   Key 1: A

80. Market segmentation recognizes consumer differences and adjusts to them.
    a. True
    b. False

    Answer: a Difficulty: 2 Page: 66   Key 1: A

81. A good example of product differentiation is when watch companies demonstrate the importance of pricing by offering fashionable watches at modest prices.
    a. True
    b. False

    Answer: a Difficulty: 2 Page: 66   Key 1: A

82. The image of a product often has little to do with the actual product features.
    a. True
    b. False

    Answer: a Difficulty: 2 Page: 66   Key 1: A

83. Positioning creates a market niche for a product.
    a. True
    b. False

    Answer: a Difficulty: 2 Page: 67   Key 1: R

84. Marketers can position a product, service or idea by price.
    a. True
    b. False

    Answer: a Difficulty: 2 Page: 67   Key 1: R

85. Integrated marketing first considers the needs of the ad agency itself.
    a. True
    b. False

    Answer: b Difficulty: 2 Page: 68   Key 1: R

86. Relationship marketing recognizes the needs of customers and responds to those needs through a coordinated marketing mix.
    a. True
    b. False

    Answer: b Difficulty: 2 Page: 68   Key 1: A

87. The product is usually not the object of the advertising, nor the reason for marketing.
    a. True
    b. False

    Answer: b Difficulty: 1 Page: 68   Key 1: A

88. The intangible, symbolic attributes of certain automobiles now offer psychological and social functions for the buyer.
    a. True
    b. False

    Answer: a Difficulty: 2 Page: 69   Key 1: R

89. Branding makes a product distinctive in the marketplace.
    a. True
    b. False

    Answer: a Difficulty: 1 Page: 70   Key 1: R

90. Brand equity refers to the name, term, design, symbol or any other feature that identifies the goods, service, institution or idea sold by a marketer.
    a. True
    b. False

    Answer: b Difficulty: 2 Page: 71   Key 1: A

91. In a self-service retailing situation, the packaging is often the primary message of a product.
    a. True
    b. False

    Answer: a Difficulty: 2 Page: 71   Key 1: R

92. The people and institutions involved in moving products from producers to consumers make up the distribution channels.
    a. True
    b. False

    Answer: a Difficulty: 2 Page: 72   Key 1: R

93. Manufacturers rarely work with wholesalers and retailers on their advertising campaigns.
    a. True
    b. False

    Answer: b Difficulty: 3 Page: 73   Key 1: R

94. A pull strategy is fueled by consumer demand.
    a. True
    b. False

    Answer: a Difficulty: 2 Page: 73   Key 1: R

95. With exclusive distribution, several distributors are allowed to sell a brand in a particular market.
    a. True
    b. False

    Answer: b Difficulty: 1 Page: 73   Key 1: R

96. Coca-Cola, Snickers and Marlboro usually use an intensive distribution approach.
    a. True
    b. False

    Answer: a Difficulty: 2 Page: 74   Key 1: A

97. The price a seller sets has little to do with the cost of making and marketing the product.
    a. True
    b. False

    Answer: b Difficulty: 2 Page: 74   Key 1: R

98. Implementing the communication mix in a coordinated manner is called integrated marketing communication.
    a. True
    b. False

    Answer: a Difficulty: 1 Page: 75   Key 1: R

99. Sales promotion is an extra incentive to buy now or soon.
    a. True
    b. False

    Answer: a Difficulty: 1 Page: 76   Key 1: R

100. The media department within an ad agency has three functions: planning, buying and research.
a. True
b. False

Answer: a Difficulty: 2 Page: 82   Key 1: R

ESSAY

101. Discuss the four types of markets, give an example for each and the predominant form of advertising used.

Answer:
Consumer markets consist of people who buy products and services for personal or household use. For example, a college student might be considered a member of the market for jeans, backpacks, along with many other products.

Industrial markets consist of companies that buy products or services to use in their own businesses or in making other products. General Electric, for example, buys computers to use in billing and inventory control, steel and wiring to use in the manufacturing of its products and cleaning supplies to use in maintaining its buildings.

Institutional markets include a wide variety of profit and non-profit organizations---such as hospitals, government agencies and schools---that provide goods and services for the benefit of society. Universities for example, are in the market for furniture, cleaning supplies, computers, etc.

Reseller markets include wholesalers, retailers and distributors who buy finished or semi-finished products and resell them for profit. Companies that sell products and services such as trucks, cartons, athletic shoes, etc. often consider resellers the market.

Each market requires a different form of advertising. Businesses usually advertise to consumers through mass media and direct-response advertising media. Businesses typically reach the other three markets through trade and professional advertising in specialized media such as trade journals, professional magazines and direct mail.
Difficulty: 2 Page: 64-65   Key 1: R/S

102. Discuss the concept of product differentiation and some of the strategies advertisers use to differentiate products.

Answer:
Product differentiation is a competitive marketing strategy designed to create product differences in the eyes of consumers that distinguish the company's product from all others. Those perceived features may be tangible or intangible. Tangible differences include unique product features, color, size, quality or available options. Price can also be a tangible distinguishing characteristic. The Swatch watch demonstrates the importance of pricing by offering a fashionable watch at a modest price. In instances where products are really the same (such as milk, gasoline or salt) marketers most often turn to intangible differences to distinguish products. They create an image, although the image may have little to do with tactual product features. Beer companies, for example, try to suggest status, enjoyment and sex appeal.

Difficulty: 1 Page:. 66-67   Key 1: R/S

103. Discuss the development of the marketing concept and the reasons for this development.

Answer:
The marketing concept suggests that marketing should focus first on the needs and wants of consumers, rather than finding ways to sell products that may or may not meet consumer needs. A handful of businesses, such as L.L. Bean and UPS, adopted this perspective early. However, according to marketing experts, most did not embrace the marketing concept until the 1980s. They had to become more market-oriented to adapt to changes because consumers have become better educated and empowered with opinions and dollars. World trade barriers have come down, allowing new competitors and better choices. Me-too products, although profitable, are no longer always acceptable to most consumers. Today, marketers know that to compete effectively, they must focus on consumer problems and try to develop products to solve them. Performing this task well promises the ultimate competitive advantage. The marketing concept suggests two marketing steps. First, determine what the customer needs and wants. Second, develop, manufacture, market and service the goods and services to fill those particular needs and wants.

Difficulty: 2 Page: 67-68   Key 1: R/S

104. Discuss branding, give examples of various types of branding and discuss their importance.

Answer:
Branding makes a product distinctive in the marketplace. However, there are subtle differences. A brand is the name, term, design, symbol or any other feature that identifies the goods, service, institution or ideas sold by a marketer. The brand name is the part of the brand that can be spoken. Hershey's is a brand name, as is K2R. The brand mark or logo is the graphic part of the brand. It can be a symbol, picture, design, distinctive lettering or color combination. For example, the Nike "Swoosh" is recognized globally. Part of Prestone's advertising strategy for the de-icer windshield fluid was to brand the product in a largely unbranded category. By creating a brand image, Prestone hoped to justify a premium pricing strategy. The importance of the brand cannot be overstated. When we talk about brand equity, we refer to the reputation that the name or symbol connotes. It is on every important message and becomes synonymous with the company. Losing brand equity through excessive discounting, substandard products, poor service or questionable ethical practices has proven disastrous for many companies. Nike's reputation suffered when it was accused of using underage labor in poor working conditions.
Difficulty: 2 Page: 70-71   Key 1: R/S

105. Discuss the effects of technological changes on advertising agencies.

Answer:
The computer has expanded the ability to collect, collate and analyze data. Single-source data is now available for many households that identify purchase patterns in retail stores and the advertising messages they have seen. The industry is flooded with more information than it can analyze. Technological changes in the media industry have also affected the advertising industry. For one thing, available media have multiplied in number, specificity and type. But more importantly, interactive and personalized media are becoming more efficient and effective in delivering one-on-one messages, which is beginning to move advertising away from its mass-media base. Computers have also changed how creative people operate: most now write and design their ads on computers and share ideas with others in the agency and sometimes even with their client through online networks.
Difficulty: 3 Page: 83-84   Key 1: R

CHAPTER 4: THE CONSUMER AUDIENCE

MULTIPLE CHOICE

1. What must advertisers do first in order to communicate to audiences in a way that persuades the consumer to purchase the product?
   a. be creative
   b. find the right media
   c. understand the consumer
   d. appeal to a complex consumer audience
   e. use target audiences

   Answer: c Difficulty: 2 Page: 90   Key 1: A

2. What is the goal of advertising?
   a. to inform the consumer
   b. to persuade the consumer to do something
   c. to create an image for a product
   d. to understand the behavior of consumers
   e. to entertain audiences

   Answer: b Difficulty: 2 Page: 90   Key 1: R

3. People who buy or use products are called:
   a. target market.
   b. market.
   c. consumers.
   d. public.

   Answer: c Difficulty: 2 Page: 91   Key 1: R

4. What are the two types of consumers?
   a. buyers and users
   b. shoppers and buyers
   c. shoppers and viewers
   d. buyers and borrowers

   Answer: a Difficulty: 2 Page: 91   Key 1: S

5. A group of people who are most likely to respond favorably to what the marketer has to offer is called:
   a. target market.
   b. market segment.
   c. market.
   d. target segment.
   e. brand loyal users.

   Answer: a Difficulty: 2 Page: 91   Key 1: R

6. The complex of tangible items such as art, literature, buildings, furniture, clothing, and music is called:
   a. social environment.
   b. culture.
   c. material culture.
   d. tangible social environment.
   e. tangible subculture.

   Answer: b Difficulty: 2 Page: 92   Key 1: R

7. Simple rules for behavior that are established by the culture are called:
   a. mores.
   b. norms.
   c. values.
   d. subcultures.
   e. social class.

   Answer: b Difficulty: 2 Page: 92   Key 1: R

8. A source for our norms is called:
   a. customs.
   b. markets.
   c. subcultures.
   d. social classes.
   e. values.

   Answer: e Difficulty: 2 Page: 92   Key 1: R

9. All of the following have been identified as core values EXCEPT:
   a. sense of belonging.
   b. excitement.
   c. fun and enjoyment in life.
   d. convenience.
   e. security.

   Answer: d Difficulty: 2 Page: 93   Key 1: S

10. Giving presents to family and friends at Christmas is a:
    a. norm.
    b. custom.
    c. value.
    d. material culture.
    e. cultural trend.

    Answer: b Difficulty: 2 Page: 93   Key 1: A

11. Overt modes of behavior which constitute culturally approved ways of behaving in specific situations are called:
    a. norms.
    b. values.
    c. customs.
    d. mores.
    e. culture.

    Answer: c Difficulty: 2 Page: 93   Key 1: R

12. The position that you and your family occupy within your society is called:
    a. norm.
    b. value.
    c. subculture.
    d. social class.
    e. custom.

    Answer: d Difficulty: 2 Page: 94   Key 1: R

13. When Mountain Dew shows young people playing together and drinking its soft drink, what is the basis of the suggestion to buy?
    a. social class strategy
    b. image strategy
    c. lifestyle strategy
    d. reference group strategy
    e. subculture strategy

    Answer: d Difficulty: 2 Page: 95   Key 1: A

14. A collection of people that you use as a guide for behavior in specific situations is called:
    a. social class.
    b. subculture.
    c. reference group.
    d. tribal clan.
    e. social group.

    Answer: c Difficulty: 2 Page: 95   Key 1: R

15. What are the functions of reference groups for consumers?
    a. control, information, and assistance
    b. comparison, emotional support, and guidance
    c. control, information, and power
    d. information, comparison and guidance
    e. guidance, control, and direction

    Answer: d Difficulty: 2 Page: 95   Key 1: S

16. All those who occupy a living unit, whether they are related or not are called:
    a. tribe.
    b. family.
    c. household.
    d. living unit.
    e. home.

    Answer: c Difficulty: 2 Page: 95   Key 1: R

17. What kinds of resources does the family provide for its members?
    a. sexual and emotional
    b. ego and emotional
    c. economic and emotional
    d. economic and power
    e. ego and power

    Answer: c Difficulty: 2 Page: 96   Key 1: R

18. The statistical representation of social and economic characteristics of people, including age, sex, income, occupation, and family size is called:
    a. demographics.
    b. descriptions.
    c. individuals.
    d. psychographics.
    e. surveys.

    Answer: a Difficulty: 2 Page: 96   Key 1: R

19. How has the shift from blue-collar occupations to white-collar occupations affected advertising?
    a. blue-collar jobs are seldom portrayed in advertisements anymore
    b. ad copy tends to be more technical
    c. women are being depicted increasingly in professional roles
    d. ad copy tends to be more scientific
    e. all of the above

    Answer: e Difficulty: 2 Page: 100   Key 1: S

20. The money available to a household after taxes and basic necessities such as food and shelter are paid for is called:
    a. net income.
    b. financial power.
    c. optional finances.
    d. discretionary income.
    e. personal spending power.

    Answer: d Difficulty: 2 Page: 100   Key 1: R

21. As total income increases, what happens to discretionary income?
    a. decreases slowly
    b. grows at a much faster rate
    c. decreases rapidly
    d. grows but very slowly
    e. remains constant

    Answer: b Difficulty: 2 Page: 100   Key 1: R

22. How does race and ethnicity affect consumer behavior?
    a. People who settle in the U.S. tend to completely assimilate.
    b. These factors do not usually affect consumer behavior.
    c. Different races and ethnicities often have consumer behavior
       different from the norm.
    d. Different races and ethnicities often have no varying consumer
       patterns.
    e. All of the above

    Answer: c Difficulty: 3 Page: 101   Key 1: S

23. Knowing consumers' geographic locations:
    a. is important to advertisers.
    b. can help reveal sales patterns in different regions.
    c. helps advertisers determine different consumer needs in different
       regions.
    d. can help predict geographic trends.
    e. all of the above

    Answer: b Difficulty: 2 Page: 101-102   Key 1: S

24. A process of receiving information through our senses and assigning
    meaning to it is called:
    a. communication.
    b. recognition.
    c. perception.
    d. screening.
    e. stimulation.

    Answer: c Difficulty: 2 Page: 102   Key 1: R

25. People's psychological variables, such as attitudes, lifestyles,
    opinions, and personality traits are called:
    a. demographics.
    b. lifestyles.
    c. personalities.
    d. psychographics.
    e. individuals.

    Answer: d Difficulty: 2 Page: 102   Key 1: R

26. Perceptions are shaped by what three sets of influences?
    a. family background, culture, and stereotypes
    b. physical characteristics of the stimuli, relation of the stimuli to their surroundings, and conditions within the individual
    c. intensity of stimuli, physical characteristics of the stimuli, characteristics of individual
    d. relation of the stimuli to their surroundings, physical characteristics of the stimuli, and the intensity of the stimuli
    e. means by which the stimuli are received, the nature of the stimuli, and the context in which the stimuli are received

    Answer: b Difficulty: 3 Page: 102   Key 1: S

27. Filtering out information that does not interest us and retaining information that does is called:
    a. selective experience.
    b. selective perception.
    c. psychological screening.
    d. informational processing.
    e. perception.

    Answer: b Difficulty: 2 Page: 103   Key 1: R

28. Which of the following is true concerning perception?
    a. we select stimuli that interest us
    b. our frame of reference changes what we perceive
    c. we perceive stimuli in ways that coincide with our view of reality
    d. perception is a personal trait
    e. all of the above

    Answer: e Difficulty: 3 Page: 103   Key 1: S

29. The process we go through in trying to save information for future use is called:
    a. selective retention.
    b. selective exposure.
    c. selective attention.
    d. selective perception.
    e. selective distortion.

    Answer: a Difficulty: 2 Page: 103   Key 1: R

30. Interpreting information in a way that is consistent with the person's existing opinion is called:
    a. selective exposure.
    b. selective perception.
    c. selective distortion.
    d. selective retention.

    Answer: c Difficulty: 2 Page: 103   Key 1: R

31. A consumer hears that an automobile gets good gas mileage, even through the salesperson has clearly indicated this is not so, but because the consumer perceives other features of the car as perfect and therefore wants very much to buy it is an example of:
    a. selective perception
    b. selective distortion
    c. selective exposure
    d. selective retention
    e. cognitive dissonance

    Answer: b Difficulty: 2 Page: 103   Key 1: R

32. How can advertising make it easier for the audience to retain the message?
    a. using repetition in ads
    b. using easily remembered brand or product names
    c. using jingles
    d. using high-profile spokespeople
    e. all of the above

    Answer: e Difficulty: 2 Page: 103   Key 1: R

33. The process of remembering only a small portion of what a person is exposed to is called:
    a. selective perception.
    b. selective exposure.
    c. selective retention.
    d. selective distortion.

    Answer: c Difficulty: 2 Page: 103   Key 1: R

34. The process we go through when we seek out messages that are pleasant or sympathetic with our views and avoid those that are painful or threatening is called:
    a. selective exposure.
    b. selective perception.
    c. selective distortion.
    d. selective retention.
    e. selective attention.

    Answer: a Difficulty: 2 Page: 103   Key 1: R

35. What means does the individual have to deal with cognitive dissonance?
    a. distort information that does not support the decision
    b. seek information to support the decision
    c. ignore information that does not support the decision
    d. all of the above

    Answer: d Difficulty: 2 Page: 103   Key 1: R

36. A tendency to compensate or justify the small or large discrepancy between what we actually received and what we perceived we would receive is called:
    a. distortion.
    b. cognitive dissonance.
    c. selective response.
    d. selective justification.
    e. cognitive distortion.

    Answer: b Difficulty: 2 Page: 103   Key 1: R

37. The cognitive school of learning emphasizes:
    a. training dogs to salivate.
    b. the importance of perception problem solving, and insight.
    c. trial-and-error process in which one behavior is rewarded more than another.
    d. the importance of people learning connections between stimuli and responses.
    e. all of the above

    Answer: b Difficulty: 2 Page: 104   Key 1: R

38. The experiments of Ivan Pavlov, in which a dog was taught to salivate at the sound of a bell, is associated with what school of learning?
    a. operant conditioning
    b. instrumental conditioning
    c. cognitive
    d. trial-and-error
    e. classical conditioning

    Answer: e Difficulty: 2 Page: 104   Key 1: R

39. An advertiser who uses the cognitive perspective of learning would concentrate on what?
    a. repetition to convince the consumer the brand rewards more than the others do
    b. role of motivation in decision making
    c. providing cues that suggest a reward
    d. reinforcement of information that leads to satisfaction
    e. conditioning that leads to the appropriate buying response

    Answer: b Difficulty: 2 Page: 104   Key 1: R

40. Reason-why ad copy, in which a consumer problem is noted, then solved by the virtues of the product, would be most closely associated with what school of learning?
   a. classical conditioning
   b. operant conditioning
   c. connectionist
   d. cognitive
   e. habit

   Answer: d Difficulty: 2 Page: 104   Key 1: A

41. If we have an ad campaign designed to remind the consumer of a pleasurable experience then try to connect it to use of our product, what school of learning would this be most closely related?
   a. classical conditioning
   b. operant conditioning
   c. instrumental conditioning
   d. trial-and-error

   Answer: a Difficulty: 2 Page: 104   Key 1: A

42. An ad campaign that works at providing information to help the consumer in solving his problems would be using the concept of what school of learning?
   a. cognitive
   b. operant learning
   c. instrumental learning
   d. trial-and-error

   Answer: a Difficulty: 2 Page: 104   Key 1: A

43. A limitation on or total absence of information seeking and evaluation of alternatives is called:
   a. habit.
   b. conditioning.
   c. selective exposure.
   d. cognitive dissonance.
   e. death.

   Answer: a Difficulty: 2 Page: 105   Key 1: R

44. What are the benefits of purchasing by habit?
   a. conformity and comfort
   b. facilitates decision making and less risk
   c. saves time and facilitates decision-making
   d. less risk and comfort
   e. none of the above

   Answer: b Difficulty: 2 Page: 105   Key 1: R

45. How can an advertiser work to help consumers break a habit?
    a. attack a competitor's message
    b. provide an extra incentive to change, such as coupons or free samples
    c. point out the weaknesses of competing products
    d. all of the above

    Answer: b Difficulty: 2 Page: 106   Key 1: R

46. What causes the motive or driving force that stimulates individuals to act in a particular way?
    a. a state of tension resulting from an unfulfilled need
    b. cognitive dissonance
    c. entertaining advertising messages
    d. coercive advertising messages
    e. none of the above

    Answer: a Difficulty: 2 Page: 106   Key 1: R

47. How can an advertiser improve learning?
    a. use music and jingles
    b. create positive associations with a brand
    c. use testimonials by well-liked celebrities
    d. use humor
    e. all of the above

    Answer: e Difficulty: 2 Page: 106   Key 1: R

48. A _____ is an internal force that stimulates you to behave in a certain manner.
    a. stimulus
    b. motive
    c. need
    d. habit
    e. condition

    Answer: b Difficulty: 3 Page: 106   Key 1: R

49. The physiological need for food, water, air, shelter, and sex is called:
    a. secondary need.
    b. basic need.
    c. innate need.
    d. life need.
    e. survival need.

    Answer: c Difficulty: 2 Page: 107   Key 1: R

50. The needs we learn in response to our culture or environment and include needs for esteem, prestige, affection, power, and learning are called:
    a. learned needs.
    b. acquired needs.
    c. primary needs.
    d. sociological needs.
    e. induced needs.

    Answer: b Difficulty: 2 Page: 107   Key 1: R

51. The needs, which are not necessary to our physical survival, are called:
    a. elementary needs.
    b. tertiary needs.
    c. social needs.
    d. primary needs.
    e. secondary needs.

    Answer: e Difficulty: 2 Page: 107   Key 1: R

52. Which of the following is a basic force that motivates you to do or to want something?
    a. need
    b. habit
    c. motive
    d. attitude

    Answer: a Difficulty: 2 Page: 107   Key 1: R

53. A learned predisposition, a feeling that you hold toward an object, a person, or an idea that leads to a particular behavior is called:
    a. attitude.
    b. principle.
    c. ethic.
    d. opinion.
    e. stereotype.

    Answer: a Difficulty: 2 Page: 107   Key 1: R

54. Because attitudes are learned:
    a. people can change them.
    b. people cannot unlearn them.
    c. people cannot replace them.
    d. people cannot adopt new ones.
    e. all of the above

    Answer: a Difficulty: 2 Page: 107   Key 1: R

55. How we look at ourselves is called:
    a. personality.
    b. self-concept.
    c. recognition.
    d. achievement.

    Answer: b Difficulty: 2 Page: 108   Key 1: R

56. A collection of traits that makes a person distinctive: how you look at the world, how you perceive and interpret what is happening around you, how you respond intellectually and emotionally, and how you form your opinions and attitudes are called:
    a. sexuality.
    b. lifestyle.
    c. image.
    d. attitudes.
    e. personality.

    Answer: e Difficulty: 2 Page: 108   Key 1: R

57. What are the two key factors now used in the VALS-2 psychographic analysis?
    a. resources and self-orientation
    b. achievement and recognition
    c. self-concept and achievement
    d. independence and self-concept
    e. self-concept and resources

    Answer: a Difficulty: 2 Page: 109   Key 1: R

58. Conceptual models that categorize people according to their values and then identify the consumer behaviors associated with those values are called:
    a. psychographics.
    b. Values and Lifestyles Systems (VALS) model.
    c. consumer profiles.
    d. lifestyle research.
    e. Lifestyle Focus System (LFS) model.

    Answer: b Difficulty: 2 Page: 109   Key 1: R

59. Complex decisions that have high personal relevance and contain a high degree of perceived risk are called:
    a. product decision process.
    b. low-involvement decision process.
    c. purchase decision process.
    d. high risk decision process.
    e. high-involvement decision process.

    Answer: e Difficulty: 2 Page: 112   Key 1: R

60. Simple decisions that require limited deliberation and require little information and virtually no evaluation are called:
    a. low-involvement decision process.
    b. right-brain decision process.
    c. purchase decision process.
    d. low-risk decision process.
    e. high-involvement decision process.

    Answer: a Difficulty: 2 Page: 112   Key 1: R

61. The process consumers go through in making a purchase is called:
    a. purchase evaluation.
    b. decision process.
    c. cognitive evaluation.
    d. cognitive dissonance.
    e. purchase decision.

    Answer: b Difficulty: 2 Page: 112   Key 1: R

62. Need recognition, information research, outlet selection and purchase decision, evaluation and comparison, and post-purchase evaluation are all part of the:
    a. judgment process.
    b. assessment process.
    c. evaluation process.
    d. decision process.

    Answer: d Difficulty: 2 Page: 112   Key 1: R

63. The stage in the decision process in which the consumer looks at alternatives, focuses on important features, and tries to reduce the alternatives to a manageable number is called:
    a. post-purchase evaluation.
    b. evaluation and comparison.
    c. need recognition.
    d. information search.
    e. purchase decision.

    Answer: b Difficulty: 2 Page: 113   Key 1: R

64. The stage in the decision process in which the consumer looks for new information and recalls information is called:
    a. post-purchase evaluation.
    b. evaluation.
    c. comparison.
    d. information search.
    e. need recognition.

    Answer: d Difficulty: 2 Page: 113   Key 1: R

65. Doubt or worry about the wisdom of a purchase even before the package is opened or the product is used is called:
a. post-purchase evaluation.
b. post-purchase guilt.
c. information search.
d. post-purchase dissonance.
e. second thoughts.

Answer: d Difficulty: 2 Page: 113   Key 1: R

66. Need recognition, information search, evaluation of alternatives, purchase decision and postpurchase evaluation are the stages in what process?
a. perception process
b. decision process
c. demographic process
d. consumer process
e. advertising process

Answer: b Difficulty: 1 Page: 113   Key 1: S

TRUE/FALSE

67. Great advertising can readily convert the users of a competitor's products.
a. True
b. False

Answer: b Difficulty: 2 Page: 90   Key 1: R

68. Changing attitudes is relatively simple for the professional advertiser.
a. True
b. False

Answer: b Difficulty: 2 Page: 90   Key 1: R

69. Advertisers look at people as an audience for messages.
a. True
b. False

Answer: a Difficulty: 2 Page: 91   Key 1: A

70. Cultural and social influences are the forces that other people exert on your behavior.
a. True
b. False

Answer: a Difficulty: 2 Page: 92   Key 1: R

71. Values are numerous and tied to specific objects or situations.
    a. True
    b. False

    Answer: b Difficulty: 2 Page: 92   Key 1: R

72. The boundaries each culture establishes are called norms.
    a. True
    b. False

    Answer: a Difficulty: 2 Page: 92   Key 1: R

73. Values are relatively easy to change.
    a. True
    b. False

    Answer: b Difficulty: 2 Page: 92   Key 1: R

74. Advertisers often refer to core values when selecting their primary appeals.
    a. True
    b. False

    Answer: a Difficulty: 2 Page: 93   Key 1: R

75. Norms and values often combine to create cultural customs.
    a. True
    b. False

    Answer: a Difficulty: 2 Page: 93   Key 1: R

76. Customs are models of behavior that establish culturally acceptable ways of behaving in certain situations.
    a. True
    b. False

    Answer: a Difficulty: 2 Page: 93   Key 1: R

77. Mother's day is not an example of a custom.
    a. True
    b. False

    Answer: b Difficulty: 2 Page: 93   Key 1: A

78. Customs remain fairly consistent around the world.
    a. True
    b. False

    Answer: b Difficulty: 2 Page: 93   Key 1: R

79. Culture has no influence on buying behavior.
   a. True
   b. False

   Answer: b Difficulty: 2 Page: 93   Key 1: R

80. A culture can be divided into subcultures based on geographic region or characteristics.
   a. True
   b. False

   Answer: a Difficulty: 2 Page: 94   Key 1: R

81. Skateboarders are an example of a subculture.
   a. True
   b. False

   Answer: a Difficulty: 2 Page: 94   Key 1: A

82. The position you and your family occupy within your society is your social class.
   a. True
   b. False

   Answer: a Difficulty: 2 Page: 94   Key 1: R

83. Social class is mostly determined by your subculture.
   a. True
   b. False

   Answer: b Difficulty: 2 Page: 94   Key 1: R

84. Marketers assume that people in different classes often buy the same goods.
   a. True
   b. False

   Answer: b Difficulty: 2 Page: 94   Key 1: R

85. Marketers can get a feel for the social class of a target market by using marketing research and census data.
   a. True
   b. False

   Answer: a Difficulty: 2 Page: 94   Key 1: R

86. A reference group is a collection of people used as a guide to determine behavior in specific situations.
    a. True
    b. False

    Answer: a Difficulty: 2 Page: 95   Key 1: R

87. An example of a reference group is a peer group.
    a. True
    b. False

    Answer: a Difficulty: 2 Page: 95   Key 1: R

88. Reference groups tend to be consistent over time.
    a. True
    b. False

    Answer: b Difficulty: 2 Page: 95   Key 1: R

89. The family is a reference group.
    a. True
    b. False

    Answer: a Difficulty: 2 Page: 95   Key 1: R

90. A household is synonymous with family.
    a. True
    b. False

    Answer: b Difficulty: 2 Page: 95   Key 1: R

91. Your age, income, sex, education, occupation, and race can affect your way of looking at the world.
    a. True
    b. False

    Answer: a Difficulty: 2 Page: 96   Key 1: R

92. Demographics is the study of those social and economic factors that influence how you behave as an individual consumer.
    a. True
    b. False

    Answer: a Difficulty: 2 Page: 96   Key 1: R

93. The elderly are not interesting to marketers because they do not have much money.
   a. True
   b. False

   Answer: b Difficulty: 2 Page: 97   Key 1: R

94. The text expects the trend toward a less-educated consumer to continue through the 1990s.
   a. True
   b. False

   Answer: b Difficulty: 2 Page: 100   Key 1: R

95. Consumers who are better educated are more likely to respond to an emotional appeal.
   a. True
   b. False

   Answer: b Difficulty: 2 Page: 100   Key 1: R

96. The number of service-related jobs is expected to increase, especially in the health-care, education, and legal and business-service sectors.
   a. True
   b. False

   Answer: a Difficulty: 2 Page: 100   Key 1: R

97. There has been a gradual movement from white-collar occupations to blue-collar occupations during the last three decades.
   a. True
   b. False

   Answer: b Difficulty: 2 Page: 100   Key 1: R

98. You are only meaningful to a marketer if you have the resources to buy the product.
   a. True
   b. False

   Answer: a Difficulty: 1 Page: 100   Key 1: A

99. Selective perception means we screen out information that does not interest us.
   a. True
   b. False

   Answer: a Difficulty: 2 Page: 103   Key 1: R

100. An ad will be perceived only if it is relevant to the consumer.
    a. True
    b. False

Answer: a Difficulty: 2 Page: 103   Key 1: R

ESSAY

101. Discuss how culture, subculture, and social class can influence advertising decisions.

    Answer:
    The culture that a person is raised in affects values and opinions. This culture also helps to establish norms and values. A example of a value is personal security. Norms that reflect this range from bars on the windows in Brooklyn, NY to unlocked cars and homes in Eau Claire, WI. Advertisers often appeal to core values when targeting certain groups of consumers. Because advertisers find it difficult, if not impossible, to change values, they seek to appeal to them in order to affect people's decisions.

    Cultures can be divided into subcultures based on geographic regions or human characteristics. Within subcultures there are similarities in people's attitudes and secondary values. Advertising aimed at a subculture such as snowboarders would probably not advertise in a magazine like "Good Housekeeping." They would probably aim more for specialty snowboard publications.

    Marketers assume that people in different social classes buy different goods from different outlets and for different reasons than people in other classes. For example, advertising directed at lower classes may emphasize practical details such as durability and low price, while a product, like a luxury automobile, might be directed at upper classes and stress prestige and status.

    Difficulty: 2 Page: 92-95   Key 1: S/A

102. Discuss how the concept of reference groups is used in advertising.

Answer:
Reference groups have three main functions: (1) They provide information, (2) they serve as a means of comparison, and (3) they offer guidance. Because people use reference groups to guide behavior, norms within that group may help determine buying habits. For example, if the reference group is a group of construction workers, norms may dictate the purchase of certain equipment---tool belts, hard hats, etc. An individual may also be attracted to a particular reference group and want to be like members of that group out of respect or admiration or a need to fit in. Advertisers use celebrity endorsement to tap into these desires. A family, the most influential reference group, may also use portrayals of different family situations to tap into the desire for certain products. For example, the advertisement might state families on the go use X brand of microwave meals. A family that recognizes itself as a family on the go might opt to purchase that product.
Difficulty: 2 Page: 95   Key 1: A

103. Compare and contrast demographics and psychographics.

Answer:
Demographics are the statistical representations of social and economic characteristics of people, including age, sex, income, occupation and family size. These factors serve as a basis for most advertising strategies knowing demographic features about a target audience helps advertisers in message design and media selection. For example, an advertisement for a brand of golf clothing might be aimed at mostly middle to upper class, middle-aged men, based on demographic research. Chances are, advertisements for these products would not appear in Spin magazine. Choosing media is only one example of how demographics can help advertisers.

Psychographics tends to deal more generally with human behavior, including areas such as perception, learning, motives, attitudes and lifestyles. Psychographics goes beyond demographics in helping to explain complex behavior patterns. For instance, demographics might explore a question like: Why does one mother with a newborn use disposable diapers, whereas another mother chooses reusable cloth diapers? To try to explain the true motivations for behavior, advertisers look at a variety of dimensions, including activities, interests, hobbies, opinions, needs, values, attitudes and personality traits. Taken together, these elements give a much broader picture of a person than do demographic data.
Difficulty: 3 Page: 96-112   Key 1: S/A

104. Discuss the cognitive and connective schools of learning and the implications of each school for advertising.

Answer:
Typically, experts rely on two schools of thought to explain the learning process. The first approach focuses on cognitive or mental processes. The second approach focuses on behavioral conditioning. Cognitive theorists stress the importance of perception, problem solving, and insight and characterize people as problem solvers who go through a complex set of mental processes to analyze information. Advertisers that adopt the cognitive learning approach try to motivate by providing information that will aid a consumer's decision-making process. They might adopt an ad with a lot of copy, explaining why their product is better. The connective school of learning argues that people learn behavior by experiencing connections between stimuli and responses through classic conditioning or operant conditioning. The person's reward for certain behaviors is instrumental in this behavior learning process, so advertisers that adopt this view tend to emphasize that their brand provides greater rewards than other brands. For example, a cola might claim that it is the best tasting.
Difficulty: 2 Page: 104-105 Key 1: S

105. Explain the difference between low- and high-involvement decision-making.

Answer:
For the most part, consumers expend a great deal of effort on more expensive, personal, or emotion-laden products (such as automobiles, medical care, clothes and vacations). For the inexpensive, less exciting products that are purchased regularly, such as milk, gum, or soda, consumers tend to put little thought and effort into their decision. The former example is called a complex, high-involvement decision process, whereas the latter is known as a simple, low-involvement decision process. Product decisions that have high personal relevance and contain a high-perceived risk are high-involvement purchases and require complex decision-making. Products that are less relevant and offer low perceived risk require simple decision-making.
Difficulty: 1 Page: 112   Key 1: S/A

CHAPTER 5: STRATEGIC RESEARCH

MULTIPLE CHOICE

1. What two major sources of information from advertising can be developed?
   a. collective experience of the advertiser and the ad agency and formal research
   b. formal research and the government
   c. the government and the media
   d. collective experience of the advertiser and the ad agency and the government
   e. competitive analysis and the government

   Answer: a Difficulty: 2 Page: 119   Key 1: R

2. The most important source of information for developing advertising is:
   a. formal research.
   b. data compiled by the U.S. government.
   c. competitive analysis.
   d. collective and personal experience of the advertiser and ad agency.
   e. data from the media.

   Answer: d Difficulty: 2 Page: 119   Key 1: R

3. Advertising research whose purpose is to collect all relevant information needed to make advertising decisions is called:
   a. evaluative research.
   b. diagnostic research.
   c. primary research.
   d. decisional research.
   e. strategic research.

   Answer: e Difficulty: 2 Page: 119   Key 1: R

4. Advertising whose purpose is to evaluate the effectiveness of advertising is called:
   a. evaluative research.
   b. diagnostic research.
   c. strategic research.
   d. secondary research.

   Answer: a Difficulty: 2 Page: 119   Key 1: R

5. Exploratory research is an example of what kind of research?
   a. investigative
   b. strategic
   c. diagnostic
   d. evaluative
   e. exploratory

   Answer: b Difficulty: 2 Page: 119   Key 1: R

6. What are the major sources of information for advertising planning?
   a. experience and formal research
   b. secondary and primary research
   c. survey and informal research
   d. records and survey research
   e. informal and formal research

   Answer: a Difficulty: 2 Page: 119   Key 1: R

7. _____ is used to identify consumer needs, develop new products, evaluate pricing levels, assess distribution methods, and test the effectiveness of various promotional strategies.
   a. Marketing research
   b. Survey research
   c. Market research
   d. Advertising research
   e. Sales research

   Answer: a Difficulty: 2 Page: 119   Key 1: R

8. What type of research is used to gather information about a specific market?
   a. market research
   b. survey research
   c. marketing research
   d. advertising research
   e. sales research

   Answer: a Difficulty: 2 Page: 119   Key 1: R

9. Research that investigates all elements of the marketing mix is called:
   a. quantitative studies.
   b. qualitative studies.
   c. market research.
   d. marketing research.
   e. consumer research.

   Answer: d Difficulty: 2 Page: 119   Key 1: R

10. Which of the following is a source of formal research for use in developing advertising?
    a. trade associations
    b. research departments of advertising agencies
    c. government departments
    d. research departments of advertisers
    e. all of the above

    Answer: e Difficulty: 2 Page: 120   Key 1: R

11. Information that was originally collected by some other organization (and usually for some other purpose) is called:
    a. primary research.
    b. marketing research.
    c. strategic research.
    d. exploratory research.
    e. secondary research.

    Answer: e Difficulty: 2 Page: 120   Key 1: R

12. What are the two most important secondary research providers?
    a. A.C. Nielsen and Simmons Market Research Bureau
    b. Mediamark Research, Inc. and Arbitron
    c. FIND/SVP and Off-The-Shelf Publications, Inc.
    d. A.C. Nielsen and Arbitron
    e. Simmons Market Research Bureau and Standard Rate & Data Service

    Answer: c Difficulty: 3 Page: 120   Key 1: R

13. Which of the following is a secondary research source?
    a. FIND/SVP
    b. Simmons Market Research Bureau
    c. Mediamark Research, Inc.
    d. Off-The-Shelf Publications, Inc.
    e. all of the above

    Answer: e Difficulty: 2 Page: 120   Key 1: R

14. Some of the most frequent sources of secondary research data include all of the following EXCEPT:
    a. personal interviews of customers.
    b. government organizations.
    c. trade associations.
    d. research departments of advertisers.
    e. primary research suppliers.

    Answer: a Difficulty: 2 Page: 120   Key 1: R

15. _____ is gathered in interviewing, observing, and recording the behavior of those who purchase, or influence the purchase of, industrial consumer goods and services.
    a. Exploratory research
    b. Primary research
    c. Secondary research
    d. Survey research
    e. Strategic research

    Answer: b Difficulty: 2 Page: 121   Key 1: R

16. Which of the following is a source of both product usage information and media usage information?
    a. A.C. Nielsen
    b. Simmons Market Research Bureau
    c. Burke, Inc.
    d. Savage, Inc.
    e. FIND/SVP

    Answer: b Difficulty: 3 Page: 121   Key 1: R

17. Why did ad agencies provide advertising and marketing research to clients in the 1950s?
    a. Advertising and marketing research were not considered very important
    b. Low profit margins of advertisers made it necessary
    c. Ad agency profit margins allowed the agencies to provide research at no extra cost
    d. Clients' advertising departments were well developed but still needed help
    e. Outside research suppliers were too expensive

    Answer: c Difficulty: 2 Page: 122   Key 1: R

18. Specialized libraries maintained by advertising agencies that provide access to reference volumes, such as dictionaries, encyclopedias, atlases, cookbooks, books of famous quotations, and trade and general newspapers and magazines and other sources of information needed in developing advertising are called:
    a. market research departments.
    b. virtual libraries.
    c. morgues.
    d. information centers.

    Answer: d Difficulty: 2 Page: 124   Key 1: R

19. The major problem with information generated through advertising research is:
    a. too much information.
    b. too little information.
    c. not specific enough.
    d. too specific.
    e. not very useful.

    Answer: a Difficulty: 2 Page: 124   Key 1: R

20. Where did the concept of the account planner originate?
    a. United States
    b. Japan
    c. England
    d. Germany
    e. France

    Answer: c Difficulty: 2 Page: 124   Key 1: R

21. Research that seeks to understand how and why people think and behave as
    they do is called:
    a. quantitative research.
    b. qualitative research.
    c. exploratory research.
    d. diagnostic research.
    e. market research.

    Answer: b Difficulty: 2 Page: 124   Key 1: R

22. If data were reported as numbers and as a percentage of the total, the
    data would be classified as which of the following types of data?
    a. primary data
    b. secondary data
    c. qualitative data
    d. quantitative data
    e. none of the above

    Answer: d Difficulty: 1 Page: 124   Key 1: R

23. The creation, implementation, and modification of the strategy on which
    creative work is based and the generation, selection, and interposition
    of the research evidence at each stage of the advertising process is the
    responsibility of the:
    a. strategic analyzer.
    b. account planner.
    c. strategy planner.
    d. creative director.
    e. research coordinator.

    Answer: b Difficulty: 1 Page: 124   Key 1: R

24. When a survey reports spontaneous comments by consumers, it is including
    what kind of data?
    a. quantitative
    b. secondary
    c. exploratory
    d. qualitative
    e. experimental

    Answer: d Difficulty: 2 Page: 124   Key 1: R

25. What is the core craft skill in account planning?
    a. collecting research from secondary sources
    b. tact in presentation of ads
    c. creativity in maintaining information centers
    d. organizing huge amounts of relevant information
    e. graphic design of advertising

    Answer: d Difficulty: 2 Page: 124   Key 1: R

26. What is another name for the strategy document?
    a. creative brief
    b. account planning document
    c. competitive analysis
    d. situation analysis
    e. marketing objective

    Answer: a Difficulty: 2 Page: 125   Key 1: R

27. What part of the strategy document deals with a product or company's competitive situation, sales history, and market share?
    a. marketing research
    b. the target audience
    c. advertising research
    d. advertising objective
    e. marketing objective

    Answer: e Difficulty: 2 Page: 125   Key 1: R

28. What are the major parts of the strategy document?
    a. marketing objective, target audience, the promise
    b. advertising objective, marketing objective, target audience, the promise, creative strategy
    c. marketing research, market objective, advertising objective, target audience, the promise
    d. marketing objective, the product, target audience, the promise, brand personality
    e. marketing research, market objective, target audience, the promise, brand personality

    Answer: d Difficulty: 2 Page: 125   Key 1: S

29. All of the following are major parts of the strategy document EXCEPT:
    a. target audience.
    b. evaluation.
    c. product.
    d. marketing objective.
    e. brand personality.

    Answer: b Difficulty: 2 Page: 125   Key 1: R

30. The product section of the strategy document includes:
    a. goal for the campaign.
    b. results of product tests.
    c. market share of the brand.
    d. review of competitive situation.

    Answer: b Difficulty: 2 Page: 125   Key 1: R

31. What part of the strategy document would include consumers' perceptions
    of the brand and its major competitors, and tests of reactions to the
    brand's and its competitors' advertisements?
    a. market research
    b. the marketing objective
    c. the product
    d. the target audience
    e. the promise

    Answer: c Difficulty: 2 Page: 125   Key 1: R

32. What part of the strategy document includes surveys that reveal the age,
    income, education, and geographical distribution of consumers who might
    be persuaded to adopt the brand?
    a. marketing research
    b. the marketing objective
    c. the target audience
    d. the promise
    e. none of the above

    Answer: c Difficulty: 2 Page: 125   Key 1: R

33. The marketing objective section of the strategy document includes:
    a. competitive situation, sales history, and market share of the brand
       and major competitors.
    b. consumer reactions to questions such as what would the product be
       like if it was a person.
    c. surveys that reveal the age, income, education, etc. of the consumers
       who might be persuaded to adopt the brand.
    d. facts about the product that are likely to make the product more
       acceptable to consumers.
    e. consumers' perceptions of the brand and its major competitors.

    Answer: a Difficulty: 2 Page: 125   Key 1: R

34. What part of the strategy document would include the reward that the consumer can obtain by buying or using the product?
    a. market research
    b. the promise
    c. the marketing objective
    d. the target audience
    e. the product

    Answer: b Difficulty: 2 Page: 126   Key 1: R

35. What part of the strategy document would include consumer reactions to questions such as "What would the product be like if it were a person?"
    a. brand image
    b. product tone
    c. product character
    d. brand personality
    e. product image

    Answer: d Difficulty: 2 Page: 126   Key 1: R

36. The brand personality section of the strategy document includes:
    a. competitive situation, sales history, and market share of the brand and major competitors.
    b. consumer reactions to questions such as what would the product be like if it was a person.
    c. surveys that reveal the age, income, education, etc., of the consumers who might be persuaded to adopt the brand.
    d. facts about the product that are likely to make the product more acceptable to consumers.
    e. consumers' perceptions of the brand and its major competitors.

    Answer: b Difficulty: 2 Page: 126   Key 1: R

37. Research used to identify the best advertising approach from a set of alternatives is called:
    a. copy testing.
    b. diagnostic research.
    c. exploratory research.
    d. concept testing.
    e. decision research.

    Answer: b Difficulty: 2 Page: 128   Key 1: R

38. The target audience's evaluation of alternative creative strategies is called:
    a. diagnostic research.
    b. audience research.
    c. early feedback.
    d. creative research.
    e. consumer research.

    Answer: c Difficulty: 2 Page: 128   Key 1: R

39. McDonald's is trying out three new advertising approaches for its breakfast biscuits in selected geographic areas. The approach that performs the best will be used nationally. McDonald's is:
    a. collecting secondary data.
    b. using a marketing research experiment.
    c. doing concept testing.
    d. conducting diagnostic research.
    e. performing copy tests.

    Answer: d Difficulty: 3 Page: 128   Key 1: A

40. The method used to collect data from people by telephone or by mail is called:
    a. contact method.
    b. intercept survey.
    c. secondary data.
    d. quantitative data.
    e. communication test.

    Answer: a Difficulty: 2 Page: 128   Key 1: R

41. When the questions are relatively simple and the questionnaire is short you can use a:
    a. mail survey.
    b. personal interview.
    c. telephone survey.
    d. direct observation.
    e. communication test.

    Answer: c Difficulty: 2 Page: 128   Key 1: R

42. In which one of the following does the researcher ask questions of the respondent in person?
    a. mail survey
    b. personal interview
    c. telephone survey
    d. direct observation
    e. all of the above

    Answer: b Difficulty: 2 Page: 128   Key 1: R

43. Which of the following is a longer and more in-depth form of data gathering?
    a. mail survey
    b. personal interview
    c. telephone survey
    d. direct observation
    e. all of the above

    Answer: a Difficulty: 2 Page: 128   Key 1: R

44. Focus groups used to assess early advertising ideas are a type of:
    a. copy test.
    b. research.
    c. concept testing.
    d. market research.
    e. communication test.

    Answer: c Difficulty: 2 Page: 128   Key 1: A

45. A garden tool company is preparing a big advertising campaign and has three possible approaches in mind. It invites 18 to 20 members of the target market in, shows them the ads, and gets their reactions. This is an example of what kind of research?
    a. market research
    b. secondary research
    c. concept testing
    d. copy test
    e. strategic research

    Answer: c Difficulty: 2 Page: 128   Key 1: A

46. Research that uses structured interview forms to ask large numbers of people the same questions is called:
    a. exploratory research.
    b. survey research.
    c. experimental research.
    d. direct observation research.
    e. market research.

    Answer: b Difficulty: 2 Page: 128   Key 1: R

47. A marketing researcher needs to know what everyone between the ages of 25 and 40 thinks about the Ford Probe. Everyone in the target group is called:
    a. the sampling frame.
    b. the sample.
    c. the universe.
    d. a focus group.
    e. the population.

    Answer: e Difficulty: 2 Page: 129   Key 1: A

48. A selection of people who are identified as representative of the larger population is called:
   a. focus group.
   b. population.
   c. sample.
   d. target audience.
   e. market.

   Answer: c Difficulty: 2 Page: 129   Key 1: R

49. What is the advantage of direct observation research?
   a. gives insight into why someone does something
   b. reveals what people actually do as opposed to what they say they do
   c. can probe feelings and attitudes
   d. reveals the cause for behavior
   e. all of the above

   Answer: b Difficulty: 2 Page: 129   Key 1: R

50. What can in-depth interview research tell advertising researchers and account executives?
   a. probe attitudes, feelings, and behaviors such as the purchase of a product
   b. general attitudes and feelings of the target audience
   c. whether one advertising approach will work better than another will in a campaign
   d. all of the above
   e. none of the above

   Answer: a Difficulty: 2 Page: 130   Key 1: R

51. What can content analysis tell advertising researchers and account executives?
   a. how people feel about the product or its advertising
   b. what people say they do rather than why they do
   c. how well an ad conveyed the intended message
   d. provide clues to what competitors are thinking through their advertising
   e. whether or not the target market noticed an ad

   Answer: d Difficulty: 2 Page: 130   Key 1: R

52. Research that analyzes various dimensions of a message such as length or type of headline is:
   a. experimental research.
   b. exploratory research.
   c. survey research.
   d. content analysis.
   e. concept testing.

   Answer: d Difficulty: 2 Page: 130   Key 1: R

53. Analyzing competitors' advertising messages including summaries of the most used slogans, appeals, and images as well as competitors' approaches and strategies is what kind of research?
    a. content analysis
    b. concept testing
    c. survey
    d. diagnostic
    e. secondary

    Answer: a Difficulty: 2 Page: 130   Key 1: R

54. What research technique uses a one-on-one interview to probe feelings, attitudes and behaviors such as decision making?
    a. focus group
    b. survey
    c. verbatim
    d. in-depth interview
    e. exploratory research

    Answer: d Difficulty: 2 Page: 130   Key 1: R

55. Which one of the following is a type of field research in which the researcher is in a natural setting where they record consumer behavior?
    a. intercept survey
    b. personal interview
    c. communication test
    d. direct observation
    e. experiment

    Answer: d Difficulty: 2 Page: 130   Key 1: R

56. An aisle study would fall under which one of the following research categories?
    a. intercept study
    b. personal interview
    c. communication test
    d. direct observation
    e. experiment

    Answer: d Difficulty: 2 Page: 130   Key 1: A

57. The biggest drawback to direct observation is that it shows:
    a. why it is happening but not what is happening.
    b. what is happening but not why.
    c. when it is happening but not why.
    d. who was doing it but not when.
    e. what is happening but not who was doing it.

    Answer: b Difficulty: 3 Page: 130   Key 1: A

58. Bob has been assigned to sit behind a stack of boxes and count the number of people who stick their finger through the toilet paper package to feel the tissues before they buy it. Bob is doing:
a. secondary research.
b. direct observation.
c. experimental research.
d. communication test.
e. intercept survey.

Answer: b Difficulty: 2 Page: 130   Key 1: A

59. _____ is a research method used to stimulate a group of people to talk candidly about some topic with one another. The interviewer sets up a general topic and then lets conversation develop as group interaction takes over.
a. Focus group
b. Telephone survey
c. Exploratory research
d. Verbatim research
e. In-depth interview

Answer: a Difficulty: 2 Page: 130   Key 1: R

60. _____ is a type of qualitative research.
a. Experimental research
b. Focus group
c. Survey research
d. Content analysis

Answer: b Difficulty: 2 Page: 130   Key 1: R

61. Which of the following is a type of quantitative research?
a. in-depth interview
b. focus group
c. communication test
d. direct observation
e. none of the above

Answer: d Difficulty: 2 Page: 130   Key 1: A

62. Which of the following is a problem with the use of focus groups?
a. samples are too large
b. outcome depends heavily on skill of the moderator
c. information is too personal to be useful
d. too much information to use effectively
e. none of the above

Answer: b Difficulty: 2 Page: 130   Key 1: A

63. What research technique is designed to answer questions such as "Did the ad convey the intended message?" or "How did consumers react to the message?" through the use of intensive interviewing and questioning about ads usually in research centers at shopping malls?
    a. focus group
    b. survey
    c. communication test
    d. experiment
    e. in-depth interview

    Answer: c Difficulty: 2 Page: 131   Key 1: R

64. Which one of the following research methods is a one-on-one interview usually conducted in a shopping mall that supplies facilities? The potential participants are asked to participate in a "study of consumers' opinions," and are sometimes offered a small fee for their cooperation.
    a. in-depth interview
    b. qualitative interview
    c. concept testing
    d. communication tests
    e. focus group

    Answer: d Difficulty: 2 Page: 131   Key 1: R

65. Communications tests can usually provide answers to which of the following questions?
    a. Did the advertisement convey the message it was intended to convey?
    b. Did the advertisement convey any messages it was not intended to convey?
    c. How did consumers react to the characters, the setting, the message, and the tone of the advertising?
    d. all of the above
    e. none of the above

    Answer: d Difficulty: 2 Page: 131   Key 1: R

66. Tests that evaluate advertisements by measuring their sales influence are known as:
    a. frame-by-frame tests.
    b. direct-response counts.
    c. persuasion tests.
    d. in-market tests.
    e. none of the above.

    Answer: d Difficulty: 2 Page: 136   Key 1: R

TRUE/FALSE

67. Understanding of consumers can come only from research.
    a. True
    b. False

    Answer: b Difficulty: 2 Page: 119   Key 1: R

68. A very important part of advertising information comes from the personal and professional experiences of the professionals who develop and evaluate advertising.
    a. True
    b. False

    Answer: a Difficulty: 2 Page: 119   Key 1: R

69. Marketing research applies to all elements of the marketing mix.
    a. True
    b. False

    Answer: a Difficulty: 2 Page: 119   Key 1: A

70. Research is the backbone of advertising and marketing.
    a. True
    b. False

    Answer: a Difficulty: 2 Page: 119   Key 1: A

71. The U.S Government is an excellent source of secondary research information.
    a. True
    b. False

    Answer: a Difficulty: 1 Page: 120   Key 1: R

72. It is very rare for a large advertiser to have a marketing research department of its own.
    a. True
    b. False

    Answer: b Difficulty: 2 Page: 122   Key 1: R

73. Mediamark Research, Inc. surveys include items on product consumption and usage as well as media usage.
    a. True
    b. False

    Answer: a Difficulty: 2 Page: 121   Key 1: R

74. Simmons Market Research Bureau is a secondary research data source.
    a. True
    b. False

    Answer: a Difficulty: 2 Page: 121   Key 1: R

75. Most large advertisers rely on research firms and do not have marketing research departments.
    a. True
    b. False

    Answer: b Difficulty: 2 Page: 121   Key 1: A

76. Primary research is information collected from original sources.
    a. True
    b. False

    Answer: a Difficulty: 2 Page: 121   Key 1: R

77. By 1950, all the major advertising agencies had a professional research department.
    a. True
    b. False

    Answer: a Difficulty: 2 Page: 122   Key 1: R

78. Prior to the 1960s many companies' marketing research departments were relatively underdeveloped and advertisers relied heavily on advertising agencies for marketing research.
    a. True
    b. False

    Answer: a Difficulty: 2 Page: 124   Key 1: A

79. By the end of the 1960s, most advertisers had effective marketing research departments that took over evaluative testing of advertising.
    a. True
    b. False

    Answer: a Difficulty: 2 Page: 124   Key 1: R

80. Surprisingly, with all the emphasis on the need and value of research, the problem in strategically planning an advertising campaign is still too little information.
    a. True
    b. False

    Answer: b Difficulty: 2 Page: 124   Key 1: A

81. In developing an ad campaign the problem is seldom too little information, but too much.
    a. True
    b. False

    Answer: a Difficulty: 2 Page: 124   Key 1: R

82. Innovations such as integrated marketing communication are making account planning obsolete.
    a. True
    b. False

    Answer: b Difficulty: 2 Page: 125   Key 1: A

83. The most important research information usually goes into a creative concept document that is, in a rough sense, a plan for the campaign.
    a. True
    b. False

    Answer: b Difficulty: 2 Page: 125   Key 1: R

84. In the strategy document the marketing objective should be specific.
    a. True
    b. False

    Answer: a Difficulty: 2 Page: 125   Key 1: R

85. Someone in the agency research department or the account group collects and organizes a vast array of facts, distills those facts into a strategy document and hands that document over to previously uninformed writers and art directors who then go off and make some advertising.
    a. True
    b. False

    Answer: b Difficulty: 1 Page: 125   Key 1: A

86. Diagnostic research provides exposure to real consumers and opens the possibility that potentially excellent ideas may be rejected.
    a. True
    b. False

    Answer: a Difficulty: 2 Page: 128   Key 1: A

87. Diagnostic research provides a valuable safeguard against the possibility that advertising will fail to convey the intended message.
    a. True
    b. False

    Answer: a Difficulty: 2 Page: 128   Key 1: R

88. Diagnostic research makes it possible to hear what real consumers think about advertising.
a. True
b. False

Answer: b Difficulty: 2 Page: 128   Key 1: R

89. Direct observation has the advantage of revealing what people actually do, as distinguished from what people say.
a. True
b. False

Answer: a Difficulty: 2 Page: 129   Key 1: R

90. A problem with focus group interviews is that assertive and articulate respondents sometimes dominate the conversation, swaying others' opinions and decreasing the likelihood that others will express their true feelings.
a. True
b. False

Answer: a Difficulty: 2 Page: 130   Key 1: R

91. The outcome of a focus group depends heavily upon the skill of the moderator.
a. True
b. False

Answer: a Difficulty: 2 Page: 130   Key 1: A

92. Memory tests are based on the assumption that an ad leaves a mental residue with people exposed to it.
a. True
b. False

Answer: a Difficulty: 2 Page: 132   Key 1: R

93. Recall tests have reliability, but may not have validity.
a. True
b. False

Answer: a Difficulty: 2 Page: 133   Key 1: R

94. Researchers first used recognition tests to evaluate TV advertising.
a. True
b. False

Answer: b Difficulty: 2 Page: 133   Key 1: R

95. Persuasion tests are also called attitude change tests.
    a. True
    b. False

    Answer: a Difficulty: 2 Page: 133   Key 1: R

96. Persuasion tests tend to be very inexpensive.
    a. True
    b. False

    Answer: a Difficulty: 2 Page: 134   Key 1: R

97. Direct-response counts and inquiry tests rely on two very different test formats.
    a. True
    b. False

    Answer: b Difficulty: 3 Page: 134   Key 1: R

98. In-market tests evaluate ads by measuring their influence on sales.
    a. True
    b. False

    Answer: a Difficulty: 2 Page: 136   Key 1: R

99. Brand tracking is a new kind of advertising research.
    a. True
    b. False

    Answer: a Difficulty: 2 Page: 137   Key 1: R

100. One weakness of frame-by-frame tests is their high cost.
     a. True
     b. False

     Answer: a Difficulty: 2 Page: 138   Key 1: R

ESSAY

101. Compare and contrast primary and secondary research. Give examples of sources for each.

Answer:
Strategic research is an information-gathering process that enhances the design of a creative strategy. It begins with a review of secondary research, which is an exploration of all available published information. When advertisers get a new account, they start by reading all available material on the product, company, industry and competition: sales reports, annual reports, complaint letters, and trade articles about the industry available from a variety of sources, including government organizations, trade associations and secondary research suppliers. They look for a new insight, which might ultimately require customized, primary research. Research firms that specialize in interviewing, observing, recording and analyzing the behavior of those who purchase or influence the purchase of a good or service are called primary research suppliers, an extremely diverse industry ranging from A.C. Nielsen, which employs more than 45,000 workers, to one-person entrepreneurs who conduct focus groups and individual interviews.

Difficulty: 2 Page: 119-122 Key 1: R/S

102. Describe the role of the account planner in a typical ad campaign.

Answer:
A typical ad campaign might be influenced by information from many sources, including outside research suppliers and the agency's account planning department. Surprisingly, the problem is not too little information, but too much. The account planner must sift through qualitative data, which seeks to understand how consumers behave and why, and quantitative data, which includes numerical data such as exposure to ads, purchases, and other market-related events. The account planner must also separate the potentially relevant material and put the outcome into a format that decision makers and creatives can use. Planners also generate the advertising strategy and its implementation in the creative work. The ability to organize huge amounts of information and to make that information relevant is one of the most important skills they can have. Account planners typically play a major role in every facet of the agency's work on his or her brand.

Difficulty: 1 Page: 124-125 Key 1: S/R

103. Describe the five parts of the strategy document.

Answer:
The strategy document consists of the marketing objective, the product section, the target audience section, the promise section and the support section.

The marketing objective reviews the competitive situation and establishes a goal for the campaign. It includes past and present sales figures; market shares of the brand and of its major competitors; competitors' advertising and promotional resources, tactics and practices; and any other information about the brand that may lead to a prediction of early success or risk of failure.

The product section includes the results of surveys, consumers' perceptions of the brand and its major competitors, and tests of or reactions to the brand's and its competitors' advertisements, promotions, retail displays, and packaging---any facts, opinions, perceptions or reactions to the product that might fuel an advertising campaign.

The target audience section provides a demographic and psychographic description of the campaign's target audience. The demographic data comes from secondary sources or from surveys. The psychographic portion comes from attitudes and opinions surveys, in-depth interviews, etc.---all of which help paint a portrait of the target consumer as a person.

The promise section tells writers and art directors which reward, out of many possibilities, the advertising should promise. The support section indicates the facts about the product or the brand's attributes that are likely to make that promise most acceptable to users.

When a brand has a winning personality, its advertising should perpetuate and reinforce that personality. When a brand has a less than desirable personality, advertising should work to remedy the problem. These issues are dealt with the in the brand personality section.

Difficulty: 2 Page: 125-127   Key 1: R/S

104. Choose three of the basic research methods (survey, experiment, content analysis, in-depth interview, or focus group). Describe each of the three you have selected, and discuss the advantages and disadvantages of each.

Answer:
Content analysis includes a systematic audit of competitors' advertisements. These audits may include only informal summaries of the slogans, appeals and images used most often or they might include more formal and systematic tabulation of competitors' approaches and strategies.

In-depth interviews are used to probe feelings, attitudes and behaviors such as decision making. The insights can reveal how typical members of the target audience respond to the product, to competitors' products, to the advertiser's marketing efforts and to competitors' advertising and marketing activities.

A focus group is another method used to structure qualitative research. It is like an in-depth interview, except that it involves a group rather than an individual. The objective is to stimulate people to talk candidly about some topic with others.

In-depth interviews and focus groups provide valuable feedback at early stages in the creative process. However, the samples of consumers are usually so small that they usually do not represent the whole audience. Results may be skewed toward a certain market segment. Also, because the advertising ideas submitted to early evaluation are usually very rough, they might omit some important element that would make them work better in the context of a full campaign. A problem specific to focus groups is the fact that one or two people may dominate the group, thus skewing opinions.

Difficulty: 2 Page: 126-131   Key 1: S

105. Discuss the thinking behind brand tracking, including how it is done.

Answer:
Brand tracking is a new kind of advertising research. The underlying assumption of this kind of research is that with fragmented media and an abundance of high-quality products, tracking the brand is more important than tracking the ad. The relationship with the customer is built in large part on the brand's values rather than the product's attributes. Instead of arguing that a product works better, advertisers should involve consumers by showing them that their brand means more. The thinking is that advertising and other marketing communications should involve customers in the brand's values so they are more favorably disposed toward it. "Brand commitment" is a spectrum that runs from rejection of the brand through various levels of consideration to commitment. The precise criteria vary by market, but the general spectrum applies for every brand in every market. In addition, this measure is considered in the context of the advertiser's purpose. There are four purpose categories: sales response, persuasion, salience and involvement.

Difficulty: 2 Page: 137   Key 1: R/S

CHAPTER 6: HOW ADVERTISING WORKS

MULTIPLE CHOICE

1. All of the following statements about a *Parade* magazine survey are true EXCEPT:
   a. 4.8% of the respondents believe advertising is very influential in motivating other people.
   b. Ads were rated first when respondents were asked what led them to try new food products.
   c. Respondents believe they are relatively immune to advertising.
   d. 13% of the respondents say advertising is very influential on their food purchases.
   e. Coupons were rated first in prompting respondents to try new food products.

   Answer: b Difficulty: 2 Page: 146   Key 1: R

2. What are the keys to effective advertising, according to Keith Reinhard, President of DDB Needham?
   a. creativity, originality, and impact
   b. originality, impact, and creativity
   c. responsibility, creativity, and impact
   d. impression, creativity, and clarity
   e. impact, originality, and relevance

   Answer: e Difficulty: 3 Page: 147   Key 1: R

3. The external factors of the advertising process includes:
   a. marketing strategy.
   b. attitudes of target consumers.
   c. other marketing communication.
   d. history of target consumers.
   e. all of the above

   Answer: e Difficulty: 2 Page: 147   Key 1: R

4. Substantial evidence suggests that many consumers hold a _____ attitude towards advertising.
   a. positive
   b. negative
   c. indifferent
   d. enthusiastic
   e. none of the above

   Answer: b Difficulty: 1 Page: 147   Key 1: R

5. What do people look for whey they watch television, browse through a magazine or read a newspaper?
   a. ads
   b. editorial information
   c. useful information
   d. striking graphics/pictures
   e. sexy pictures

   Answer: c Difficulty: 2 Page: 148   Key 1: R

6. Most people give _____ attention to advertising.
   a. high level
   b. undivided
   c. minimal
   d. scant
   e. none of the above

   Answer: d Difficulty: 1 Page: 148   Key 1: R

7. Media messages become entangled in what cognitive psychologists call our:
   a. fragmented mind set.
   b. data bit confusion.
   c. flash in the pan syndrome.
   d. information processing.
   e. unprocessed sector snarl.

   Answer: d Difficulty: 2 Page: 148   Key 1: R

8. When we see editorial information and advertisements we:
   a. do not treat them much differently.
   b. tune in the editorial first.
   c. tune in the advertisement first.
   d. develop a cognitive discourse.
   e. process our fragmented mind set.

   Answer: a Difficulty: 2 Page: 148   Key 1: A

9. When people do not even scan the ads that do not interest them, this is called:
   a. disjointed mind set.
   b. avoidance.
   c. repression.
   d. transference.
   e. transmutation.

   Answer: b Difficulty: 2 Page: 150   Key 1: A

10. The ability of a particular advertising message to reach a target audience depends mostly on:
    a. the effectiveness of the media plan and strategy.
    b. the geographic location of the audience.
    c. the geographic distribution of the ad campaign.
    d. effective ad copy and images.
    e. all of the above

    Answer: a Difficulty: 2 Page: 150   Key 1: R

11. The creation of an advertisement begins with:
    a. an analysis of the marketing strategy.
    b. an analysis of the marketing target.
    c. an analysis of the target audience.
    d. an analysis of the media strategy.
    e. all of the above

    Answer: e Difficulty: 2 Page: 150   Key 1: S

12. All of the following are basic psychological categories EXCEPT:
    a. memorability.
    b. persuasion.
    c. understanding.
    d. attention.
    e. perception.

    Answer: d Difficulty: 2 Page: 151   Key 1: S

13. One of the biggest challenges for advertisers is:
    a. to purchase effective media.
    b. to get consumers to notice their messages.
    c. to be nonintrusive.
    d. to avoid stopping power.
    e. all of the above.

    Answer: b Difficulty: 2 Page: 151   Key 1: A

14. What is the first step in perception?
    a. attention
    b. exposure
    c. intrusion
    d. memory
    e. awareness

    Answer: b Difficulty: 2 Page: 152   Key 1: R

15. First the message has to be in a medium that your target sees, reads, watches, or listens to. In addition, the message must survive the initial scan-and-avoid decision. This is called:
    a. attention.
    b. exposure.
    c. awareness.
    d. impression.
    e. impact.

    Answer: b Difficulty: 2 Page: 152   Key 1: R

16. When the mind is engaged, and focusing on something, this is called:
    a. attention.
    b. awareness.
    c. recognition.
    d. impression.
    e. impact.

    Answer: a Difficulty: 1 Page: 152   Key 1: R

17. A trigger:
    a. catches the target audience's attention.
    b. encourages avoidance.
    c. is the minimum requirement of perception.
    d. can often alienate audience attention.
    e. all of the above

    Answer: a Difficulty: 1 Page: 152   Key 1: R

18. Something in the message that "catches" attention or something within the reader or viewer that makes him or her "lock onto" a particular message is called:
    a. peg.
    b. impact.
    c. intrusiveness.
    d. tag.
    e. trigger.

    Answer: e Difficulty: 2 Page: 152   Key 1: R

19. Ads that stop consumers from scanning are:
    a. high in intrusiveness.
    b. relevant to the consumer.
    c. very original.
    d. all of the above

    Answer: d Difficulty: 2 Page: 153   Key 1: R

20. Which of the following would catch someone's attention and get them to read the ad?
   a. sound effects
   b. startling illustration
   c. strong headline
   d. music
   e. all of the above

   Answer: e Difficulty: 2 Page: 153   Key 1: R

21. Getting attention involves more than just attracting the notice of the viewer. To nail down consumers' attention while they are in the scanning mode, an ad needs:
   a. pulling power.
   b. locking power.
   c. creativity.
   d. stopping power.
   e. all of the above

   Answer: d Difficulty: 2 Page: 153   Key 1: R

22. Which of the following is characteristic of intrusive advertising?
   a. use bold effects
   b. short
   c. use captivating ideas
   d. use contrasting techniques
   e. all of the above

   Answer: e Difficulty: 2 Page: 153   Key 1: R

23. The quality of a message that is designed to get and force attention is called:
   a. impressiveness.
   b. originality.
   c. intrusiveness.
   d. contrast.
   e. impact.

   Answer: c Difficulty: 2 Page: 153   Key 1: R

24. What is the function of originality in great advertising?
   a. to make an impression
   b. to catch attention
   c. to ensure memorability
   d. to produce understanding
   e. to hold attention

   Answer: b Difficulty: 2 Page: 153   Key 1: R

25. When impact is created with a fresh, novel and unusual advertisement designed to capture attention, this is called:
    a. association.
    b. contrast.
    c. originality.
    d. interest.
    e. all of the above

    Answer: c Difficulty: 2 Page: 153   Key 1: R

26. This was a program that allowed copywriters and art directors to have their ideas informally tested by researchers in the early stages of concept development.
    a. The Risk's clinic
    b. The Clinic
    c. The Proving Grounds
    d. The Risk Lab
    e. none of the above

    Answer: d Difficulty: 2 Page: 153   Key 1: R

27. What is the purpose of Young and Rubicam's Risk Lab?
    a. allow creative people to test ideas informally early in their development
    b. decide the best approach from among several alternative creative approaches
    c. get feedback from actual target audience members
    d. provide live copy testing in a real market
    e. all of the above

    Answer: a Difficulty: 2 Page: 153   Key 1: R

28. When the message has made an impression on the viewer this is called:
    a. attention.
    b. relevance.
    c. interest.
    d. awareness.
    e. perception.

    Answer: d Difficulty: 2 Page: 153   Key 1: R

29. What usually creates interest?
    a. relevance and personal involvement
    b. personal involvement and curiosity
    c. human interest and relevance
    d. curiosity and creativity
    e. creativity and human interest

    Answer: b Difficulty: 2 Page: 153   Key 1: R

30. We pay attention to advertisements that:
    a. speak to our personal concerns.
    b. are entertaining.
    c. are different.
    d. provide useful information.
    e. all of the above

    Answer: e Difficulty: 2 Page: 153   Key 1: S

31. What is the ultimate objective of an advertisement?
    a. attention to the ad
    b. originality
    c. awareness of the product
    d. memorability of the ad
    e. creativeness of the ad

    Answer: c Difficulty: 2 Page: 153   Key 1: R

32. When people want to hear or read about themselves and the things they care about, it is called:
    a. product interest.
    b. cognition.
    c. human interest.
    d. built-in interest.
    e. relevance.

    Answer: e Difficulty: 2 Page: 155   Key 1: R

33. Advertising for low-involvement products usually provides:
    a. demonstrations.
    b. lots of factual information.
    c. detailed explanations.
    d. simple slogans.
    e. all of the above

    Answer: d Difficulty: 2 Page: 156   Key 1: R

34. The intensity of the consumer's interest in a product refers to:
    a. understanding.
    b. conviction.
    c. involvement.
    d. persuasion.
    e. relevance.

    Answer: c Difficulty: 2 Page: 156   Key 1: R

35. Advertising for high-involvement products usually provides:
    a. simple slogans.
    b. lots of factual information.
    c. images.
    d. emotional information.
    e. all of the above

    Answer: b Difficulty: 2 Page: 156   Key 1: R

36. _____ is a conscious effort to make sense of the information being presented. While attention can be a relatively passive response, this involves an active response from the audience.
    a. Learning
    b. Information processing
    c. Interest
    d. Understanding
    e. Association

    Answer: d Difficulty: 2 Page: 156   Key 1: R

37. _____ makes a connection in the consumers' mind. Advertisers use it to get people to know something by linking the product with something such as an envied lifestyle or person—something they aspire to, respect, value, or appreciate.
    a. Understanding
    b. Association
    c. Memory
    d. Comparison

    Answer: b Difficulty: 2 Page: 157   Key 1: R

38. Literary tools such as definition, explanation, demonstration, comparison and contrast are designed to stimulate:
    a. understanding.
    b. interest.
    c. memory.
    d. knowledge.

    Answer: a Difficulty: 2 Page: 156   Key 1: A

39. If understanding is a key objective in the design of an advertising message, with what kind of information will you probably use?
    a. emotional
    b. human interest
    c. outrageous effects
    d. factual
    e. all of the above

    Answer: d Difficulty: 3 Page: 153   Key 1: A

40. Something that moves people by making the product attractive or interesting is called a/an:
    a. theme.
    b. persuasion.
    c. sales message.
    d. mnemonic.
    e. appeal.

    Answer: e Difficulty: 2 Page: 158   Key 1: R

41. People's opinions are built on a complex structure of attitudes. Advertising that seeks to affect this complex structure of attitudes will usually attempt to accomplish one of three things. Which of the following is NOT one of the three things listed by the text?
    a. attack the opinion one has of a competing product
    b. establish a new opinion where none has existed before
    c. reinforce an existing opinion
    d. change an existing opinion

    Answer: a Difficulty: 1 Page: 158   Key 1: A

42. Entertainment is important to advertising in developing:
    a. relevance.
    b. likability.
    c. originality.
    d. persuasion.
    e. understanding.

    Answer: b Difficulty: 2 Page: 159   Key 1: R

43. An existing positive opinion held by customers about the product or service that leads to repeat sales is called:
    a. customer loyalty.
    b. product personality.
    c. brand appeal.
    d. brand loyalty.
    e. brand image.

    Answer: d Difficulty: 2 Page: 159   Key 1: R

44. What most affects the intensity of consumer response to an advertising message, especially in terms of memorability?
    a. argument
    b. music
    c. emotion
    d. likability
    e. reason-why

    Answer: c Difficulty: 3 Page: 160   Key 1: A

45. Doing this is very difficult and may require complete rebuilding of the entire attitude structure.
    a. destroying the opinion one has of a competing product
    b. establishing a new opinion where none has existed before
    c. reinforcing an existing attitude
    d. changing an opinion based on conviction

    Answer: d Difficulty: 3 Page: 160   Key 1: R

46. A particularly strong belief has been anchored firmly in consumers' attitude structure. Which one of the following is built on strong rational arguments that use such techniques as test results, before and after visuals, and demonstrations to prove something?
    a. goals
    b. conviction
    c. incentives
    d. emotions
    e. an argument

    Answer: b Difficulty: 2 Page: 160   Key 1: R

47. Which of the following is important to build conviction?
    a. demonstration
    b. test results
    c. strong rational arguments
    d. before and after visuals
    e. all of the above

    Answer: e Difficulty: 2 Page: 160   Key 1: R

48. What three kinds of power might an ad have?
    a. attention power, exposure power, and creative power
    b. locking power, pulling power, and stopping power
    c. creativity, originality, and impact
    d. stopping power, holding power, and persuasion power
    e. originality, relevance, and impact

    Answer: b Difficulty: 3 Page: 160   Key 1: R

49. The ability to remember specific information content of a message is called:
    a. recall.
    b. recognition.
    c. awareness.
    d. impression.
    e. attention.

    Answer: a Difficulty: 2 Page: 161   Key 1: R

50. The "umbrella" theme that connects a series of ads in a campaign for a brand is called:
    a. tagline.
    b. jingle.
    c. repetition.
    d. slogan.
    e. mnemonic.

    Answer: d Difficulty: 2 Page: 161   Key 1: R

51. Clever phrases that are used at the end of an ad to summarize the point of the ad's message in a highly memorable way are called:
    a. slogans.
    b. jingles.
    c. taglines.
    d. mnemonic.
    e. logos.

    Answer: c Difficulty: 2 Page: 161   Key 1: R

52. Devices such as rhyme, rhythmic beats, and repeating sound to improve recall are called:
    a. jingles.
    b. slogans.
    c. taglines.
    d. logos.
    e. mnemonics.

    Answer: e Difficulty: 2 Page: 161   Key 1: R

53. Which of the following allows the advertiser to ensure the memorability of the ad message?
    a. repetition
    b. tagline
    c. jingle
    d. key visual
    e. all of the above

    Answer: e Difficulty: 2 Page: 161   Key 1: R

54. When major rock stars appear in song-and-dance extravaganzas for soft drinks, many viewers cannot remember which star is associated with which product. This is called:
    a. breakthrough creativity.
    b. transformational creativity.
    c. impact creativity.
    d. transactional creativity.
    e. vampire creativity.

    Answer: e Difficulty: 2 Page: 161   Key 1: A

55. When the advertising is more memorable than the product, this is called:
    a. breakthrough advertising.
    b. great creativity.
    c. vampire creativity.
    d. transformational creativity.
    e. creative advertising.

    Answer: c Difficulty: 2 Page: 161   Key 1: R

56. Psychologists maintain that you need to hear something three times before it crosses the threshold of perception and enters into:
    a. understanding.
    b. interest.
    c. ambiguity.
    d. knowledge.
    e. memory.

    Answer: e Difficulty: 2 Page: 161   Key 1: R

57. Which of the following is a device for ensuring repetition of a key point in an ad?
    a. tagline
    b. jingle
    c. slogan
    d. mnemonic
    e. all of the above

    Answer: e Difficulty: 2 Page: 161   Key 1: S

58. A dominant image around which the commercial's message is planned is called:
    a. logo.
    b. key visual.
    c. signature.
    d. mnemonic.
    e. graphic center.

    Answer: b Difficulty: 1 Page: 161   Key 1: R

59. What part of the advertising message is most important for attracting attention?
    a. beginning
    b. middle
    c. closing
    d. none of the above
    e. all of the above

    Answer: a Difficulty: 2 Page: 161   Key 1: R

60. What part of the advertising message is most important for memorability?
    a. beginning
    b. middle
    c. closing
    d. none of the above
    e. all of the above

    Answer: c Difficulty: 2 Page: 161   Key 1: R

61. A distinctive mark that identifies the product, company, or brand is called a:
    a. signature.
    b. key visual.
    c. tagline.
    d. logo.
    e. mnemonic.

    Answer: d Difficulty: 2 Page: 162   Key 1: R

62. The name of the company or product written in a distinctive type style is called:
    a. logo.
    b. tagline.
    c. signature.
    d. brand name.
    e. key visual.

    Answer: c Difficulty: 2 Page: 162   Key 1: R

63. Branding is especially important for what kinds of products?
    a. mass market products
    b. parity products
    c. specialty products
    d. generic products
    e. direct market products

    Answer: b Difficulty: 2 Page: 163   Key 1: R

64. A product which has only a few, if any, major differences in features from competitors, such as soap, is called a:
    a. parity product.
    b. branded product.
    c. mass market product.
    d. differentiated product.

    Answer: a Difficulty: 2 Page: 163   Key 1: R

65. A mental image that reflects the way a brand is perceived, including all the identification elements, the product personality, and the emotions and associations evoked in the mind of the consumer is called the:
    a. brand image.
    b. association.
    c. product image.
    d. product personality.
    e. brand loyalty.

    Answer: a Difficulty: 2 Page: 163   Key 1: R

66. The idea of accumulating a reservoir of goodwill and good impressions is called:
    a. brand loyalty.
    b. brand equity.
    c. brand promise.
    d. public relations.
    e. brand image.

    Answer: b Difficulty: 2 Page: 164   Key 1: R

TRUE/FALSE

67. Many advertisers believe that the more consumers are aware of an ad, the higher the sales will be.
    a. True
    b. False

    Answer: a Difficulty: 1 Page: 146   Key 1: R

68. A "soft" affect of advertising includes awareness and brand image.
    a. True
    b. False

    Answer: a Difficulty: 2 Page: 146   Key 1: R

69. Relevance is a key element of effective advertising.
    a. True
    b. False

    Answer: a Difficulty: 1 Page: 147   Key 1: R

70. Humor is a key element of effective advertising.
    a. True
    b. False

    Answer: b Difficulty: 1 Page: 147   Key 1: R

71. A distrust of advertising can occur when ads do not speak to the needs or wants of certain individuals.
    a. True
    b. False

    Answer: a Difficulty: 1 Page: 147   Key 1: R

72. Once an advertiser thoroughly understands the external environment of the advertising process, it can begin creating the advertising plan.
    a. True
    b. False

    Answer: a Difficulty: 2 Page: 147   Key 1: R

73. Most advertisements just "wash over" their audiences without any effect.
    a. True
    b. False

    Answer: a Difficulty: 1 Page: 148   Key 1: A

74. While it is clear that the communication environment is terribly cluttered, the clutter is not particularly significant because people attend carefully to well-prepared ads.
    a. True
    b. False

    Answer: b Difficulty: 2 Page: 148   Key 1: A

75. Most people do not see much difference between editorial information and advertisements.
    a. True
    b. False

    Answer: a Difficulty: 2 Page: 148   Key 1: R

76. Most consumers react negatively to most advertising.
    a. True
    b. False

    Answer: a Difficulty: 2 Page: 148   Key 1: R

77. The new generation of consumers accepts advertising more than previous generations did.
    a. True
    b. False

    Answer: b Difficulty: 2 Page: 148   Key 1: R

78. Human concentration happens in quick bursts. Most media messages can only count on a few seconds of concentrated time.
    a. True
    b. False

    Answer: a Difficulty: 1 Page: 148   Key 1: R

79. A few ads may break through and receive total concentration, but that is very rare.
    a. True
    b. False

    Answer: a Difficulty: 2 Page: 148   Key 1: A

80. More than half of all advertisements are read thoroughly.
    a. True
    b. False

    Answer: b Difficulty: 2 Page: 148   Key 1: R

81. The actual information that usually gets attended to in an advertisement is nothing more than a message fragment.
    a. True
    b. False

    Answer: a Difficulty: 2 Page: 150   Key 1: A

82. Even though consumers are bombarded by TV commercials, avoidance is often difficult.
    a. True
    b. False

    Answer: b Difficulty: 1 Page: 150   Key 1: R

83. The ability of a particular ad to reach a target audience depends on an effective media plan.
    a. True
    b. False

    Answer: a Difficulty: 2 Page: 150   Key 1: R

84. Advertisers can use the same media regardless of the target audience.
    a. True
    b. False

    Answer: b Difficulty: 1 Page: 150   Key 1: R

85. Creating an ad begins with an analysis of the marketing and ad strategy, the target audience and the media strategy.
    a. True
    b. False

    Answer: a Difficulty: 1 Page: 150   Key 1: R

86. When a person perceives an idea, the message has registered.
    a. True
    b. False

    Answer: a Difficulty: 2 Page: 151   Key 1: R

87. Consumers miss more than half of the messages directed at them.
    a. True
    b. False

    Answer: a Difficulty: 2 Page: 151   Key 1: R

88. Advertising can never communicate several messages in several areas simultaneously.
    a. True
    b. False

    Answer: b Difficulty: 2 Page: 151   Key 1: R

89. Exposure is the minimum requirement for perception.
    a. True
    b. False

    Answer: a Difficulty: 1 Page: 152   Key 1: R

90. The function of originality in advertising is to catch attention.
    a. True
    b. False

    Answer: a Difficulty: 1 Page: 152   Key 1: R

91. Exposure is mainly a media buying problem.
    a. True
    b. False

    Answer: a Difficulty: 1 Page: 152   Key 1: R

92. Awareness can be achieved only if there is some measure of attention.
    a. True
    b. False

    Answer: a Difficulty: 2 Page: 152   Key 1: R

93. A trigger can distract a viewer's attention away from an ad's message.
    a. True
    b. False

    Answer: b Difficulty: 2 Page: 152   Key 1: R

94. Advertising can transform the experience of buying and using a product.
    a. True
    b. False

    Answer: a Difficulty: 2 Page: 153   Key 1: A

95. Interest in an ad is usually based on something personal or something intriguing.
    a. True
    b. False

    Answer: a Difficulty: 2 Page: 153   Key 1: A

96. Understanding is a relatively passive response from the audience.
    a. True
    b. False

    Answer: b Difficulty: 2 Page: 153   Key 1: R

97. Recognition in advertising means top-of-mind awareness.
    a. True
    b. False

    Answer: a Difficulty: 2 Page: 153   Key 1: R

98. Interest is a momentary thing.
    a. True
    b. False

    Answer: a Difficulty: 2 Page: 155   Key 1: R

99. Arousing interest is more difficult than maintaining it.
    a. True
    b. False

    Answer: b Difficulty: 2 Page: 155   Key 1: R

100. Understanding is the intensity of the consumer's interest in a product message or medium.
     a. True
     b. False

     Answer: b Difficulty: 1 Page: 156   Key 1: R

ESSAY

101. Discuss the main elements of the external advertising environment.

Answer:
Essentially, the external factors of the advertising process are the marketing strategy, the history and attitudes of the target consumer and other marketing communication. Marketing elements such as the product, price and distribution have a direct bearing on whether advertising is used to achieve marketing objectives.

The target consumer's history and attitudes strongly influence whether and how consumers process an advertisement. For example, we know that consumers who already use a product tend to note and respond more favorably to ads for that product. In contrast, consumers who are loyal to another brand are less likely to pay attention to advertising for the brand they don't use.

The other marketing communication tactics, include sales promotion, public relations, personal selling, packaging, signage and so forth. Blending all of these external elements creates a synchronized message that is the foundation for integrated marketing communication.

Difficulty: 2 Page: 147   Key 1: R/S

102. Discuss the four elements of the internal advertising environment.

Answer:
The internal advertising environment consists of four major elements: noise, target audience, media strategy and creative strategy.

Any factor that interferes with or distorts the correct delivery of the advertising message is noise. The interference can be technical, such as an unreadable newspaper ad or a preempted TV ad. Noise can also occur in the consumer's environment, as when he or she sees a TV ad in a noisy bar. The advertising environment is also seriously cluttered by other media, other ads and promotions and news stories that get in the way of an advertiser's message (these other ads are called "clutter").

The target audience is a second factor. The actual information that gets attention is often nothing more than a quick impression or a message fragment. Much depends on how relevant the consumer feels the ad is, how the consumer processes information and whether consumers avoid the ad.

The ability of a particular advertising message to reach an identified target audience depends on the effectiveness of the media plan and strategy. Simply put, the media plan produces the best set of media to reach the target audience. For example, an HBO TV commercial delivered through prime-time cable may be appropriate when creating perception and providing relevant information to new users. However, when HBO wants to prompt consumers to subscribe to its service, it often wages direct mail campaigns in conjunction with local cable systems.

Answer:

In the execution phase, copywriters and art directors execute the creative strategy by writing and designing ads. The final phase is the production phase. The creative strategy outlines what type of message must be developed.

Difficulty: 2 Page: 147-151   Key 1: R/S

103. What factors contribute to making consumer notice an advertiser's message? How do each of these factors work to break through consumers' inattention to advertisements?

Answer:
The first step in perception is exposure. Exposure is mainly a media-buying problem because advertisers must place a message in a medium that the target audience sees, read, watches or listens to. Exposure is the minimum requirement for perception to take place.

Once the audience has been exposed to the message, the next step is to keep their attention, meaning that the mind is engaged and focussed on something. Attention is aroused by a trigger, something that catches the target's interest. The trigger can be something in the message or something within the reader or viewer that makes him or her lock onto a particular message. For example, in print, the trigger might be a sale price in large type, a startling illustration or a strong headline.

The final factor is stopping power. Getting attention involves more than just attracting attention or notice of the viewer or reader. Consumers who scan ads have wandering attention. Nailing down attention requires stopping power. Ads that stop the consumer from scanning are usually high in intrusiveness and originality. What creates this kind of impact? Many intrusive ads use loud, bold effects to attract viewer attention. The function of originality is the same as intrusiveness. People notice things that are new, novel or surprising.

Difficulty: 3 Page: 151-153   Key 1: S

104. Once a message has been perceived and has caught your attention, your perceptual process can move on to the next step which is awareness of the message and the product. Discuss some of the factors that influence awareness and attention.

Answer:
Attention is a message design problem. The advertising message can, and must, compete with other messages in the same medium. Low levels of attention can create a minimal level of awareness. If the objective is simply a brand or product reminder, then the attention level doesn't need to be as high as it does when the objective calls for the understanding of a copy point. Attention is obtained by providing relevance, information and involvement.

Relevance aids awareness. People pay attention to advertising only if it's worth their while to do so. We pay attention to ads that speak to our personal concerns and interests by providing information about such things as work, hobbies, roles and relationships. Because many type of relevance exist, many types of interest exist. You might be interested in the product advertised or in some element in the ad itself: the model or the star, the promise, or by an unusual graphic. Interest is usually created by one of two things: personal involvement or curiosity. You are predisposed to be aware of things that interest or apply to you. Curiosity provides the cognitive nudge that engages your mind. Whenever you are confronted with something new, there is a period of curiosity, usually accompanied by some kind of doubt or questioning.

Difficulty: 3 Page: 153-156 Key 1: S

105. One of the great advertising challenges is to create memorability. Discuss a potential drawback to this challenge. Give an example.

Answer:
Memorability is necessary if a consumer is to remember a product. However, testing has proven that people often remember a commercial, but not the advertised product. This problem, called vampire creativity, occurs primarily with advertisements that are too original, too entertaining or too involving The story of the commercial can be so mesmerizing that it gets in the way of the product. Celebrity advertising can have this problem. When major rock stars appear in song-and-dance extravaganzas for soft drinks, many viewers cannot remember which star is associated with which product. It is essential that the commercial establish a strong link between the message and the product so that remembering the advertisement also means remembering the brand. Fortunately, for Maytag, the recurring Maytag repairman did not detract from the product.

Difficulty: 1 Page: 161 Key 1: R/A

CHAPTER 7: STRATEGY AND PLANNING

MULTIPLE CHOICE

1. What does the statement, "advertising is a disciplined art" mean?
   a. Ad messages are created to achieve objectives.
   b. Ad messages are a sudden flash of inspirations.
   c. Ad messages must be well written.
   d. Ad messages are intended to entertain audiences.
   e. Ad messages must be exciting.

   Answer: a Difficulty: 2 Page: 169   Key 1: A

2. The process by which messages are developed to accomplish specific objectives and then strategies are developed specifically to achieve those objectives is called:
   a. strategy.
   b. planning.
   c. marketing.
   d. advertising.
   e. creativity.

   Answer: b Difficulty: 1 Page: 170   Key 1: R

3. In strategic planning, what do we call the execution tools that make the plan come to life?
   a. tactics
   b. strategy
   c. objective
   d. goal
   e. creativity

   Answer: a Difficulty: 2 Page: 170   Key 1: R

4. What a plan seeks to accomplish is called:
   a. strategy.
   b. tactic.
   c. plan.
   d. objective.

   Answer: d Difficulty: 2 Page: 170   Key 1: R

5. In strategic planning, what do we call the means by which the firm will accomplish objectives?
   a. strategy
   b. objective
   c. plan
   d. tactic
   e. execution

   Answer: a Difficulty: 2 Page: 170   Key 1: R

6. The process of determining objectives, deciding on strategies, and implementing the tactics within a specific time frame is called:
   a. marketing management.
   b. execution planning.
   c. strategic planning.
   d. market planning.
   e. tactical planning.

   Answer: c Difficulty: 2 Page: 170   Key 1: R

7. A demonstration, a testimonial, an emotional or funny story, or a straightforward fact-based story are examples of a/an:
   a. objective.
   b. strategy.
   c. plan.
   d. tactic.

   Answer: d Difficulty: 2 Page: 170   Key 1: A

8. Reinforcing brand loyalty for the product is an example of a/an:
   a. tactic.
   b. objective.
   c. strategy.
   d. plan.
   e. opportunity.

   Answer: b Difficulty: 2 Page: 171   Key 1: A

9. An advertising plan is an example of a:
   a. marketing plan.
   b. functional plan.
   c. specific plan.
   d. business plan.
   e. creative plan.

   Answer: c Difficulty: 2 Page: 172   Key 1: R

10. _____ is a statement of the broad aims of the company, such as its aspiration to technological leadership or short-term growth.
    a. Marketing strategy
    b. Marketing goal
    c. Business strategy
    d. Corporate objective
    e. Business mission statement

    Answer: e Difficulty: 2 Page: 172   Key 1: R

11. A trend or development in the environment that will erode the company's business position unless it takes purposeful marketing action is called a/an:
    a. threat.
    b. opportunity.
    c. objective.
    d. position.
    e. competitive priority.

    Answer: a Difficulty: 2 Page: 172   Key 1: R

12. An area in which a business has a competitive advantage is called:
    a. a strategic goal.
    b. a marketing objective.
    c. an opportunity.
    d. a position.
    e. competitive parity.

    Answer: c Difficulty: 3 Page: 172   Key 1: R

13. Which of the following is a characteristic of appropriate business goals?
    a. consistent
    b. prioritized
    c. stated quantitatively
    d. realistic
    e. all of the above

    Answer: e Difficulty: 2 Page: 173   Key 1: R

14. What is the time frame for evaluating and developing a marketing plan?
    a. semi-annually
    b. annually
    c. bi-annually
    d. every 5 years
    e. every 10 years

    Answer: b Difficulty: 1 Page: 174   Key 1: R

15. A company's profit objectives are stated in its:
    a. marketing plan.
    b. advertising plan.
    c. campaign plan.
    d. business plan.
    e. copy strategy.

    Answer: a Difficulty: 2 Page: 174   Key 1: R

16. All the marketing mix elements—product, pricing, distribution, and marketing communication (which includes advertising)—are coordinated in the:
    a. marketing plan.
    b. advertising plan.
    c. campaign plan.
    d. corporate plan.
    e. copy strategy.

    Answer: a Difficulty: 2 Page: 174   Key 1: R

17. Why is marketing strategy the key element of the marketing plan to the advertising manager?
    a. It outlines what advertising must do
    b. It identifies marketing opportunities
    c. It links overall business plan with advertising
    d. It pinpoints key problems to be solved by advertising
    e. It describes the target market

    Answer: c Difficulty: 3 Page: 174   Key 1: R

18. The percentage of market share sought by the company is an example of a/an:
    a. marketing strategy.
    b. marketing objective.
    c. marketing tactic.
    d. advertising objective.
    e. business mission statement.

    Answer: b Difficulty: 2 Page: 174   Key 1: A

19. The marketing manager predicts his brand will sell 600, 000 units next year for a total sales of $1.2 million. This is 4.8% of all sales in the category. This 4.8% of all sales would be called:
    a. marketing objective.
    b. advertising objective.
    c. marketing strategy.
    d. media objective.
    e. sales objective.

    Answer: a Difficulty: 2 Page: 174   Key 1: A

20. What is the process of figuring out what all the information and data mean in strategic planning? The text calls it the heart of strategic planning.
    a. strategy
    b. analysis
    c. planning
    d. creativity
    e. thinking

    Answer: b Difficulty: 2 Page: 174   Key 1: R

21. When the planner analyzes the mountain of information uncovered in any planning situation, what is the planner trying to spot?
    a. objectives
    b. tactics
    c. strategies
    d. problem/opportunities
    e. advertising messages

    Answer: d Difficulty: 2 Page: 174   Key 1: R

22. A group of consumers having one or more similar characteristics that make it unique from other groups who use the product is called a:
    a. target market.
    b. marketing prospects.
    c. principle target.
    d. benefit segment.
    e. market segment.

    Answer: e Difficulty: 2 Page: 175   Key 1: R

23. A group of cat food consumers subdivided on the basis of cat breed would be a/an:
    a. opportunity.
    b. position.
    c. market segment.
    d. copy platform.

    Answer: c Difficulty: 2 Page: 175   Key 1: A

24. Target markets are the:
    a. best prospects for the product.
    b. market segments selected for the marketing plan.
    c. market segments that can be best served from a competitive standpoint.
    d. focus of the marketing plan.
    e. all of the above

    Answer: e Difficulty: 2 Page: 175   Key 1: R

25. A group of people identified as the best prospects for a product or service is called a:
    a. market segment.
    b. target market.
    c. benefit segment.
    d. differentiated segment.
    e. market.

    Answer: b Difficulty: 2 Page: 175   Key 1: R

26. Stouffer's failure to get input from retailers about a new food product is a problem with:
    a. creative strategy.
    b. marketing strategy.
    c. implementation.
    d. marketing objectives.

    Answer: c Difficulty: 2 Page: 176   Key 1: A

27. A sound evaluation for a marketing plan:
    a. compares actual performance with planned performance.
    b. is done at least annually.
    c. determines why particular results have occurred.
    d. determines if the gap between planned and actual performance is enough to require corrective action.
    e. all of the above

    Answer: e Difficulty: 2 Page: 176   Key 1: R

28. What type of plan matches the right audience to the right message and presents the message in the right medium to reach the audience?
    a. marketing
    b. copy
    c. advertising
    d. copy platform
    e. business

    Answer: c Difficulty: 1 Page: 177   Key 1: R

29. What basic elements lie at the heart of advertising strategy?
    a. target audience, advertising objective, and creative strategy
    b. advertising objective and creative strategy
    c. target audience, message strategy, and media strategy
    d. advertising objective, creative strategy, and media strategy
    e. target audience and creative strategy

    Answer: c Difficulty: 2 Page: 177   Key 1: S

30. What section, standard at the beginning of the advertising plan and most marketing plans, summarizes relevant information about the product, marketplace, competition, demand, consumer behavior, distribution channels, costs and environmental factors?
    a. research
    b. market research
    c. market analysis
    d. situation analysis
    e. background

    Answer: d Difficulty: 2 Page: 177   Key 1: R

31. All of the following are steps in the DAGMAR hierarchy of effects model EXCEPT:
    a. awareness.
    b. interest.
    c. conviction.
    d. action.
    e. comprehension.

    Answer: b Difficulty: 2 Page: 178   Key 1: R

32. A statement of the intended effect of the advertising message on the audience is called the:
    a. market objective.
    b. advertising strategy.
    c. advertising objective.
    d. message effect.
    e. advertising tactic.

    Answer: c Difficulty: 2 Page: 178   Key 1: R

33. The stages in the AIDA hierarchy of effects model are (in the proper order):
    a. analysis, information, decision, action
    b. attention, interest, desire, action
    c. action, information, decision, attitude
    d. attitude, interest, desire, action
    e. analysis, interest, decision, action

    Answer: b Difficulty: 2 Page: 178   Key 1: R

34. The stage in the hierarchy of effects at which the target audience knows it has a possible desire for the product is called:
    a. interest.
    b. recognition.
    c. awareness.
    d. recall.
    e. comprehension.

    Answer: c Difficulty: 2 Page: 178   Key 1: R

35. When consumers' curiosity is aroused and they are willing to hear more about the product, this is called:
    a. awareness.
    b. interest.
    c. comprehension.
    d. liking.
    e. recognition.

    Answer: b Difficulty: 2 Page: 178   Key 1: R

36. When the target audience is interested in the product and understands the value from the information, this is called:
    a. comprehension.
    b. recognition.
    c. awareness.
    d. recall.
    e. preference.

    Answer: a Difficulty: 2 Page: 178   Key 1: R

37. When the target audience wants to try the product, this is called:
    a. credibility.
    b. comprehension.
    c. conviction.
    d. preference.
    e. interest.

    Answer: c Difficulty: 2 Page: 178   Key 1: R

38. What are the three categories of message effects in the Lavidge and Steiner model?
    a. cognitive, affective, and emotional
    b. emotional, rational, and attitudinal
    c. cognitive, affective, and conative
    d. rational, attitudinal, and perceptual
    e. perceptual, mental, and decisional

    Answer: c Difficulty: 2 Page: 178   Key 1: S

39. In the Lavidge and Steiner model of analysis of message effect, "affective" effects are also called:
    a. mental.
    b. deciding.
    c. action.
    d. emotional.
    e. rational.

    Answer: d Difficulty: 2 Page: 178   Key 1: R

40. In the Lavidge and Steiner model of analyzing message effects, "cognitive" effects are also called:
    a. emotional.
    b. deciding.
    c. rational.
    d. attitudinal.
    e. action.

    Answer: c Difficulty: 2 Page: 178   Key 1: R

41. In the Lavidge and Steiner model of analyzing message effect, "conative" effects are also called:
    a. emotional.
    b. rational.
    c. mental.
    d. attitudinal.
    e. action.

    Answer: e Difficulty: 2 Page: 178   Key 1: R

42. A group of people who can be reached with a particular medium and message is called a:
    a. market segment.
    b. target market.
    c. benefit segment.
    d. target audience.

    Answer: d Difficulty: 2 Page: 179   Key 1: R

43. What main characteristics are used to identify target audiences?
    a. demographic, personality, and lifestyle
    b. sociological, psychological, and behavioral
    c. personality, social, and economic
    d. demographic, social, and behavioral
    e. economic, social, and behavioral

    Answer: a Difficulty: 2 Page: 179   Key 1: S

44. What kind of model is the high-involvement model of message effects?
    a. think-feel-do
    b. feel-think-do
    c. do-think-feel
    d. think-do-feel
    e. do-feel-think

    Answer: a Difficulty: 3 Page: 179   Key 1: R

45. What kind of model is the low-involvement model of message effects?
    a. feel-think-do
    b. think-feel-do
    c. do-think-feel
    d. think-do-feel
    e. do-feel-think

    Answer: d Difficulty: 3 Page: 179   Key 1: R

46. What kind of model is the rationalization model of effects?
    a. feel-think-do
    b. think-feel-do
    c. do-think-feel
    d. think-do-feel
    e. do-feel-think

    Answer: e Difficulty: 3 Page: 179   Key 1: R

47. The think-feel-do model is called the high-involvement model because it depicts a series of standard responses for:
    a. an emotional consumer.
    b. a consumer purchasing for a family.
    c. a consumer with little interest in the product.
    d. a consumer who actively participates in getting information and making decisions.
    e. all of the above

    Answer: d Difficulty: 2 Page: 179   Key 1: R

48. Why is the think-do-feel model called the low-involvement model?
    a. describes consumers with little interest in the product
    b. describes impulse buying
    c. describes purchasing that requires little decision-making
    d. all of the above
    e. none of the above

    Answer: d Difficulty: 2 Page: 179   Key 1: R

49. What does the analysis of the target audience allow the advertising planner to do?
    a. pinpoint the most responsive audience
    b. determine the best message for the audience
    c. identify the product's competitive advantage
    d. describe the target market
    e. all of the above

    Answer: a Difficulty: 2 Page: 180   Key 1: R

50. When the advertising agency staff prepares a life-like personality sketch of a typical prospect in the targeted audience to help make the target audience come to life, this is called a:
    a. target analysis.
    b. feature analysis.
    c. positioning.
    d. principal target.
    e. profile.

    Answer: e Difficulty: 2 Page: 180   Key 1: R

51. When the product to be advertised as pertaining to a particular area that matters to the target and in which the competition is weak or lacking, this is called:
    a. competitive advantage.
    b. position.
    c. feature analysis.
    d. opportunity.
    e. advertising objective.

    Answer: a Difficulty: 2 Page: 180   Key 1: R

52. A comparison of one product's features against the features of competing products is called:
    a. positioning.
    b. feature analysis or benefit analysis.
    c. competitive advantage analysis.
    d. differentiation.
    e. benefit segmentation.

    Answer: b Difficulty: 2 Page: 180   Key 1: R

53. The two dimensions on which a feature analysis of competitive advantage would be based are:
    a. product performance and image.
    b. price and product performance.
    c. importance to target and relevant product benefits.
    d. price and importance to target.
    e. image and importance to target.

    Answer: c Difficulty: 2 Page: 180   Key 1: S

54. Why does the advertising plan include a profile of the target audience?
    a. to help creative people
    b. to make messages more believable
    c. to make writing messages easier
    d. to help writers associate the target audience with someone they know
    e. all of the above

    Answer: e Difficulty: 2 Page: 180   Key 1: R

55. An important step in figuring out a product's competitive advantage is:
    a. to analyze the product compared to competitor products.
    b. to make a chart for the product's and competitor's product features.
    c. to do feature analysis.
    d. to evaluate how important each feature is to the target audience.
    e. all of the above

    Answer: e Difficulty: 2 Page: 180   Key 1: R

56. The way in which the consumers perceive a product in the marketplace is called:
    a. image.
    b. brand image.
    c. perceptual map.
    d. positioning.
    e. competitive advantage.

    Answer: d Difficulty: 2 Page: 181   Key 1: R

57. Changing the consumer's perception of a product is called:
    a. repositioning.
    b. product differentiation.
    c. remapping.
    d. image makeover.
    e. persuasion.

    Answer: a Difficulty: 2 Page: 181   Key 1: R

58. A map that shows where consumers locate various category products in terms of several important features is called:
    a. position.
    b. mental map.
    c. perceptual map.
    d. product space.
    e. feature analysis.

    Answer: c Difficulty: 2 Page: 181   Key 1: R

59. Where does positioning research start?
    a. feature analysis
    b. perceptual mapping
    c. product space analysis
    d. mental mapping
    e. all of the above

    Answer: a Difficulty: 2 Page: 181   Key 1: R

60. The last section of the advertising plan includes:
    a. the evaluation plan.
    b. the budget.
    c. schedules.
    d. implementation.
    e. all of the above

    Answer: e Difficulty: 2 Page: 182   Key 1: S

61. On what is an advertising budget based?
    a. marketing budget
    b. marketing communication budget
    c. marketing mix
    d. marketing plan
    e. all of the above

    Answer: e Difficulty: 2 Page: 183   Key 1: R

62. A budgeting method that builds a budget by asking what it will cost to achieve a stated objectives is called:
    a. percent-of-sales method.
    b. competitive parity method.
    c. share-of-mind method.
    d. task-objective method.
    e. share-of-market method.

    Answer: d Difficulty: 2 Page: 183   Key 1: R

63. A budgeting method that uses previous advertising expenditures as a basis for establishing an advertising budget is called:
    a. task-objective method.
    b. competitive parity method.
    c. standard year basis method.
    d. advertising level method.
    e. historical method.

    Answer: e Difficulty: 2 Page: 183   Key 1: R

64. In the last year, sales for a company were $10 million and the advertising budget was $1 million. Next year, sales are predicted to be $15 million so the advertising budget will be $1.5 million. What budgeting method is being used?
    a. task-objective
    b. historical
    c. percent-of-sales
    d. competitive parity

    Answer: c Difficulty: 3 Page: 184   Key 1: A

65. A company wants to increase its market share to 25% so it sets its advertising budget as 25% of total advertising expenditures in the category. What budgeting method is being used?
    a. percent-of-sales
    b. share-of-mind
    c. task objective
    d. competitive parity

    Answer: d Difficulty: 3 Page: 184   Key 1: A

66. In the "share-of-mind" concept, share-of-media-voice equals what?
    a. advertising objective
    b. total sales
    c. share of market
    d. brand image
    e. position

    Answer: c Difficulty: 3 Page: 185   Key 1: R

TRUE/FALSE

67. The art of advertising comes from strategic thinking.
    a. True
    b. False

    Answer: b Difficulty: 2 Page: 169   Key 1: R

68. Advertisers often create messages by relying on sudden flashes of inspiration.
    a. True
    b. False

    Answer: b Difficulty: 1 Page: 170   Key 1: R

69. A strategy is how an advertiser will accomplish objectives.
    a. True
    b. False

    Answer: a Difficulty: 2 Page: 170   Key 1: R

70. Tactics make an advertising plan come to life.
    a. True
    b. False

    Answer: a Difficulty: 2 Page: 170   Key 1: R

71. Even experienced advertising people have trouble telling the difference between an objective and strategy.
    a. True
    b. False

    Answer: a Difficulty: 3 Page: 171   Key 1: A

72. Strategic thinking means weighing the alternatives and identifying the best approach to solving a problem.
    a. True
    b. False

    Answer: a Difficulty: 2 Page: 171   Key 1: R

73. Reinforcing brand loyalty is an example of an ad campaign goal.
    a. True
    b. False

    Answer: a Difficulty: 2 Page: 171   Key 1: R

74. An opportunity is a market area in which the company would enjoy a competitive advantage.
    a. True
    b. False

    Answer: a Difficulty: 2 Page: 172   Key 1: R

75. Most businesses pursue only one goal at a time.
    a. True
    b. False

    Answer: b Difficulty: 2 Page: 173   Key 1: R

76. After business managers have defined the mission and examined the external and internal environment, they can develop specific objectives and goals for the planning period.
    a. True
    b. False

    Answer: a Difficulty: 2 Page: 173   Key 1: R

77. Once a business develops its key strategies for attaining goals, it must develop tactics for carrying out these strategies.
    a. True
    b. False

    Answer: a Difficulty: 2 Page: 173   Key 1: R

78. Only the poorest business plans run a risk of failure if there is poor implementation.
    a. True
    b. False

    Answer: b Difficulty: 2 Page: 173   Key 1: R

79. A marketing plan is a hypothetical plan that proposes strategies for using the elements of the marketing mix to achieve marketing objectives.
    a. True
    b. False

    Answer: b Difficulty: 1 Page: 174   Key 1: R

80. Companies are finding that marketing plans need to be updated more often than once a year.
    a. True
    b. False

    Answer: a Difficulty: 2 Page: 174   Key 1: R

81. The typical time frame for developing and evaluating a marketing plan is one year.
    a. True
    b. False

    Answer: a Difficulty: 2 Page: 174   Key 1: E

82. The heart of strategic planning is analysis—the process of figuring out what all the information and data mean.
    a. True
    b. False

    Answer: a Difficulty: 2 Page: 174   Key 1: R

83. When marketers target consumer segments, they ignore the interests of other customers in order to produce a meaningful effect with the targeted segment.
    a. True
    b. False

    Answer: a Difficulty: 3 Page: 175   Key 1: A

84. An advertising plan matches the right audience to the right message and presents it in the right medium to reach that audience.
    a. True
    b. False

    Answer: a Difficulty: 2 Page: 177   Key 1: R

85. The advertising plan begins with a statement of objectives.
    a. True
    b. False

    Answer: b Difficulty: 2 Page: 177   Key 1: R

86. Great advertising can solve problems related to the price and
    availability of the product as well as solving message-related problems.
    a. True
    b. False

    Answer: b Difficulty: 2 Page: 178   Key 1: R

87. Advertising cannot solve problems related to the price of the product.
    a. True
    b. False

    Answer: a Difficulty: 1 Page: 178   Key 1: R

88. The crucial point in the discussion of turning problems into
    opportunities in advertising planning is to use advertising to solve
    marketing problems.
    a. True
    b. False

    Answer: b Difficulty: 2 Page: 178   Key 1: A

89. The target audience is always the same as the target market.
    a. True
    b. False

    Answer: b Difficulty: 2 Page: 179   Key 1: R

90. Target audience analysis allows the advertiser to pinpoint the most
    responsive audience.
    a. True
    b. False

    Answer: a Difficulty: 2 Page: 179   Key 1: R

91. A product's position is determined by its principal characteristics.
    a. True
    b. False

    Answer: b Difficulty: 2 Page: 181   Key 1: A

92. Evaluation in the advertising plan examines how well the plan meets its objectives.
   a. True
   b. False

   Answer: a Difficulty: 1 Page: 182   Key 1: R

93. The share of media voice always equals market shares in the long run.
   a. True
   b. False

   Answer: b Difficulty: 2 Page: 185   Key 1: R

94. Probably the least effective message strategy is a product-centered strategy.
   a. True
   b. False

   Answer: b Difficulty: 3 Page: 186   Key 1: R

95. The benefit is strictly in the mind of the consumer.
   a. True
   b. False

   Answer: a Difficulty: 2 Page: 187   Key 1: A

96. A benefit statement that looks to the future is called a promise.
   a. True
   b. False

   Answer: a Difficulty: 2 Page: 188   Key 1: R

97. Execution of the strategy is the heart of the advertising creative process.
   a. True
   b. False

   Answer: a Difficulty: 3 Page: 188   Key 1: A

98. The focus of support is to make the selling premise believable.
   a. True
   b. False

   Answer: a Difficulty: 2 Page: 188   Key 1: R

99. A reason why you should buy something is another form of a benefit statement.
    a. True
    b. False

    Answer: a Difficulty: 2 Page: 188   Key 1: R

100. The heart of the unique selling proposition is a promise that states a specific and unique benefit you will get from using the product.
    a. True
    b. False

    Answer: a Difficulty: 2 Page: 188   Key 1: R

ESSAY

101. Discuss the difference between the objectives, strategies and tactics. Explain why even experienced marketing and advertising professionals sometimes get them confused.

    Answer:
    Strategic planning is the process of determining objectives (what you want to accomplish), deciding on strategies (how to accomplish objectives), and implementing the tactics (which make the plan come to life). Marketing and advertising strategies are chosen from an array of possible alternatives. Intelligent decision making means weighing these alternatives and sorting out the best approach. Often there is no one right way, but there may be a best way to accomplish these objectives.

    Even those experienced in advertising sometimes have a hard time telling the difference between an objective and a strategy. Both are important to successful marketing and advertising plans; they are related to each other, but they also serve different purposes. An objective is a goal or task to accomplish (the destination). A strategy is the means by which the goal is accomplished (the route to the destination).

    Difficulty: 2 Page: 170-171 Key 1: S/A

102. Discuss the key elements of the marketing plan.

Answer:
A marketing plan is a written document that proposes strategies for using the elements of the marketing mix to achieve marketing objectives. It analyzes the marketing situation, identifies the problems, outlines the marketing opportunities, sets the objectives, and proposes strategies and tactics to solve these problems and meet objectives. A marketing plan is developed and evaluated annually, although sections dealing with long-term goals might operate for a number of years. To a large extent, the marketing plan parallels the business strategic plan and contains many of the same components. For advertising managers, the most important part of the marketing plan is the marketing strategy, which links the overall strategic business plan with specific marketing programs, including advertising.

Difficulty: 1 Page: 174-176 Key 1: S

103. Discuss the key elements and main sections of the advertising plan.

Answer:
An advertising plan matches the right audience to the right message and presents it in the right medium to reach that audience. Three basic elements summarize the heart of advertising strategy: targeting the audience, message strategy and media strategy.

The introduction provides a summary and overview of the plan. The next section, the situation analysis, consists of backgrounding: researching and reviewing the current state of the business that is relevant to advertising communication. This section details the search for and analysis of important information and trends affecting the marketplace.

The key strategy decisions section deals with issues that are crucial to developing advertising strategy: how to set objectives and identify the target audience, create a competitive advantage, position a product and establish brand image and brand personality.

The last section of an advertising plan contains details of the implementation of the tactics, including scheduling, the budget and techniques for evaluating the effectiveness of the plan. Executing the advertising plan is undoubtedly the most difficult part of the plan. There are thousands of details and missing even one deadline might mean scrapping an entire campaign.

Difficulty: 2 Page: 177-183 Key 1: S/R

104. Discuss positioning and give an example.

Answer:
How consumers perceive a product relative to its competition is called positioning. Positioning is a marketing strategy, but businesses can position through advertising. To overcome the Weather Channel's commodity image and to give it a distinct market position, ad agency TBWA Chiat/Day repositioned TWC around its passion for weather, rather than focusing on its forecasting expertise. But market research suggested that to completely reposition TWC, the advertising had to do more than convey TWC's passion. It also had to celebrate the viewer's passion for weather in such a way that it made it alright for them to "come out of the closet" and to make TWC socially acceptable to a broader audience.

Difficulty: 1 Page: 181   Key 1: R/A

105. Discuss the key elements in the creative platform.

Answer:
Advertisers may develop a message strategy for an individual advertisement. The document that sets out the message strategy is the creative platform. Not all agencies use such a document, but all copywriters work from some kind of systematic analysis of the problem at hand. A creative platform structures this kind of analysis.

The first element is the message strategy. Advertisers can sell the product in a generic way, a strategy that only works when the product dominates the market, or they can sell the brand, a strategy that usually is considered more effective. Another message option considers the information content of the ad and its associations or emotional impact.

Different people and different situations require different strategies and salespeople generally are more comfortable with some approaches than with others. The same is true in advertising. The various approaches to the logic of the sales message are called selling premises. The most common premises are categorized as either product centered or prospect centered.

Difficulty: 2 Page: 185-188   Key 1: R/S

CHAPTER 8: MEDIA STRATEGY AND PLANNING

MULTIPLE CHOICE

1. What is the ultimate goal of media planning?
   a. find the lowest cost media vehicles
   b. find new media through which to expose advertising messages
   c. deliver the message to as many different people as possible
   d. place the advertising message before a target audience

   Answer: d Difficulty: 2 Page: 194   Key 1: R

2. A problem-solving process leading to the use of advertising time and space to assist in the achievement of marketing objectives is called:
   a. advertising plan.
   b. media strategy.
   c. media planning.
   d. media objective.
   e. media analysis.

   Answer: c Difficulty: 2 Page: 194   Key 1: R

3. What planning decisions does media planning involve?
   a. audiences, creative strategy, timing, campaign length, and type of media
   b. audiences, geographic emphasis, timing, campaign length, and intensity of exposure
   c. available media, media characteristics, creative strategy, timing, and cost
   d. audiences, available media, creative strategy, campaign length, and cost
   e. type of media, geographic emphasis, campaign length, creative strategy and intensity of exposure

   Answer: b Difficulty: 3 Page: 194   Key 1: S

4. The ideal moment for exposing consumers to an advertising message when their interest and attention are high is called:
   a. critical timing.
   b. mnemonic.
   c. awareness.
   d. aperture.
   e. perceptual timing.

   Answer: d Difficulty: 2 Page: 196   Key 1: R

5. Which of the following has the greatest impact on successful message placement?
   a. marketing research, appreciation of message concept, and understanding of media channels
   b. skillful statistical analysis, understanding of media channels, and attention to detail
   c. marketing research, understanding of media channels, and problem-solving ability
   d. computer skill, experience in the media, and appreciation of message concept
   e. analytical skill, creativity, and understanding of media channels

   Answer: a Difficulty: 3 Page: 196   Key 1: R

6. Finding the aperture opportunity is a major responsibility of which one of the following people?
   a. campaign coordinator
   b. media procurement supervisor
   c. media planner
   d. advertising creativity supervisor

   Answer: c Difficulty: 1 Page: 196   Key 1: R

7. When is advertising most effective?
   a. when people find the information in the advertising interesting
   b. when it reaches large numbers of the target audience
   c. when the humor in the advertising causes the target to pay attention
   d. when it stops the target audience
   e. when people are exposed at a time whey they are most receptive to the information

   Answer: e Difficulty: 3 Page: 196   Key 1: A

8. In many ad agencies, account planners:
   a. gather and analyze large amounts of data and information.
   b. collect market and creative information.
   c. analyze information about target audiences.
   d. analyze message design of a campaign.
   e. all of the above

   Answer: e Difficulty: 2 Page: 197   Key 1: R

9. What major challenges face media planners searching media for target audience opportunities?
   a. discrepancies between the language of internal research and external media research.
   b. a lack of reliable audience research for new media.
   c. providing profiles of a firm's valued customers and prospects.
   d. both a and b
   e. both b and c

   Answer: d Difficulty: 2 Page: 197   Key 1: R

10. When the media plan varies the amount of advertising for each sales territory, what marketing factor is influencing the media decision?
    a. the competitor's advertising pattern
    b. the monthly sales patterns
    c. the distribution patterns
    d. the territoriality
    e. the area sales pattern

    Answer: e Difficulty: 2 Page: 198   Key 1: A

11. When the media plan varies the amount of advertising to account for fluctuations in sales for different periods, what marketing factor is influencing the media decision?
    a. the competitor's advertising patterns
    b. the regionality of sales
    c. the monthly sales patterns
    d. the area sales patterns
    e. the distribution patterns

    Answer: c Difficulty: 2 Page: 198   Key 1: A

12. When the media plan varies the amount of advertising to account for the varying levels of advertising by competing products, what marketing factor is influencing the media decision?
    a. price analysis
    b. competitor's advertising patterns
    c. distribution patterns
    d. competitor's promotion analysis
    e. area sales patterns

    Answer: b Difficulty: 2 Page: 199   Key 1: A

13. What are the most important issues that direct media strategy?
    a. whom to advertise to, geographic coverage, timing, campaign duration, length of the ad
    b. whom to advertise to, media characteristics, timing, geographic coverage
    c. whom to advertise to, timing, geographic coverage, cost
    d. whom to advertise to, creative strategy, cost, ad campaign duration

    Answer: a Difficulty: 3 Page: 199   Key 1: S

14. All of the following are factors in making correct media planning timing decisions EXCEPT:
    a. competitor advertising.
    b. seasonal buying patterns.
    c. product-use segmentation.
    d. how often the product is bought.
    e. month-to-month buying patterns.

    Answer: c Difficulty: 2 Page: 199   Key 1: R

15. Which of the following affects the decision about how long the advertisement should run?
    a. competitive strategies
    b. advertising budget
    c. consumer use cycles
    d. none of the above
    e. all of the above

    Answer: e Difficulty: 2 Page: 200   Key 1: R

16. The percentage of advertising messages in a medium or the percentage of vehicles owned by one brand among all messages for that product or service is called:
    a. brand development index.
    b. competitor development index.
    c. share of market.
    d. share of voice.
    e. pattern of competitive advertising.

    Answer: d Difficulty: 2 Page: 200   Key 1: R

17. How is traffic to a website measured?
    a. how many URLs were opened.
    b. how many different people visit a site during a given period.
    c. how many times people returned to the site.
    d. the total number of pages people looked at while at a site.
    e. all of the above methods.

    Answer: e Difficulty: 2 Page: 201   Key 1: R

18. The formula planners use to allocate advertising dollars may rely on what market statistics?
    a. target populations
    b. distribution
    c. media costs
    d. company sales results
    e. all of the above

    Answer: d Difficulty: 2 Page: 201   Key 1: R

19. Planners typically don't make heavy allocations in weak sales areas unless:
    a. the company is being bought out by another company.
    b. proportional increases indicate good sales management.
    c. strong marketing reasons indicate significant growth potential.
    d. all of the above
    e. none of the above

    Answer: c Difficulty: 2 Page: 202   Key 1: R

20. The strategy and tactics used to schedule advertising messages over the time span of the advertising campaign are called:
    a. media plan.
    b. continuity.
    c. frequency.
    d. advertising plan.
    e. coverage.

    Answer: b Difficulty: 1 Page: 203   Key 1: R

21. Advertising spending that remains relatively constant during the campaign period follows:
    a. a pulse pattern.
    b. a continuous pattern.
    c. flighting.
    d. a carry-over pattern.
    e. a continuity.

    Answer: b Difficulty: 2 Page: 203   Key 1: R

22. An advertising pattern in which time and space are scheduled on a continuous but uneven pattern, and lower levels are followed by burst or peak periods of intensified activity is called:
    a. flighting.
    b. continuous pattern.
    c. pulsing.
    d. interval.
    e. impact.

    Answer: c Difficulty: 2 Page: 203   Key 1: R

23. Which one of the following is a popular alternative to continuous advertising?
    a. aperture
    b. pulsing
    c. fragmenting
    d. impact

    Answer: b Difficulty: 3 Page: 203   Key 1: R

24. Pulsed schedules cover what part of a media plan time?
    a. less than a week
    b. a month
    c. three months
    d. six months
    e. most of the year

    Answer: e Difficulty: 2 Page: 203   Key 1: R

25. Andre Breton's Deli runs ads two days a week in the daily newspaper. Every three months, Andre Breton's also runs a week of radio ads. Andre Breton's is using a _____ strategy.
    a. flighting
    b. continuous
    c. pulsing
    d. wave
    e. reach

    Answer: c Difficulty: 2 Page: 203   Key 1: A

26. An advertising pattern characterized by a period of intensified activity, followed by periods of no advertising is called:
    a. pulsing.
    b. continuous.
    c. interval.
    d. impact.
    e. flighting.

    Answer: e Difficulty: 2 Page: 203   Key 1: R

27. A measure of residual effect (awareness or recall) of the advertising message some time after the advertising period has ended is called:
    a. a residual effect.
    b. a discontinuous pattern.
    c. continuity.
    d. a carry-over effect.
    e. retention.

    Answer: d Difficulty: 2 Page: 203   Key 1: R

28. The period following a flight in a flighting schedule is called a/an:
    a. hiatus.
    b. residual.
    c. residue.
    d. carry-over.
    e. impact.

    Answer: a Difficulty: 2 Page: 203   Key 1: R

29. Planners discuss gross impressions when dealing with:
    a. one vehicle in a schedule.
    b. no more than two vehicles in a schedule.
    c. multiple vehicles in a schedule.
    d. all of the above.
    e. none of the above

    Answer: c Difficulty: 2 Page: 203   Key 1: R

30. Data on the most effective size of a particular message within a medium:
    a. is inconclusive.
    b. indicates that bigger is better.
    c. indicates that size does count.
    d. indicates that smaller and more colorful is the best strategy.
    e. none of the above

    Answer: a Difficulty: 2 Page: 204   Key 1: R

31. Setting objectives and recommending strategies help focus the media plan, but planners must consider what other factor(s) to select the specific advertising medium for the message?
    a. the number of different people exposed to the message
    b. the degree of exposure repetition
    c. the efficiency
    d. none of the above
    e. all of the above

    Answer: e Difficulty: 2 Page: 204   Key 1: R

32. A person's opportunity to be exposed to the advertising message is called:
    a. impression.
    b. gross recall.
    c. carry-over effect.
    d. top-of-mind awareness.
    e. pulse.

    Answer: a Difficulty: 2 Page: 204   Key 1: R

33. What is the sum of all the media vehicles used in a certain time spot?
    a. impressions
    b. gross impressions
    c. reach
    d. frequency
    e. none of the above

    Answer: b Difficulty: 2 Page: 205   Key 1: R

34. What do impressions measure?
    a. impact of advertising message
    b. size of the media audience for an ad
    c. efficiency of the media plan
    d. degree of exposure repetition
    e. all of the above

    Answer: b Difficulty: 2 Page: 205   Key 1: R

35. If a medium has an audience of 50,000 and five ads run in that medium, what are the gross impressions?
    a. 50,000
    b. 100,000
    c. 250,000
    d. 500,000
    e. 1 million

    Answer: c Difficulty: 2 Page: 205   Key 1: A

36. The sum of the audiences of all media vehicles used within a designated time span is called:
    a. gross rating points.
    b. gross impressions.
    c. weight.
    d. coverage.
    e. penetration.

    Answer: b Difficulty: 2 Page: 205   Key 1: R

37. The summary figure in gross impressions is called gross because:
    a. The figure is so large it often becomes distorted.
    b. The figure is so inaccurate it is often useless.
    c. It makes no attempt to calculate how many different people viewed the show.
    d. It is taken from raw data that have yet to be compiled and verified.

    Answer: c Difficulty: 2 Page: 205   Key 1: R

38. A month-long advertising campaign exposes 80,000 people in the target audience (which is 70% of the total population) an average of 6 times each. The campaign has produced _____ gross impressions and _____ gross rating points.
    a. 80,000 . . . 12
    b. 80,000 . . . 70
    c. 80,000 . . . 420
    d. 480,000 . . . 70
    e. 480,000 . . . 420

    Answer: e Difficulty: 2 Page: 206   Key 1: A

39. What are the gross rating points in the following situation? There are two newspapers in a city with a population of 900,000. The circulation of the papers are 300,000 and 150,000. If a media plan calls for using five ads each in both papers, what are the gross rating points?
    a. 200
    b. 250
    c. 450
    d. 500
    e. 2,000

    Answer: d Difficulty: 2 Page: 206   Key 1: A

40. The sum of the total exposure potential of a series of media vehicles expressed as a percentage of the audience population is called:
    a. gross impressions.
    b. weight.
    c. coverage.
    d. gross rating points.

    Answer: d Difficulty: 2 Page: 206   Key 1: R

41. If a medium has an audience of 500,000 and the total number of TV households is 1,000,000, what is the gross rating point total for four messages delivered in that medium?
    a. 20
    b. 50
    c. 80
    d. 200
    e. 4,000

    Answer: d Difficulty: 3 Page: 206   Key 1: A

CHAPTER 8:   MEDIA STRATEGY AND PLANNING

42. A method of calculating gross ratings points is to multiply what two audience measurements?
a. weight and frequency
b. frequency and gross impressions
c. reach and frequency
d. gross impressions and frequency

Answer: c Difficulty: 2 Page: 206   Key 1: S

43. The percentage of different homes or people exposed to a media vehicle or vehicles at least once during a specific period of time is called:
a. frequency.
b. weight.
c. gross rating points.
d. reach.
e. gross impressions.

Answer: d Difficulty: 2 Page: 206   Key 1: R

44. In media planning, what does reach times frequency equal?
a. continuity
b. gross impressions
c. gross rating points
d. average frequency

Answer: c Difficulty: 2 Page: 206   Key 1: R

45. What is the reach in the following situation? There are two newspapers in a city with a population of 900,000. The circulations of the papers are 220,000 and 140,000. Research has revealed that 60,000 households subscribe to both papers. If a media plan calls for using both papers, what is the reach?
a. 30%
b. 33%
c. 40%
d. 50%
e. 67%

Answer: b Difficulty: 3 Page: 206   Key 1: A

46. How do most mass media calculate the unduplicated audience for their medium?
a. audience diaries reporting media use and purchase
b. in-home surveys
c. media audience data
d. through media planning computer calculations of statistical probability

Answer: d Difficulty: 2 Page: 206   Key 1: R

47. The number of times an audience has an opportunity to be exposed to a media vehicle or vehicles in a specified time span is called:
    a. reach.
    b. continuity.
    c. repetition.
    d. gross rating points.
    e. frequency.

    Answer: e Difficulty: 2 Page: 207   Key 1: R

48. Which of the media planning "yardsticks" measures the degree of exposure repetition?
    a. frequency
    b. gross impressions
    c. continuity
    d. gross rating points
    e. reach

    Answer: a Difficulty: 2 Page: 207   Key 1: A

49. If the media planner divides the gross rating points by the reach, what calculation results?
    a. effective frequency
    b. continuity
    c. average frequency
    d. frequency distribution
    e. gross impressions

    Answer: c Difficulty: 2 Page: 207   Key 1: R

50. The city in question has a population of 100,000. There are two newspapers. Paper one has a circulation of 40,000 and paper two has a circulation of 20,000. 10,000 people subscribe to both papers. The media plan calls for running 15 ads in the paper with 40,000 circulation and 5 ads in the paper with 20,000 circulation. What is the average frequency?
    a. 7
    b. 8.6
    c. 11.7
    d. 12
    e. 14

    Answer: d Difficulty: 3 Page: 207   Key 1: A

51. _____ shows the pattern of exposures for each target audience member.
    a. Average frequency
    b. Reach
    c. Gross rating points
    d. Effective frequency
    e. Frequency distribution

    Answer: e Difficulty: 2 Page: 208   Key 1: R

52. Which of the following is a formula to compute of frequency?
    a. gross rating points divided by reach
    b. cost of message unit divided by gross impressions
    c. gross audience impressions divided by continuity
    d. reach divided by gross rating points
    e. none of the above

    Answer: a Difficulty: 2 Page: 208   Key 1: R

53. Which of the following is the preferred method for calculating the
    frequency of a schedule?
    a. frequency distribution
    b. unduplicated frequency
    c. gross frequency
    d. effective frequency
    e. average frequency

    Answer: a Difficulty: 2 Page: 208   Key 1: R

54. A recent concept in planning that determines a range (minimum and
    maximum) of repeat exposure for a message is called:
    a. average frequency.
    b. frequency distribution.
    c. reach.
    d. effective frequency.
    e. continuity.

    Answer: d Difficulty: 2 Page: 208   Key 1: R

55. What is the recommended level for effective frequency?
    a. more than once
    b. 5
    c. 10
    d. 15
    e. 20 or more

    Answer: a Difficulty: 2 Page: 208   Key 1: R

56. The cost of exposing 1,000 members of the target audience to the advertising message is called:
a. cost per thousand.
b. cost per reach.
c. unit cost.
d. average media cost.
e. cost per rating point.

Answer: a Difficulty: 1 Page: 209   Key 1: R

57. What is the typical means of comparing the efficiency of different media?
a. cost per thousand
b. cost per medium
c. cost per hundred
d. cost per million
e. cost per exposure

Answer: a Difficulty: 2 Page: 209   Key 1: R

58. A method of comparing media vehicles by relating the cost of the message unit to the audience rating is called:
a. cost per thousand.
b. gross rating point.
c. comparative cost.
d. cost per rating point.
e. average media cost.

Answer: d Difficulty: 2 Page: 209   Key 1: R

59. The process of measuring the target audience size against the cost to reach that audience is called:
a. relative cost.
b. efficiency.
c. cost per medium audience.
d. effectiveness.
e. media cost analysis.

Answer: b Difficulty: 1 Page: 209   Key 1: R

60. Suppose a newspaper has 50,000 readers who could be considered a target audience. The cost for a one-page ad is $2,000. What is the paper's cost per thousand?
a. $4
b. $25
c. $40
d. $250
e. $400

Answer: a Difficulty: 2 Page: 209   Key 1: A

61. Which of the following is a formula to compute cost per thousand?
    a. cost of message unit times program or issue rating
    b. (cost of message unit divided by gross impressions) times 1,000
    c. (gross audience impressions times unduplicated impressions) times 1,000
    d. cost of message unit times gross impressions times 1,000
    e. (gross impressions divided by cost of message unit) times 1,000

    Answer: b Difficulty: 2 Page: 209   Key 1: R

62. Which of the following measures efficiency?
    a. gross impressions
    b. effective frequency
    c. gross rating point
    d. cost per thousand
    e. reach

    Answer: d Difficulty: 2 Page: 209   Key 1: R

63. Which of the media planning "yardsticks" for media decisions measures the efficiency of the selected media vehicles?
    a. cost per impression
    b. cost per thousand
    c. cost per million
    d. cost per medium
    e. all of the above

    Answer: b Difficulty: 2 Page: 209   Key 1: R

64. Suppose a magazine has a circulation of 200,000 readers who could be considered a target audience. The total target audience is 1,000,000. The cost of a 4-color, one-page ad is $10,000. Calculate the cost per rating point.
    a. 20 cents
    b. $5
    c. $50
    d. $200
    e. $500

    Answer: c Difficulty: 2 Page: 209   Key 1: A

65. Which of the following is a formula to compute cost per rating point?
    a. cost of message unit divided by program or issue rating
    b. cost of message unit divided by gross impressions times 1000
    c. gross audience impressions divided by unduplicated impressions times 1000
    d. cost of message unit divided by target audience readers

    Answer: a Difficulty: 2 Page: 209   Key 1: R

TRUE/FALSE

66. The media planning field has undergone a metamorphosis because of the proliferation of new media.
    a. True
    b. False

    Answer: a Difficulty: 1 Page: 195   Key 1: R

67. An effective advertisement must expose the consumer to the product when interest and attention are high.
    a. True
    b. False

    Answer: a Difficulty: 2 Page: 196   Key 1: R

68. The goal of the media planner is to expose consumer prospects to the advertiser's message at the point when prospects are in the purchasing mode.
    a. True
    b. False

    Answer: a Difficulty: 2 Page: 196   Key 1: R

69. Aperture means reaching the right audience with the right message at the right time.
    a. True
    b. False

    Answer: a Difficulty: 2 Page: 196   Key 1: R

70. Timing is the least important element of successful advertising.
    a. True
    b. False

    Answer: b Difficulty: 2 Page: 196   Key 1: S

71. Media choices may either improve or limit message effectiveness.
    a. True
    b. False

    Answer: a Difficulty: 2 Page: 197   Key 1: S

72. Message characteristics such as a testimonial or use of humor should have no influence on media vehicle selection.
    a. True
    b. False

    Answer: b Difficulty: 2 Page: 197   Key 1: A

73. Media planners operate on the periphery of an ad campaign.
    a. True
    b. False

    Answer: b Difficulty: 2 Page: 197   Key 1: R

74. Company research can often provide profiles of the firm's valued
    customers and prospects.
    a. True
    b. False

    Answer: a Difficulty: 2 Page: 197   Key 1: R

75. Sales geography is a negligible part of most advertising plans.
    a. True
    b. False

    Answer: b Difficulty: 1 Page: 198   Key 1: R

76. Advertising is most effective when people are most receptive to the
    product information.
    a. True
    b. False

    Answer: a Difficulty: 1 Page: 198   Key 1: R

77. The advertising budget, consumer use cycles and competitive strategies
    influence the selection of advertising patterns.
    a. True
    b. False

    Answer: a Difficulty: 2 Page: 198   Key 1: R

78. Only the largest advertisers can advertise every day.
    a. True
    b. False

    Answer: b Difficulty: 3 Page: 199   Key 1: R

79. Consumer use cycles refer to the time between purchase and repurchase.
    a. True
    b. False

    Answer: a Difficulty: 2 Page: 200   Key 1: R

80. Crowded product categories allow advertisers to ignore competitors' advertising activity.
    a. True
    b. False

    Answer: b Difficulty: 2 Page: 200   Key 1: R

81. Final media strategies reflect advertising objectives.
    a. True
    b. False

    Answer: a Difficulty: 2 Page: 200   Key 1: R

82. Media planners are never limited by mass media audience research.
    a. True
    b. False

    Answer: b Difficulty: 2 Page: 200   Key 1: R

83. Marketing mix modeling enables marketers to determine the precise impact of a media plan on product sales.
    a. True
    b. False

    Answer: a Difficulty: 2 Page: 200   Key 1: R

84. Measuring traffic to an Internet site is based on a single standard approach.
    a. True
    b. False

    Answer: b Difficulty: 1 Page: 201   Key 1: R

85. Media planners must often balance uneven regional or national sales with market-by-market advertising investments.
    a. True
    b. False

    Answer: a Difficulty: 2 Page: 201   Key 1: R

86. Geographic ad strategies are useless in helping local businesses fight national corporations' power.
    a. True
    b. False

    Answer: b Difficulty: 2 Page: 201   Key 1: R

87. Successful allocation strategies entail only the media planner's efforts.
a. True
b. False

Answer: b Difficulty: 1 Page: 202   Key 1: R

88. Media continuity means that the ads run continuously or evenly.
a. True
b. False

Answer: b Difficulty: 1 Page: 203   Key 1: R

89. Gross rating points apply only to broadcast-audience measurements.
a. True
b. False

Answer: b Difficulty: 1 Page: 206   Key 1: R

90. Reach represents the percentage of unduplicated audience.
a. True
b. False

Answer: a Difficulty: 2 Page: 206   Key 1: R

91. Reach for newspapers in a city can be found by adding the circulations of the newspapers.
a. True
b. False

Answer: b Difficulty: 2 Page: 203   Key 1: R

92. Planners compare media on the basis of the size of the audience delivered.
a. True
b. False

Answer: b Difficulty: 2 Page: 204   Key 1: A

93. Most mass media do special research to calculate the part of their audience that is not duplicated in other media.
a. True
b. False

Answer: b Difficulty: 2 Page: 206   Key 1: R

94. Planners who consider frequency in a functional way will not accept average frequency if a frequency distribution is available.
a. True
b. False

Answer: a Difficulty: 2 Page: 207   Key 1: R

95. The frequency distribution method is less revealing and thus less valuable than the average frequency method of reporting repetition.
a. True
b. False

Answer: b Difficulty: 2 Page: 208   Key 1: R

96. The efficiency of the media plan is measured in terms of cost per thousand audience members.
a. True
b. False

Answer: a Difficulty: 2 Page: 209   Key 1: R

97. Nothing is considered more crucial in media buying than securing the lowest possible price for media placements.
a. True
b. False

Answer: b Difficulty: 2 Page: 211   Key 1: R

98. Once an advertising campaign is completed, the buyer's duties are completed.
a. True
b. False

Answer: b Difficulty: 2 Page: 212   Key 1: R

99. Open pricing in media negotiations reduces risk.
a. True
b. False

Answer: b Difficulty: 2 Page: 213   Key 1: R

ESSAY

100. Discuss the aperture concept in media planning.

Answer:
Prospective customers for a product or service have ideal times and places at which they can be reached with an advertising message. This point can occur when the consumer is in the "search corridor"---the purchasing mode---or it can occur when the consumer is seeking more information before entering the corridor. The goal of the media planner is to expose the target audience to the advertiser's message at these critical points. This ideal opening is called the aperture. The most effective advertisement should expose the consumer to the product when interest and attention are high. Aperture can be thought of as the home run swing in baseball: The ball meets the bat at the right spot and at the precise instant for maximum distance. Locating the aperture opportunity is a major responsibility for media planners.

Difficulty: 1 Page: 196-197 Key 1: R

101. Compare and contrast the timing and duration of continuous, pulsing, and flighting strategies.

Answer:
The question of when to advertise can mean seasons, months or parts of the day or week, but it all fits within the aperture concept. The strategy for meeting time and duration objectives involves a balance between the available advertising dollars and the length of the campaign. A continuity strategy spreads advertising continuously and evenly over the length of the campaign. Planners who cannot afford or do not want continuous scheduling have two other options: pulse patterns or flight patterns.

Pulsing is designed to intensify advertising before an open aperture and then reduce advertising to much lower levels until the aperture opens again. The pulse pattern has peaks and valleys unlike the straight line pattern of continuity strategies.

The flighting strategy is the most severe type of continuity adjustment. It is characterized by alternating periods of intense advertising activity and periods of no advertising (hiatus). This on-and-off schedule allows for a longer campaign without making the advertising schedule too light. Unlike the continuity and pulsing schedule, the advertiser hopes consumers will remember the message without reminders for long periods of time.

Difficulty: 3 Page: 203 Key 1: A/S

102. Discuss the three secondary factors---reach, frequency and CPM---that planners consider when selecting the specific advertising media for the message and how they calculate each when considering them.

Answer:
Setting objectives and recommending strategies help focus the media plan, but planners must consider three other factors to select the specific advertising media for the message: reach, frequency and cost per thousand.

Reach is the percentage of the target population exposed at least once to the advertiser's message during a specific time frame. The media planner calculates the reach of a schedule according to research estimates that forecast the unduplicated audience. Planners measure most mass media this way, although for some media, the estimate is only a statistical probability. This means the reach is not based on actual data, but is calculated based on laws of chance. Reach can be calculated only when the planner has access to media audience research or projections from statistical models.

As important as the reach is the frequency or number of times people are exposed to a message. Whereas the reach estimate is based on only a single exposure, frequency estimates the number of times the exposure is expected to happen. To measure the frequency of a schedule, planners use two methods: a shorthand summary called average frequency and the preferred frequency method, which shows the percentage of audience reached at each level of repetition (exposed once, twice, and so on).

The process of measuring the target audience size against the cost of reaching that audience is called efficiency or cost per thousand (CPM). It is best to use CPM analysis to compare vehicles within a single medium rather than across media. It is also important to base it only on the portion of the audience that has target characteristics. To calculate the CPM you only need two figures: the cost per unit and the estimated target audience. We divide the target audience's gross impressions into the cost per unit to determine the advertising dollars needed to expose 1,000 members of the target.

Difficulty: 3 Page: 204-210   Key 1: R/S

103. Discuss the five most important media buyer functions. Give examples.

Answer:
The most important buyer functions are: providing information to media planners, selecting the media, negotiating costs, monitoring the media choices and evaluating the media choices after the campaign.

Media buyers are close enough to day-to-day changes in media popularity and pricing to be a constant source of inside information to media planners. For example, if a radio time buyer discovers that a top disk jockey is leaving the station, this could influence the strategy and tactics of current and future advertising plans.

One essential part of buying is choosing the best media vehicles to fit the target audience's aperture. The media planner lays out the direction, but the buyer is responsible for choosing specific vehicles. For example, an advertisement for a new brand of jeans aimed at Gen-Xers might do well in a magazine like *Alternative Press*.

Aside from finding aperture-related target audiences, nothing is considered more crucial in media buying than securing the lowest possible price for placements. Time and space charges make up the largest portion of the advertising budget, so there is continuous pressure to keep costs as low as possible.

Not every vehicle in a campaign performs at or above expectations---underperformance and schedule problems are facts of life. The buyer's response to problems must be swift and decisive. For example, poorly performing vehicles must be replaced or costs must be modified; Production and schedule difficulties must be rectified.

Once a campaign is completed, the buyer's duty is to compare the plan's expectations and forecasts with what actually happened. For example, they might ask, "Did the plan actually achieve GRP, reach, frequency and CPM objectives?" These five tasks are the highlights of media buying.

Difficulty: 2 Page: 210-213   Key 1: S/R

104. Discuss and describe the major sections of the typical media plan.

Answer:
Typical media plans begin with the general and work down to more
specific questions. Similarly, they begin with the most important
decisions and work down to those of lesser priority.

The background and situation analysis is the marketing perspective. It
may discuss media options and opportunities to narrowly target consumers
using niche channels and programs. It also describes the target
audience, their psychographics and the best way to reach them.

The media objective and aperture opportunities section discusses the
goals or tasks the plan should accomplish. Objectives are relevant to
the brand's strategy, detailed, measurable and realistic in terms of a
time frame. The objective should be limited to goals that the media can
accomplish.

The strategy section explains why a single medium or set of media is
appropriate for the campaign objectives. A sound strategy should anchor
each dimension to the recommendation. Because planning typically occurs
months before the campaign actually begins, some detail is omitted.

Finally, the scheduling and budget allocation illustrates most of the
media recommendations. It uses graphics to show month-by-month placement
of messages, details the anticipated impact through forecasted levels of
GRPs and illustrates how the campaign budget is allocated by medium and
by month. It is a concise blueprint of the media plan.

Difficulty: 1 Page: 216-220   Key 1: R

CHAPTER 9: PRINT MEDIA

MULTIPLE CHOICE

1. All of the following are true about print media EXCEPT:
   a. selective targeting.
   b. delivering messages one topic at a time.
   c. moving toward online media.
   d. is the dominant media form in our society.
   e. has more credibility than broadcast media.

   Answer: d Difficulty: 2 Page: 226   Key 1: R

2. What is a key benefit of print media?
   a. simultaneous delivery of a great deal of information
   b. interactivity
   c. selective targeting of audiences
   d. unstructured information processing style
   e. all of the above

   Answer: c Difficulty: 2 Page: 226   Key 1: R

3. Which of the following is an advantage of print media?
   a. selectivity
   b. deliver one thought at a time
   c. credibility
   d. deliver one message at a time
   e. all of the above

   Answer: e Difficulty: 2 Page: 226   Key 1: R

4. All of the following are true about newspapers EXCEPT:
   a. provide information faster than broadcast.
   b. no longer the nation's medium of choice.
   c. have poor production quality.
   d. major newspaper owners have become publishing empires.
   e. most cities have one daily newspaper.

   Answer: a Difficulty: 2 Page: 227   Key 1: R

5. All of the following characteristics of weekly newspapers are correct EXCEPT:
   a. they appear in towns, suburbs, and smaller cities.
   b. they represent an administrative headache for national advertisers.
   c. they emphasize news of a relatively restricted area.
   d. they occupy a unique circulation niche different from dailies or Sunday papers.
   e. they tend to ignore national news and sports.

   Answer: d Difficulty: 2 Page: 228   Key 1: R

6. Daily newspapers are usually found in:
   a. smaller cities.
   b. large cities.
   c. suburbs.
   d. towns.
   e. all of the above

   Answer: b Difficulty: 2 Page: 228   Key 1: R

7. Why do national advertisers shun weekly newspapers?
   a. they contain mostly local news
   b. they avoid national news
   c. they are relatively expensive
   d. they serve towns, suburbs, and smaller cities
   e. they have too much advertising clutter

   Answer: c Difficulty: 2 Page: 228   Key 1: R

8. Weekly newspapers usually are found in:
   a. towns.
   b. neighborhoods.
   c. suburbs.
   d. smaller cities.
   e. all of the above

   Answer: e Difficulty: 2 Page: 228   Key 1: R

9. What is the most common size/format for newspapers?
   a. metro
   b. gatefold
   c. double spread
   d. tabloid
   e. broadsheet

   Answer: e Difficulty: 2 Page: 228   Key 1: R

10. Which of the following is used by U.S. Today to adjust to consumer tastes in information?
    a. more use of full color
    b. charts and graphs to simplify information
    c. brief and breezy stories
    d. pages dressed up with flashy graphics
    e. all of the above

    Answer: e Difficulty: 2 Page: 228   Key 1: R

11. What has the newspaper industry done recently to encourage national advertisers to use newspapers more?
    a. reduced advertising cost to national advertisers
    b. increased penetration
    c. introduced the Standard Advertising Unit
    d. standardized the news format of newspapers
    e. all of the above

    Answer: c Difficulty: 2 Page: 228   Key 1: R

12. What major problem has plagued the newspaper industry historically and has discouraged national advertisers from using newspapers?
    a. declining penetration
    b. high cost
    c. lack of standardization of news format
    d. lack of format and selectivity
    e. lack of standardization and advertising format

    Answer: e Difficulty: 1 Page: 228   Key 1: R

13. A measure of the number of copies sold is called:
    a. coverage.
    b. circulation.
    c. penetration.
    d. audience.
    e. readership.

    Answer: b Difficulty: 1 Page: 228   Key 1: R

14. What percentage of adults receive a Sunday or weekend newspaper?
    a. nearly 10%
    b. nearly 25%
    c. nearly 50%
    d. nearly 67%
    e. nearly 75%

    Answer: c Difficulty: 2 Page: 230   Key 1: R

15. The Audit Bureau of Circulation:
    a. provides newspaper research data.
    b. verifies circulation statistics.
    c. set advertising rates.
    d. provides information on competitive advertising.
    e. all of the above

    Answer: b Difficulty: 2 Page: 231   Key 1: R

16. Newspapers verify their circulation by:
    a. belonging to the Audit Bureau of Circulation.
    b. a sworn statement called a publisher's statement.
    c. an annual statement called a Post Office statement.
    d. all of the above
    e. none of the above

    Answer: d Difficulty: 2 Page: 231   Key 1: R

17. Which company provides the only consistent measurement of popular newspaper audiences in individual markets?
    a. Audit Bureau of Circulation
    b. Simmons-Scarborough
    c. Advertising Checking Bureau
    d. National Advertising Bureau
    e. Marketing Research, Inc.

    Answer: b Difficulty: 2 Page: 231   Key 1: R

18. Research indicates that the rate differential charged national advertisers is:
    a. relatively constant.
    b. decreasing.
    c. increasing.

    Answer: c Difficulty: 2 Page: 231   Key 1: S

19. Commercial messages arranged in the newspaper according to reader interests are called:
    a. local advertising.
    b. national advertising.
    c. supplements.
    d. display advertising.
    e. classified advertising.

    Answer: e Difficulty: 2 Page: 231   Key 1: R

20. Sponsored messages that can be of any size and location within the newspaper, with the exception of the editorial page are called:
    a. supplements.
    b. display advertising.
    c. free-standing insert advertising.
    d. classified advertising.
    e. specialty advertising.

    Answer: b Difficulty: 2 Page: 232   Key 1: R

21. What is the dominant form of newspaper advertising?
    a. classified advertising
    b. supplements
    c. free-standing insert advertising
    d. display advertising
    e. specialty advertising

    Answer: d Difficulty: 2 Page: 232   Key 1: A

22. What are the three general types of newspaper advertising?
    a. national, local, and supplements
    b. display, inserts, and supplements
    c. general, retail, and institutional
    d. classified, display, and supplements
    e. local, suburban, and national

    Answer: d Difficulty: 2 Page: 232   Key 1: S

23. What are the two types of display advertising?
    a. local and national
    b. retail and local
    c. special and general
    d. syndicated and local
    e. special and national

    Answer: a Difficulty: 1 Page: 232   Key 1: R

24. The difference between what is charged for local display advertising and national display advertising is referred to as:
    a. local display rate.
    b. cooperative advertising.
    c. milline rate.
    d. rate differential.
    e. rip-off.

    Answer: d Difficulty: 2 Page: 232   Key 1: R

25. Approximately 85 percent of all display advertising in daily newspapers is:
    a. national.
    b. local.
    c. regional.
    d. syndicated.

    Answer: b Difficulty: 3 Page: 232   Key 1: R

26. All of the following are reasons given by newspapers to justify the different rates charged local and national advertisers EXCEPT:
    a. newspapers must allow a commission to the ad agencies normally used by national advertisers.
    b. national advertisers ask for more help.
    c. national advertisers are unlikely to change the number of ads placed regardless of rate.
    d. national advertisers are less reliable.
    e. all of the above

    Answer: a Difficulty: 2 Page: 232   Key 1: R

27. What is the relative comparison of the rates paid for display advertising by national and local advertisers?
    a. local advertisers pay slightly more
    b. national advertisers and local advertisers pay about the same
    c. local advertisers pay nearly twice as much as national advertisers
    d. national advertisers pay over 50% more than local advertisers
    e. national advertisers pay slightly more

    Answer: d Difficulty: 2 Page: 232   Key 1: R

28. An arrangement between the advertiser and the retailer whereby both parties share the cost of placing an ad is called:
    a. syndicated advertising.
    b. local contract.
    c. co-op advertising.
    d. sponsorship advertising.
    e. participation advertising.

    Answer: c Difficulty: 2 Page: 232   Key 1: R

29. Preprinted advertisements that are placed loosely within the newspaper are called:
    a. classified advertising.
    b. display advertising.
    c. supplements.
    d. free-standing insert advertising.

    Answer: d Difficulty: 2 Page: 233   Key 1: R

30. A full-color advertisement insert that is published by independent publishers and distributed to newspapers throughout the country such as *Parade* and *USA Weekend* is called:
    a. magazine supplement.
    b. syndicated supplement.
    c. local supplement.
    d. free-standing insert advertising.
    e. advertising supplement.

    Answer: b Difficulty: 3 Page: 233   Key 1: R

31. Which of the following is a reason for using cooperative advertising?
    a. makes it easier to use coupons
    b. allows national advertisers to pay the local advertising rate
    c. makes advertising more credible
    d. to get more help from the newspaper
    e. all of the above

    Answer: b Difficulty: 2 Page: 233   Key 1: R

32. *Parade* magazine is a well-known example of which of the following?
    a. tabloid newspaper
    b. free-standing insert
    c. local supplement
    d. syndicated supplement
    e. online magazine

    Answer: d Difficulty: 2 Page: 233   Key 1: A

33. What is the greatest advantage of advertising in newspapers?
    a. flexibility
    b. quality production
    c. comparison shopping
    d. extensive market coverage
    e. positive consumer attitudes

    Answer: d Difficulty: 3 Page: 233   Key 1: R

34. Which of the following is a reason free-standing insert advertising is growing in popularity with retail advertisers?
    a. allows greater control over reproduction quality of ads
    b. allows national advertisers to pay local advertising rates
    c. more flexible
    d. more credible
    e. readers like them better

    Answer: a Difficulty: 2 Page: 234   Key 1: R

35. Which of the following is an advantage of newspapers?
    a. mental imagery
    b. minimal advertising clutter
    c. production flexibility
    d. national market coverage
    e. product demonstration

    Answer: c Difficulty: 2 Page: 234   Key 1: R

36. In newspaper advertising, what term is used to refer to the fact that newspapers allow advertisers to advertise in some geographic markets and not in others?
    a. market coverage
    b. segmentation
    c. targeting
    d. flexibility
    e. reach

    Answer: d Difficulty: 2 Page: 234   Key 1: R

37. Which of the following is a disadvantage of newspapers?
    a. clutter
    b. poor reproduction
    c. short life span
    d. limited coverage of the elderly
    e. all of the above

    Answer: e Difficulty: 2 Page: 234   Key 1: R

38. Which of the following groups are not frequent readers of the newspaper?
    a. well-educated
    b. white-collar professionals
    c. under-20 age group
    d. higher income group
    e. all of the above

    Answer: c Difficulty: 2 Page: 234   Key 1: R

39. All of the following would have difficulty making an impact in the newspaper EXCEPT:
    a. professional services.
    b. trades people services.
    c. product demonstrations.
    d. coupons.
    e. all of the above

    Answer: d Difficulty: 2 Page: 234   Key 1: S

40. A critical factor in the poor reproduction quality of newspapers is:
    a. time pressures.
    b. lack of printing technology.
    c. lack of good color inks.
    d. not enough quality press professionals.
    e. all of the above

    Answer: a Difficulty: 2 Page: 235   Key 1: R

41. The most consistent characteristic of magazines is:
    a. mass circulation.
    b. weekly publication cycle.
    c. aimed at specific audiences.
    d. literary content.
    e. all of the above

    Answer: c Difficulty: 2 Page: 236   Key 1: R

42. In the magazine industry, to what does the "age of skimming" refer?
    a. high introductory prices for new magazines to take the cream off the
       market
    b. magazine readers requiring 80% of the information from story titles,
       subheadings, captions, and pictures rather than editorial content
    c. magazine's executives taking profit off the top in the form of lavish
       benefits and salaries before declaring dividends for stockholders
    d. practice in the magazine industry of targeting upscale audiences and
       ignoring others
    e. all of the above

    Answer: b Difficulty: 2 Page: 236   Key 1: R

43. What are the three types of magazines that are categorized by audience?
    a. farm, consumer, and business
    b. consumer, retailer, and manufacturer
    c. professional, institutional, and homemaker
    d. urban, suburban, and rural
    e. consumer, distributor, and industrial

    Answer: a Difficulty: 2 Page: 237   Key 1: R

44. In the magazine industry, magazines that are directed to people who buy
    products for their personal use are called:
    a. general magazines.
    b. people magazines.
    c. horizontal magazines.
    d. consumer magazines.
    e. demographic magazines.

    Answer: d Difficulty: 2 Page: 237   Key 1: R

45. Which category of magazines is divided into "trade papers,"
    "professional magazines," and "industrial magazines"?
    a. consumer
    b. business
    c. professional
    d. vertical
    e. horizontal

    Answer: b Difficulty: 2 Page: 237   Key 1: R

46. What are magazines which are directed to retailers, wholesalers, and other distributors called?
    a. people magazines
    b. vertical magazines
    c. distribution magazines
    d. horizontal magazines
    e. trade papers

    Answer: e Difficulty: 2 Page: 237   Key 1: R

47. _____ presents stories and information about an entire industry.
    a. Horizontal publication
    b. Industrial publication
    c. Trade papers
    d. Vertical publication
    e. Producer publications

    Answer: d Difficulty: 2 Page: 237   Key 1: R

48. _____ deals with a business function that cuts across industries, such as Direct Marketing.
    a. Horizontal publication
    b. Trade papers
    c. Vertical publication
    d. Consumer publication
    e. Industrial publication

    Answer: a Difficulty: 2 Page: 237   Key 1: R

49. The text suggests what primary reason for geographic editions of magazines?
    a. allows localizing of editorial content
    b. encourages local retail support
    c. simplifies distribution
    d. reduces production costs
    e. improves image of magazine

    Answer: b Difficulty: 2 Page: 237   Key 1: R

50. What is the traditional delivery system in the magazine industry?
    a. through professionals
    b. through newsstands or to a home via mail
    c. within newspapers
    d. hanging bagged copies on doorknobs
    e. handed out at shopping malls

    Answer: b Difficulty: 1 Page: 238   Key 1: R

51. Which of the following is a nontraditional delivery system used in the magazine industry?
    a. delivery through professionals
    b. free distribution
    c. delivery within newspapers
    d. hanging bagged copies on doorknobs
    e. all of the above

    Answer: e Difficulty: 2 Page: 238   Key 1: R

52. The distribution of magazines through nontraditional delivery systems for free is called:
    a. controlled circulation.
    b. fee distribution.
    c. paid circulation.
    d. non-traditional distribution.
    e. guaranteed circulation.

    Answer: a Difficulty: 2 Page: 238   Key 1: R

53. How much time is spent reading the average magazine?
    a. almost 1 hour
    b. 2 hours
    c. 3 hours
    d. 4 hours
    e. 5 or more hours

    Answer: a Difficulty: 3 Page: 239   Key 1: R

54. The number of readers that a magazine publisher promises to provide for an ad is called:
    a. controlled circulation.
    b. guaranteed circulation.
    c. paid circulation.
    d. publisher's statement.
    e. magazine circulation.

    Answer: b Difficulty: 2 Page: 239   Key 1: R

55. Which of the following represents readers' attitudes toward magazine advertising?
    a. pay more attention to magazine advertising than TV advertising
    b. have a positive attitude toward advertising
    c. most adults consider magazine advertising helpful for buying
    d. most adults have a positive attitude about the amount of information carried in magazines
    e. all of the above

    Answer: e Difficulty: 2 Page: 239   Key 1: R

56. On what are magazine advertising rates based?
    a. circulation
    b. publication costs
    c. distribution costs
    d. editorial costs
    e. production costs

    Answer: a Difficulty: 2 Page: 239   Key 1: A

57. What organization is responsible for establishing the official circulation of magazines on which advertising rates are based?
    a. Simmons Market Research Bureau
    b. Market Research Incorporated
    c. National Advertising Bureau
    d. Audit Bureau of Circulation
    e. MediaMark

    Answer: d Difficulty: 2 Page: 239   Key 1: R

58. What research service provides an analysis of magazine audiences that is relied on by most advertisers and agencies and that relates readership patterns to purchase habits?
    a. Audit Advertising Bureau
    b. National Advertising Bureau
    c. MediaMark
    d. Standard Rate and Data Service
    e. Birch Scarborough-VNU

    Answer: c Difficulty: 2 Page: 239   Key 1: R

59. Simmons Market Research Bureau:
    a. provides information relating reading habits to purchasing habits.
    b. verifies circulation statistics.
    c. analyzes television viewing habits.
    d. sets advertising rates for publishers.
    e. all of the above

    Answer: a Difficulty: 2 Page: 239   Key 1: R

60. A new technology that allows magazines to combine information on subscribers kept in a data-base with a computer program so that the end result is a magazine that includes special sections for subscribers based on their demographic profiles is called:
    a. desktop publishing.
    b. selective binding.
    c. ink-jet printing.
    d. data-base manager.
    e. integrated distribution.

    Answer: b Difficulty: 2 Page: 240   Key 1: R

61. A new technology that allows a magazine such as *U.S. News & World Report* to personalize its renewal form so that each issue contains a renewal card already filled out with the subscriber's name, address, and so on is called:
    a. ink-jet printing.
    b. data-base manager.
    c. desktop publishing.
    d. offset printing.
    e. selective binding.

    Answer: a Difficulty: 2 Page: 240   Key 1: R

62. A new technology, which allows magazines to close pages just hours before press time and thus to eliminate a long lead-time, a serious drawback long associated with magazine advertising, is called:
    a. data-base manager.
    b. electronic mail.
    c. selective binding.
    d. desktop publishing.
    e. ink-jet printing.

    Answer: d Difficulty: 2 Page: 240   Key 1: R

63. What does data-base management allow magazine publishers to do for their readers?
    a. combine information available from exact subscriber lists of other public and private lists to write complete consumer profiles for advertisers
    b. include special inserts for individual subscribers
    c. personalize renewal forms so that each issue contains a renewal card already filled out with the subscriber's name, address, etc.
    d. include special sections for particular subscribers in which there is information based on the subscriber's demographic profile
    e. all of the above

    Answer: e Difficulty: 2 Page: 240   Key 1: R

64. Normally, what is the largest unit of space sold by magazines?
    a. fractional page space
    b. 3-page spread
    c. gatefold
    d. double-page spread

    Answer: d Difficulty: 2 Page: 240   Key 1: R

65. A single or double page broken into a variety of units is called:
    a. bleed page.
    b. gatefold.
    c. fractional page space.
    d. gutter.
    e. page spread.

    Answer: c Difficulty: 2 Page: 240   Key 1: R

66. What is the primary advantage of magazines today?
    a. long life span
    b. ability to reach specialized audiences
    c. visual quality
    d. production quality
    e. ability to teach a wide, general audience

    Answer: b Difficulty: 2 Page: 241   Key 1: A

TRUE/FALSE

67. Print media are moving toward going online.
    a. True
    b. False

    Answer: a Difficulty: 2 Page: 226   Key 1: R

68. Print media have more credibility than broadcast media.
    a. True
    b. False

    Answer: a Difficulty: 2 Page: 226   Key 1: R

69. Print media deliver messages one topic at a time and one thought at a time and deliver them with credibility unmatched by broadcast advertising.
    a. True
    b. False

    Answer: a Difficulty: 1 Page: 226   Key 1: A

70. Weekday editions of daily newspapers normally have greater circulations than do Sunday newspapers.
    a. True
    b. False

    Answer: b Difficulty: 2 Page: 227   Key 1: R

71. High costs of competition and increased costs of newspaper production have resulted in consolidation within the newspaper industry.
    a. True
    b. False

    Answer: a Difficulty: 2 Page: 227   Key 1: R

72. *The Christian Times* is an example of special-interest newspapers.
    a. True
    b. False

    Answer: a Difficulty: 2 Page: 227   Key 1: A

73. Newspapers can be classified by frequency of publication (daily, weekly, etc.).
    a. True
    b. False

    Answer: a Difficulty: 2 Page: 228   Key 1: R

74. Newspapers are usually not classified by their circulation.
    a. True
    b. False

    Answer: b Difficulty: 2 Page: 228   Key 1: R

75. Daily newspapers report on the events of the day they are distributed.
    a. True
    b. False

    Answer: b Difficulty: 2 Page: 228   Key 1: R

76. Approximately 90 percent of daily papers publish a Sunday edition.
    a. True
    b. False

    Answer: b Difficulty: 3 Page: 228   Key 1: R

77. Tabloid size is the standard size for newspapers.
    a. True
    b. False

    Answer: b Difficulty: 2 Page: 228   Key 1: R

78. Until the 1980s national advertisers shied away from using newspapers because they had no Standard Advertising Unit.
    a. True
    b. False

    Answer: a Difficulty: 2 Page: 228   Key 1: R

79. The word circulation refers to the number of newspapers sold.
    a. True
    b. False

    Answer: a Difficulty: 2 Page: 229   Key 1: R

80. Most newspapers only have a national circulation.
    a. True
    b. False

    Answer: b Difficulty: 2 Page: 229   Key 1: R

81. Newspapers in the U.S. are only published in English in accordance with federal legislation.
    a. True
    b. False

    Answer: b Difficulty: 2 Page: 229   Key 1: R

82. Newspaper readership increases with age.
    a. True
    b. False

    Answer: a Difficulty: 2 Page: 230   Key 1: A

83. On Sundays, two-thirds of adults read the newspaper.
    a. True
    b. False

    Answer: a Difficulty: 2 Page: 230   Key 1: R

84. Any newspaper, paid for or free, can be a member of the Auditing Bureau of Circulation.
    a. True
    b. False

    Answer: b Difficulty: 2 Page: 231   Key 1: R

85. Simmons-Scarborough is one of many consistent measurements of popular audiences in individual markets.
    a. True
    b. False

    Answer: b Difficulty: 3 Page: 231   Key 1: R

86. Classified ads are offered free by most newspapers.
    a. True
    b. False

    Answer: b Difficulty: 2 Page: 232   Key 1: R

87. Newspaper ad rates are set by the official circulation audits of the Audit Bureau of Circulation.
    a. True
    b. False

    Answer: b Difficulty: 3 Page: 232   Key 1: A

88. National advertisers pay less than local advertisers for display advertising because of the higher purchase volume of national advertisers.
    a. True
    b. False

    Answer: b Difficulty: 2 Page: 232   Key 1: R

89. The dominant form of newspaper advertising is display advertising.
    a. True
    b. False

    Answer: a Difficulty: 2 Page: 232   Key 1: R

90. Most newspaper display advertising is local.
    a. True
    b. False

    Answer: a Difficulty: 2 Page: 232   Key 1: R

91. Cooperative advertising helps the national advertiser avoid the higher rates that newspapers charge national advertisers.
    a. True
    b. False

    Answer: a Difficulty: 1 Page: 232   Key 1: A

92. The traditional delivery of magazines to readers is through newsstands or home delivery.
    a. True
    b. False

    Answer: a Difficulty: 1 Page: 238   Key 1: R

93. About 92 percent of American adults (male and female) read at least one magazine per month.
    a. True
    b. False

    Answer: a Difficulty: 2 Page: 239   Key 1: R

94. On average American adults read nine different issues of magazines per month.
    a. True
    b. False

    Answer: a Difficulty: 2 Page: 239   Key 1: R

95. While Americans are avid readers of magazines, they don't have a particularly positive attitude toward magazine advertising.
    a. True
    b. False

    Answer: b Difficulty: 2 Page: 239   Key 1: R

96. In general, the text suggests that Americans pay relatively more attention to television advertising than to magazine advertising.
    a. True
    b. False

    Answer: b Difficulty: 2 Page: 239   Key 1: A

97. Magazines are becoming less specialized.
    a. True
    b. False

    Answer: b Difficulty: 2 Page: 239   Key 1: R

98. Magazines have the longest life span of all media.
    a. True
    b. False

    Answer: a Difficulty: 2 Page: 241   Key 1: R

99. Magazines offer excellent reproduction of quality visual images such as color photographs.
    a. True
    b. False

    Answer: a Difficulty: 1 Page: 241   Key 1: R

100. General audience magazines have a relatively high cost per thousand compared to other media.
    a. True
    b. False

    Answer: a Difficulty: 2 Page: 242   Key 1: R

CHAPTER 9:   PRINT MEDIA

ESSAY

101. Discuss the advantages and disadvantages of using newspapers as an advertising medium.

Answer:
Newspapers have many advantages. First, because of the range of market coverage, advertisers can reach many different consumer groups. Also, consumers use newspapers for comparison shopping, so they are particularly useful for products with an obvious competitive advantage. Thirdly, consumers usually perceive newspapers, and their ads, as current and credible. Newspapers also offer geographic flexibility: advertisers can choose to advertise in some markets and not others. Finally, newspapers provide a bridge between the national advertiser and the local retailer.

Like every other advertising medium, newspapers also have disadvantages. First of all, the average lifespan of a daily newspaper is only about 24 hours, so the life span of the ad is limited. Most newspapers are also cluttered with ads, particularly on supermarket advertising days and on Sundays. Although newspapers have wide market coverage, certain market groups are not frequent readers. For example, newspapers traditionally do not reach the under-20 age group. Newspapers also suffer the same limitations shared by all print media. Certain products should not be advertised, such as products that require demonstration. Finally, the reproduction quality of newspapers is often poor.

Difficulty: 2 Page: 234   Key 1: R/S

102. Discuss the types of audiences that magazines targets. What kind of products might you advertise in each?

Answer:
The three main types of audiences that magazines target are consumer, business and farm audiences.

Consumer magazines, directed at consumers who buy products for personal consumption, are distributed through the mail, newsstands or stores. Examples are *Reader's Digest, Lear's, Time* and *People*. A large variety of products can be advertised, especially if the main goal is to target a general audience. Ads for products like frozen dinners, health and beauty products are all likely to be found in consumer magazines.

Business magazines target business readers. There are three types: trade papers, industrial magazines and professional magazines. In a trade paper like *Chain Store Age*, you might find ads for new products that a chain store might carry. Industrial magazines like *Concrete Construction* may have ads for new construction equipment available to contractors. In a professional magazines such as one aimed at dentists might also advertise new technology in dental care.

Farm magazines, the third audience category, target farmers and those engaged in farm-related activities. *Peanut Farmer* is an example of a farm magazine and might carry ads for a new line of tractors.

Difficulty: 2 Page: 237   Key 1: A/S

103. Discuss how the audiences of newspapers and magazines are measured.

Answer:

Newspapers need to measure their audiences to assess performance and spot growth opportunities. They also use the measurements to attract advertisers that want to reach their readers. Newspapers obtain objective measures of readership by subscribing to one or both of these auditing companies: The Auditing Bureau of Circulations and Simmons-Scarborough. The ABC verifies statements about newspapers circulation statistics and provides detailed analysis of the paper by state, town and country. Simmons-Scarborough provides a syndicated newspaper readership study that annually measures readership profiles in approximately 70 of the nation's largest cities. The study covers readership of a single issue and the estimated unduplicated readers for a series of issues.

Magazine rates are based on the number of readers, which correlates with the guaranteed circulation. A single copy of a magazine might be read by one or several people, depending on its contents. As with newspapers, the ABC is responsible for collecting and evaluating these data to ensure that guaranteed circulation was obtained. The ABC audits subscriptions as well as newsstand sales. The Simmons marketing Research Bureau goes one step further by relating readership patterns to purchasing habits. The bureau provides data on who reads which magazines and which products these readers buy and consume.

Difficulty: 3 Page: 230-239   Key 1: S/R

104. Discuss the advantages and disadvantages of using magazines as an advertising medium.

Answer:

Magazine advertising has many advantages. The ability to reach specialized audiences has become a primary advantage. Also, magazines have a high level of audience receptivity. The editorial environment of a magazine lends authority and credibility to an ad. Also, magazines have the longest life-span of all the media, as well as the fact that an initial reader may pass the magazine on for others to read. The format allows advertisers to use detailed copy and more creative variety through multiple pages, inserts and other features. The visual quality of magazines also tends to be excellent because they are printed on high-quality paper that provides superior photo reproduction. Finally, Advertisers can distribute various sales promotion devices, such as coupons, product samples and information cards.

Several factors also limit magazines. Limited flexibility is one drawback---advertisers must submit ads well in advance of publication. Magazines also limit the choices for ad locations---prime locations, such as the back cover or inside front cover may be sold months in advance. Some readers do not look at an issue of a magazine until long after it has reached their homes, so the ad's effect may take a long time to affect the reader. The third disadvantage is the high cost of advertising---for a general audience magazine like *Newsweek*, the cost per thousand is quite high. Finally, the limited distribution, which the exception of some (like *People*) is a disadvantage.

Difficulty: 2 Page: 241-42   Key 1: S/R

105. Discuss the three overriding issues that help develop a sound media strategy: integration, culture and technology. Be sure to give examples.

Answer:

Integration means that advertisers need to understand which media fit particular situations, which media are complementary, and which detract from each other. An example of this is Sears' "Umpteen Appliances" campaign. The plan called for the initial use of mass reach weekly magazines such as *People* and *Time* to launch the campaign. As the campaign progressed, it added monthly magazines and finally TV advertising to reach a broad adult audience.

Advertisers, print media buyers, and media planners must create print ads that correctly reflect the values of the culture in which they appear and adhere to the laws and mores of a particular medium. In Denmark, for instance, headlines that contain superlatives are frowned upon and print ads cannot carry coupons.

Technology has injected uncertainty into the future of print media. Moving too soon into interactive technology options may alienate current readers and add to media costs. Moving too late may mean that ads aren't reaching the selected target audience as effectively as a competitor's ads. For example, Apple computers would probably want to advertise extensively online as opposed to a new brand of deodorant. In either case, interactive technology may create a form of print media that is similar to broadcast, and its advantages and disadvantages may change dramatically.

Difficulty: 3 Page: 249-50   Key 1: R/S

CHAPTER 10:   BROADCAST MEDIA

MULTIPLE CHOICE

1. Print is a _____ medium while broadcast is a _____ medium.
   a. cheap...expensive
   b. time...space
   c. rational...emotional
   d. space...time
   e. specialized...mass

   Answer: d Difficulty: 1 Page: 255   Key 1: A

2. In what type of television advertising does the advertiser contract with either a national or regional company to show commercials on a group of stations?
   a. network scheduling
   b. participation
   c. network syndication
   d. sponsorship

   Answer: a Difficulty: 2 Page: 256   Key 1: S

3. A station that is contracted with a national network to carry network-originated programming during part of its schedule is called:
   a. cable.
   b. a syndicate.
   c. an affiliate.
   d. an associate.

   Answer: c Difficulty: 1 Page: 256   Key 1: R

4. A network exists:
   a. whenever two or more stations are able to broadcast the same program that originates from a single source.
   b. whenever a station broadcasts a program originating from a source other than itself.
   c. whenever a station sells its own creation to another station.
   d. whenever a cable station and an "over-the-air" station broadcast the same show.

   Answer: a Difficulty: 2 Page: 256   Key 1: R

5. The primary source of affiliate station revenues is:
   a. a percentage of advertising revenue paid to national networks and selling advertising time during network programs and between programs.
   b. selling advertising time during local programs and between programs.
   c. creating advertisements for local programs.
   d. selling programming rights to cable networks.

   Answer: a Difficulty: 2 Page: 257   Key 1: R

6. _____ is basically a sales representative organization, which represents large market stations on a commission basis to simplify the task of buying advertising on the group of stations represented.
   a. Wired network
   b. Syndicate
   c. Cable network
   d. Unwired network
   e. Affiliate association

   Answer: d Difficulty: 2 Page: 257   Key 1: R

7. Current FCC guidelines concerning advertising on public television say:
   a. No advertising allowed on public television at all.
   b. Advertising on public television can appear during program breaks only.
   c. Whatever advertising appears is the choice of the local public television station.
   d. Local public television viewers get to vote on whether to have advertising.
   e. Federal law does not restrict advertising on public television.

   Answer: b Difficulty: 3 Page: 257   Key 1: R

8. All of the following are true about advertising on public television EXCEPT:
   a. Businesses can sponsor programs.
   b. FCC rules about advertising have been liberalized.
   c. Businesses can underwrite programs.
   d. Stations are allowed to interpret rules on advertising.
   e. Advertising messages can appear between programs.

   Answer: a Difficulty: 2 Page: 257   Key 1: R

9. Why do advertisers find PBS stations so attractive?
   a. reach minority consumers
   b. PBS has a refined image
   c. advertisers come-off as good corporate citizens
   d. all of the above

   Answer: d Difficulty: 2 Page: 257   Key 1: R

10. What is the source of most of the programming shown on cable television?
    a. cable operators
    b. independent cable networks
    c. pay networks
    d. network television

    Answer: b Difficulty: 2 Page: 258   Key 1: R

11. A form of subscription television in which the signals are carried to households by coaxial, electrical wiring is called:
    a. multi-point distribution TV.
    b. interconnect TV.
    c. subscription TV.
    d. wired TV.
    e. cable TV.

    Answer: e Difficulty: 1 Page: 258   Key 1: R

12. Which of the following most closely reflects the percentage of U.S. households that currently subscribe to cable television, according to A.C. Nielsen data?
    a. 10%
    b. 25%
    c. 50%
    d. 66%
    e. 90%

    Answer: d Difficulty: 1 Page: 258   Key 1: R

13. A local ad for air conditioners is run on one or a few local cable systems and is scheduled at the same time as national ads. This is:
    a. cable syndication.
    b. local patching.
    c. hard interconnect.
    d. local-point distribution.
    e. soft interconnect.

    Answer: e Difficulty: 2 Page: 259   Key 1: A

14. HBO and Showtime are examples of:
    a. pay cable networks.
    b. syndicated cable programming.
    c. independent cable networks.
    d. pay-per-view programming.
    e. independent superstations.

    Answer: a Difficulty: 1 Page: 258   Key 1: R

15. Which of the following is considered the most important reason for the decline in audience shares of the big three networks?
    a. growth of Fox TV Broadcasting
    b. growth of superstations
    c. growth in cable industry
    d. growth in advertising on PBS stations
    e. growth of direct-broadcasting satellite industry

    Answer: c Difficulty: 1 Page: 262   Key 1: R

16. Most advertisers on local television are:
    a. national manufacturers.
    b. direct marketing companies.
    c. local retailers.
    d. specialty advertisers.
    e. national retailers.

    Answer: c Difficulty: 3 Page: 260   Key 1: R

17. All of the following are forms of interactive television EXCEPT:
    a. simulcast, in which viewers can control the programming itself.
    b. video-on-demand, in which viewers controls what they watch and when.
    c. storing programming at TV set that allows viewer to choose programs.
    d. recording programming on a VCR for future viewing.
    e. using high-speed modems to access programming on the World Wide Web.

    Answer: d Difficulty: 2 Page: 261   Key 1: R

18. What are the two primary types of syndicated programming?
    a. first-run and affiliate
    b. off-network and re-run
    c. independent and network
    d. off-network and first-run
    e. re-run and original

    Answer: d Difficulty: 2 Page: 260   Key 1: R

19. A syndicated show that appears daily at the same time is called a/an:
    a. re-run.
    b. strip.
    c. off-network.
    d. package.
    e. syndicated series.

    Answer: b Difficulty: 1 Page: 260   Key 1: R

20. How many episodes must a network show produce before it can be syndicated?
    a. 25
    b. 40
    c. 65
    d. 88
    e. 100

    Answer: d Difficulty: 1 Page: 260   Key 1: R

21. The type of syndication that includes reruns of network shows such as *Star Trek*, *The Bob Newhart Show*, and *Remington Steele* is called:
    a. re-run.
    b. original.
    c. off-network.
    d. first-run.

    Answer: c Difficulty: 1 Page: 260   Key 1: R

22. What has fueled the boom in television syndication?
    a. growth of independent television stations
    b. growth of cable television
    c. decline of the three major networks
    d. growth of public television

    Answer: a Difficulty: 2 Page: 260   Key 1: R

23. When television or radio shows that are reruns or original programs are purchased by local stations to fill in during open hours, this is called:
    a. affiliation.
    b. local programming.
    c. syndication.
    d. cable television.

    Answer: c Difficulty: 1 Page: 260   Key 1: R

24. The prime-time access rule:
    a. forbids network affiliates in the 50 major TV markets from broadcasting more than three hours of prime-time network programming in any one four-hour slot.
    b. forbids network affiliates in the 50 major TV markets from carrying more than 22 minutes of advertising in any hour.
    c. requires network affiliates in the 50 major TV markets to carry at least two hours of family programming in prime-time.
    d. requires network affiliates in the 50 major TV markets to carry at least one hour of syndicated programming in prime-time.
    e. all of the above

    Answer: a Difficulty: 3 Page: 260   Key 1: R

25. When station directors bid on the shows available for syndication at the winter National Association of TV Program Executives meeting, this is called the:
    a. syndication auction.
    b. off-network syndication.
    c. upfront buying process.
    d. syndication bartering process.

    Answer: c Difficulty: 2 Page: 260   Key 1: R

26. Sometimes network shows that did not meet the minimal number of episodes such as *Too Close for Comfort*, *It's a Living*, and *What's Happening* are purchased from the networks and moved into syndication even as they continue to produce new episodes. This is referred to as:
    a. original syndication.
    b. first-run syndication.
    c. independent syndication.
    d. current syndication.
    e. off-network syndication.

    Answer: b Difficulty: 2 Page: 261   Key 1: R

27. When a show is offered to a station at a reduced price or free of charge with pre-sold national spots, this is called:
    a. cash syndication.
    b. off-network syndication.
    c. cable syndication.
    d. barter syndication.

    Answer: d Difficulty: 2 Page: 261   Key 1: R

28. What is the largest part of the syndication industry?
    a. cash syndication
    b. syndication
    c. credit syndication
    d. barter syndication

    Answer: a Difficulty: 1 Page: 261   Key 1: R

29. All of the following are different arrangements through which TV ads can be aired EXCEPT:
    a. unwired networks.
    b. Internet scheduling.
    c. cable scheduling.
    d. over-the-air network scheduling.
    e. local scheduling.

    Answer: b Difficulty: 1 Page: 262   Key 1: R

30. What are two forms of network advertising?
    a. spot announcements and local sponsorships
    b. syndication and participation
    c. contract and spot announcement
    d. sponsorship and participation
    e. syndication and sponsorship

    Answer: d Difficulty: 2 Page: 263   Key 1: S

31. What are two forms of local affiliated advertising?
    a. participation and sponsorship
    b. spot announcement and local sponsorship
    c. syndication and contract
    d. spot announcement and syndication
    e. sponsorship and participation

    Answer: b Difficulty: 2 Page: 263   Key 1: S

32. What is the most common type of network advertising arrangement?
    a. sponsorship
    b. spot announcement
    c. participation
    d. local sponsorship
    e. syndication

    Answer: c Difficulty: 2 Page: 263   Key 1: R

33. An arrangement in which a TV advertiser buys commercial time from a network is called:
    a. spot announcements.
    b. contract.
    c. participation.
    d. syndication.
    e. sponsorship.

    Answer: c Difficulty: 2 Page: 263   Key 1: R

34. What type of advertising dominates spot buys?
    a. regional
    b. local
    c. national
    d. international
    e. special

    Answer: b Difficulty: 1 Page: 264   Key 1: R

35. Breaks between programs that local affiliates sell to advertisers who want to show their ads locally are called:
    a. participation.
    b. sponsorships.
    c. spot announcements.
    d. contracts.
    e. syndication.

    Answer: c Difficulty: 1 Page: 264   Key 1: R

36. All of the following are benefits of sponsorship advertising EXCEPT:
    a. increased control over ad placement.
    b. lower cost.
    c. increased content control.
    d. more powerful impact on viewing public.
    e. control of length of ads.

    Answer: b Difficulty: 2 Page: 263   Key 1: S

37. The Hallmark Hall of Fame and the Kraft Music Hour are examples of what network advertising arrangement?
    a. participation
    b. syndication
    c. spot announcements
    d. unwired network
    e. sponsorship

    Answer: e Difficulty: 1 Page: 263   Key 1: R

38. All of the following are problems with using spot announcements EXCEPT:
    a. great deal of clutter.
    b. inflexibility in scheduling.
    c. impact.
    d. viewers often take a break from TV.
    e. none of the above

    Answer: c Difficulty: 2 Page: 263   Key 1: R

39. What company provides the most frequently used measure of national television audiences?
    a. Arbitron
    b. Birch
    c. Simmons
    d. A.C. Nielsen
    e. Radar

    Answer: d Difficulty: 1 Page: 264   Key 1: R

40. What is the primary method for measuring national TV audiences?
    a. diary
    b. people meters
    c. survey
    d. personal interviews
    e. audimeter

    Answer: b Difficulty: 1 Page: 266   Key 1: R

41. A/an _____ can record when the television set is used and which station it is turned to but cannot identify who is watching the program.
    a. People meter
    b. Visimeter
    c. Telimeter
    d. Audimeter

    Answer: d Difficulty: 2 Page: 266   Key 1: R

42. All of the following are advantages of television as an advertising medium EXCEPT:
    a. impact.
    b. absolute cost.
    c. influence.
    d. mass audience.
    e. wide reach.

    Answer: b Difficulty: 2 Page: 266   Key 1: R

43. A new source of audience information provided by A.C. Nielsen in which each of the nation's 250,000 census block groups is assigned to one of 47 distinct types of neighborhoods based upon the block's demographic and socioeconomic make-up is called:
    a. a television market.
    b. a ClusterPLUS grouping.
    c. a metropolitan statistical area.
    d. the Nielsen index.
    e. a designated market area.

    Answer: b Difficulty: 2 Page: 266   Key 1: R

44. Television reaches people in urban and rural areas, people of all ages and backgrounds, and people of varying opinions and preferences. This illustrates which major advantage of television?
    a. impact
    b. cost efficiency
    c. influence
    d. wide reach
    e. selective audience

    Answer: d Difficulty: 3 Page: 266   Key 1: A

45. What is the average CPM for a 30-second spot on one of the three major network evening news programs?
    a. 5 cents
    b. 50 cents
    c. $5
    d. $50
    e. $500

    Answer: c Difficulty: 3 Page: 267   Key 1: R

46. A landscaping business is interested in creating a TV ad. What is the most serious limitation of placing an ad on television?
    a. high absolute cost
    b. clutter
    c. nonselective targeting
    d. inflexibility
    e. inattentiveness

    Answer: a Difficulty: 2 Page: 269   Key 1: A

47. What is the average cost for a 30-second spot in television's prime time?
    a. $2,000
    b. $20,000
    c. $185,000
    d. $55,000
    e. $430,000

    Answer: c Difficulty: 3 Page: 269   Key 1: R

48. During an hour of television, over 30 ads may compete for a viewer's attention. This problem of competition for attention is called:
    a. non-selectivity.
    b. lack of impact.
    c. inattentiveness.
    d. inflexibility.
    e. clutter.

    Answer: e Difficulty: 1 Page: 269   Key 1: A

49. Advertisers for the Peace Corps have little assurance that their targeted audience is viewing the message. This is a problem of what?
    a. inflexibility
    b. mass coverage
    c. cost inefficiency
    d. waste coverage
    e. clutter

    Answer: d Difficulty: 2 Page: 269   Key 1: A

50. One of the drawbacks to television is the difficulty in making last-minute adjustments in terms of scheduling, copy, or visuals. What is this disadvantage called?
    a. scheduling difficulties
    b. inflexibility
    c. clutter
    d. rigidity of schedules
    e. high absolute cost

    Answer: b Difficulty: 1 Page: 269   Key 1: R

51. Why are FM stations doing better than AM stations both in terms of revenues and audience?
    a. more power
    b. cheaper
    c. perception of better sound quality
    d. greater broadcast range
    e. all of the above

    Answer: c Difficulty: 2 Page: 270   Key 1: S

52. The AM radio station WIZE uses nearly 50,000 watts of power, which classifies it as a:
    a. superstation.
    b. clear channel station.
    c. satellite station.
    d. national station.
    e. powerhouse station.

    Answer: b Difficulty: 2 Page: 270   Key 1: A

53. What new broadcast medium was launched in 1990?
    a. cable radio
    b. interactive television
    c. specialty television
    d. subscription television
    e. digital audio broadcast (DAB) radio

    Answer: a Difficulty: 2 Page: 270   Key 1: R

54. Why is the popularity of network radio increasing with advertisers?
    a. complete market coverage
    b. better sound through satellite transmission
    c. quality programming
    d. specialized programming
    e. all of the above

    Answer: e Difficulty: 1 Page: 271   Key 1: R

55. What are the three types of radio advertising?
    a. local, regional, and national
    b. spot and network
    c. network, spot, and local
    d. participation, spot, and network
    e. sponsorship, participation, and spot

    Answer: b Difficulty: 1 Page: 271-273   Key 1: S

56. An ad for pet deodorant is placed with an individual station rather than through a network. This is called:
    a. vertical programming.
    b. unwired network advertising.
    c. spot radio advertising.
    d. network syndication.
    e. local radio advertising.

    Answer: c Difficulty: 2 Page: 273   Key 1: A

57. What does it mean when we say, "radio is a highly segmented medium"?
    a. content and audience of a particular station reflect distinct differences in audience tastes
    b. content is transmitted to audience via amplitude modulation or frequency modulation
    c. audience receives message through personal radios
    d. nature of listening experience is such that people are usually doing something else
    e. audience listens in short time segments rather than spending extended periods listening

    Answer: a Difficulty: 2 Page: 273   Key 1: R

58. 30,000 homes around Missoula, Montana can pick up a certain station clearly. The geographical area in which these homes are located is referred to as the:
    a. reach.
    b. radio market.
    c. area of dominant influence.
    d. coverage.
    e. circulation.

    Answer: d Difficulty: 1 Page: 274   Key 1: R

59. _____ measures the number of homes that are actually tuned in to the particular radio station.
    a. Coverage
    b. Penetration
    c. Audience
    d. Circulation
    e. Range

    Answer: d Difficulty: 2 Page: 274   Key 1: R

60. What are the three major research firms that measure radio audiences?
    a. Nielsen, RADAR, and Arbitron
    b. Arbitron, Birch, and RADAR
    c. Nielsen, Arbitron, and Simmons
    d. Burke, Arbitron, and Nielsen
    e. Arbitron, RADAR, and Simmons

    Answer: b Difficulty: 3 Page: 274   Key 1: R

61. What is the most important advantage of radio?
    a. low cost
    b. mental imagery
    c. specific audience reach
    d. flexibility
    e. speed

    Answer: c Difficulty: 3 Page: 274   Key 1: R

62. The type of media that has the shortest closing period, and offers high reach at low cost is:
    a. television.
    b. magazines.
    c. newspapers.
    d. radio.
    e. outdoor.

    Answer: d Difficulty: 3 Page: 275   Key 1: S

63. All of the following are advantages of radio EXCEPT:
    a. high level of acceptance.
    b. attentiveness.
    c. cost.
    d. flexibility.
    e. mental imagery.

    Answer: b Difficulty: 1 Page: 276   Key 1: S

64. The advantage of radio in which words, sound effects, music and tonality enable listeners to create their own picture of what is happening is called:
    a. dramatic effect.
    b. mental imagery.
    c. imagination.
    d. attentiveness.
    e. impact.

    Answer: b Difficulty: 1 Page: 275   Key 1: R

65. In radio advertising, extensive repetition is possible because of:
    a. simplicity of messages.
    b. ease of creating messages.
    c. relatively low costs.
    d. flexibility.
    e. availability of time slots.

    Answer: c Difficulty: 1 Page: 275   Key 1: R

66. What advantage of radio is involved when messages delivered by radio are retained more readily because the passive nature of radio is not normally perceived as an irritant?
    a. attentiveness
    b. influence
    c. impact
    d. high acceptance levels
    e. mental imagery

    Answer: d Difficulty: 1 Page: 276   Key 1: R

67. One of the most serious drawbacks to radio as an advertising medium is that listeners tend to view radio as pleasant background noise and don't listen carefully. What is this called?
    a. lack of influence
    b. little impact
    c. lack of mental imagery
    d. inattentiveness
    e. low acceptance

    Answer: d Difficulty: 1 Page: 276   Key 1: R

TRUE/FALSE

68. In 1984, the FCC liberalized rules on advertising and allowed PBS stations to interpret exactly what would be defined as sponsorship or underwriting.
    a. True
    b. False

    Answer: a Difficulty: 2 Page: 257   Key 1: R

69. PBS stations are allowed to have businesses sponsor programs.
    a. True
    b. False

    Answer: b Difficulty: 1 Page: 257   Key 1: A

70. No PBS stations can carry advertising that appears on commercial TV stations.
    a. True
    b. False

    Answer: b Difficulty: 1 Page: 257   Key 1: R

71. Pay networks such as HBO and Showtime do not currently sell advertising time.
    a. True
    b. False

    Answer: a Difficulty: 2 Page: 258   Key 1: R

72. Current FCC guidelines allow ads to appear on public TV only during local program breaks.
    a. True
    b. False

    Answer: a Difficulty: 3 Page: 257   Key 1: R

73. Current FCC guidelines forbid advertising on public television stations.
    a. True
    b. False

    Answer: b Difficulty: 3 Page: 257   Key 1: R

74. According to current Nielsen data, the majority of U.S. households subscribe to cable television.
    a. True
    b. False

    Answer: a Difficulty: 1 Page: 258   Key 1: R

75. Most of the programming on cable TV is provided through network syndicated programming.
    a. True
    b. False

    Answer: b Difficulty: 3 Page: 258   Key 1: R

76. The next generation of televisions will be digital.
    a. True
    b. False

    Answer: a Difficulty: 2 Page: 262   Key 1: R

77. In 1992, the FCC began to allow telephone companies to operate cable television systems.
    a. True
    b. False

    Answer: a Difficulty: 2 Page: 262   Key 1: R

78. Total cable advertising is declining and is expected to continue to decline.
    a. True
    b. False

    Answer: b Difficulty: 1 Page: 263   Key 1: R

79. Local television stations carry both network programming and locally originated shows.
    a. True
    b. False

    Answer: a Difficulty: 1 Page: 263   Key 1: R

80. Large national advertisers dominate network advertising schedules.
    a. True
    b. False

    Answer: a Difficulty: 2 Page: 263   Key 1: R

81. Interactive television has been very successful but only in limited trials.
    a. True
    b. False

    Answer: b Difficulty: 2 Page: 261   Key 1: R

82. By FCC rules, syndicated shows must be re-runs of shows broadcasted previously.
    a. True
    b. False

    Answer: b Difficulty: 3 Page: 261   Key 1: R

83. The television syndication boom has been fueled mainly by the growth of independent television stations that require programming.
    a. True
    b. False

    Answer: a Difficulty: 2 Page: 260   Key 1: R

84. Some TV shows are produced exclusively for first-run syndication.
 a. True
 b. False

 Answer: a Difficulty: 2 Page: 261   Key 1: R

85. Television spot buys are dominated by local advertising.
 a. True
 b. False

 Answer: a Difficulty: 2 Page: 264   Key 1: R

86. Research shows that interesting and unique TV commercials get zapped just as often as messages that were useful and factual in content.
 a. True
 b. False

 Answer: b Difficulty: 2 Page: 267   Key 1: R

87. Nielsen's audience measurement service covers every television market at least once a month.
 a. True
 b. False

 Answer: b Difficulty: 2 Page: 266   Key 1: R

88. The use of people meters has been very controversial for Nielsen Media Research.
 a. True
 b. False

 Answer: a Difficulty: 1 Page: 266   Key 1: R

89. Television reaches mass audiences but is not very cost efficient.
 a. True
 b. False

 Answer: b Difficulty: 1 Page: 266   Key 1: R

90. A major advantage of television is its wide reach.
 a. True
 b. False

 Answer: a Difficulty: 3 Page: 266   Key 1: A

91. The most serious limitation of television advertising is the extremely high cost per person.
   a. True
   b. False

   Answer: b Difficulty: 3 Page: 266   Key 1: A

92. The average cost for a 30-second spot on prime-time network TV is about $185,000.
   a. True
   b. False

   Answer: a Difficulty: 3 Page: 267   Key 1: R

93. Television should be used as a primary medium if the objective is to reach a mass audience simultaneously with a visual impact.
   a. True
   b. False

   Answer: a Difficulty: 1 Page: 267   Key 1: A

94. The use of the 15-second spot appears to be declining.
   a. True
   b. False

   Answer: a Difficulty: 2 Page: 269   Key 1: R

95. Spot advertising dominates radio scheduling.
   a. True
   b. False

   Answer: a Difficulty: 2 Page: 273   Key 1: R

96. Arbitron uses people meters exclusively to measure TV viewing.
   a. True
   b. False

   Answer: b Difficulty: 2 Page: 274   Key 1: R

97. The most important advantage offered by radio is that it reaches specific types of audiences.
   a. True
   b. False

   Answer: a Difficulty: 1 Page: 274   Key 1: A

98. Radio offers high reach but at a high cost.
    a. True
    b. False

    Answer: b Difficulty: 2 Page: 275   Key 1: A

99. Local advertisers are able to show their commercials to highly restricted geographic audiences through interconnects.
    a. True
    b. False

    Answer: a Difficulty: 1 Page: 259   Key 1: R

100. Local television stations are connected with a network and carry only network programming.
    a. True
    b. False

    Answer: b Difficulty: 1 Page: 260   Key 1: R

101. A 30-second advertising spot during prime time in a large city may cost ten times more than the same spot in a small town.
    a. True
    b. False

    Answer: a Difficulty: 1 Page: 260   Key 1: A

102. Hotels and restaurants use multipoint distribution systems and subscription stations to give guests access to special movies without incurring the cost of cable.
    a. True
    b. False

    Answer: a Difficulty: 2 Page: 260   Key 1: R

103. Between the 1994/1995 and 1996/1997 television seasons, adult viewing of kid shows was up 17%.
    a. True
    b. False

    Answer: b Difficulty: 3 Page: 264   Key 1: R

104. The whole "Nielson family" and the rating process remain more or less a mystery to most people.
    a. True
    b. False

    Answer: a Difficulty: 2 Page: 264   Key 1: R

105. In the 1970s, Nielsen began to measure not only what is being watched on television, but also who is watching which shows nationally.
    a. True
    b. False

    Answer: b Difficulty: 2 Page: 266   Key 1: R

106. People are more likely to believe in a company that advertises on television and sponsors educational programs than a company that does not.
    a. True
    b. False

    Answer: a Difficulty: 2 Page: 268   Key 1: A

107. An AM station produces ground waves during the day and sky waves at night.
    a. True
    b. False

    Answer: a Difficulty: 3 Page: 270   Key 1: R

108. An FM station differs from an AM station in that FM adjusts its amplitude rather than its frequency.
    a. True
    b. False

    Answer: b Difficulty: 3 Page: 270   Key 1: R

109. Network radio is connected to one or more of the national networks through telephone wires and satellites.
    a. True
    b. False

    Answer: a Difficulty: 2 Page: 271   Key 1: R

110. Local advertising revenues account for about 60 percent of radio's advertising.
    a. True
    b. False

    Answer: b Difficulty: 2 Page: 273   Key 1: R

111. The three methods of measuring the radio audience are Arbitron, RADAR, and Birch/Scarborough-VNU.
    a. True
    b. False

    Answer: a Difficulty: 1 Page: 274   Key 1: R

ESSAY

112. Compare and contrast the forms of advertising available when using a network, local or cable scheduling.

Answer:
The form of a television commercial depends on whether network, local, or cable scheduling is used. For networks, sponsorships, participations, or spot announcements can be used. Local affiliates allow spot announcements, local sponsorships, and national spots. System (national) spots and local spots can be used on cable.

In sponsorships, which represent about 10% of network advertising, the advertiser takes full financial responsibility for producing the program and providing the accompanying commercials. Sponsorship has a powerful effect on viewers, because the advertisers can control the content and quality of the program as well as the placement and length of commercial. Though the costs of production make this option too expensive for most advertisers, one alternative is a joint production, which is common with sporting events.

Participations represent most of network advertising. Advertisers pay for 15, 30, or 60 second commercials during one or more programs. This approach reduces the costs and risks of sponsorships, and provides more flexibility in market coverage, target audiences, scheduling and budgeting. Participations do, however, have lower impact, and the advertiser has no control over program content. Available time slots for the most popular programs are usually purchased by large advertisers, leaving fewer good time slots for small advertisers.

Spot announcements appear in the breaks between programs. Commercials of 10, 20, 30, and 60 seconds are sold on a station-by-station basis to local, regional, and national advertisers, though most go to local advertisers. Program breaks are not always the best time slots because of clutter, station breaks, public service announcements and other distractions. The price of the spot depends on the rating of the programs and the "daypart" during which the commercial is shown.

Difficulty: 2 Page: 362-364 Key 1: R

113. Discuss A.C. Nielsen's approaches to measuring television audience and the information collected by these measurements.

Answer:
A.C. Nielsen currently dominates the industry and provides the most commonly used measure of national and local television audiences. Nielsen measures television audiences at network and spot levels. For local measurement, Neilsen uses two devices: the audimeter and the viewing diary. The audimeter records when the TV set is used and which station it is tuned to, but cannot identify who is watching. The view diary provides data on who is watching shows. Diaries are mailed weekly during survey months to sample homes in each of the 211 television markets, adding up to about one million diaries returned each year.

In 1987 Nielsen replaced the two above methods with people meters, which provide information on what television shows are being watched, the number of households that are watching, and which family members are viewing. Household members only have press a button to indicate their presence. The 5,000 people meters have become the main method for measuring national television audiences. Digital television has presented a new ratings challenge. Nielsen has spent almost 30 million developing a new digital meter, but there is no guarantee that it will be adopted.

Neilsen also provides data for 47 ClusterPlus geodemographic groupings. According to Nielsen, these groupings are distinct types of neighborhoods, categorized by their demographic and socioeconomic makeup. These distinctions help advertisers zero in on their target audience.

Difficulty: 1   Page: 265-266   Key 1: R

114. List and discuss the advantages and disadvantages of television as an advertising medium.

Answer:
The advantages of television as an advertising medium are its cost efficiency, impact, and influence. It's cost efficient because television reaches millions of people, including people who are not reached effectively by print media. For an advertiser attempting to reach an undifferentiated market, a 30-second spot on a top-rated show may cost a penny or less for each person reached. Television's second advantage is its strong impact, which comes from the interaction of sight and sound. This interaction compares to the experience of shopping, including the persuasive salesperson. Television also allows for great flexibility because of the many possible combinations of sight, sound, color, motion, and drama. Television has great dramatic capacity, and can create a positive association with the sponsor. The final advantage is television's strong effect on our culture. Television is a critical source of news, entertainment, and education for most Americans. It is so much a part of our daily lives that we are more likely to believe companies that advertise on television and sponsor dramas and educational programs, than we are to believe those who don't.

The disadvantages of television as an advertising medium are expense, clutter, nonselective audience, and inflexibility. The most serious limitation is the high cost of producing and running commercials. Though the per-person cost is low, the absolute cost can be restrictive, especially for smaller companies. Costs include filming and paying the talent. Television also suffers from a high level of commercial clutter. The high number of commercials, station break announcements, credits, public service announcements, and stations promoting their own programming are responsible. Although the recent growth of the 15-second spot has been responsible for much of the clutter, 1990 marked the beginning of the decline of these shorter commercials. Another problem is nonselective audience. Despite technology to better target consumers, television remains nonselective. Network television advertising includes a lot of waste coverage: communication directed at an unresponsive audience. The final disadvantage is inflexibility in scheduling. Most network television is bought in the spring and summer for the next fall season. If an advertiser is unable to make this up-front buy, only limited time-slot alternatives remain available. Also, last-minute adjustments to scheduling, copy, or visuals are difficult to make. (Cable, on the other hand, is much more targeted and has far less waste than network and spot television, though cable cannot cover a mass audience and is probably even more cluttered than network TV.)
Difficulty: 3 Page: 266-269   Key 1: R

115. Discuss the radio advertising by examining both network radio and spot radio, stating qualities of each that an advertiser would consider important.

Answer:
Radio advertising is available on national networks and on local markets. Complete market coverage combined with high-quality programming has increased the popularity of network radio concerts, talk show, sports events, and dramas. Satellite transmission has produced important technological improvements, such as better sound and allowing transmission of multiple programs with different formats. Network radio is a viable national advertising medium, especially for advertisers of food, automobiles, and over-the-counter drugs. Network radio has grown, and as the number of affiliates increase, so has the number of syndicated radio shows, creating more advertising opportunities for companies eager to reach new markets. Syndication has been beneficial by offering advertisers a variety of high-quality, specialized programs.

In spot radio advertising, an advertiser places an ad with an individual station rather than through a network. Spot radio advertising represents nearly 80 percent of all radio advertising. Its popularity is result of the flexibility it offers the advertiser. With over 8,000 available stations, messages can be tailored for particular audiences. In large cities such as New York, Chicago, and Los Angeles, 40 or more radio stations are available. Local stations also offer flexibility through their willingness to run unusual ads, allow last minute changes, and negotiate rates. Buying spot radio and coping with its nonstandardized rate structures can be very cumbersome, however.

Difficulty: 2 Page: 271-273   Key 1: R

116. List and discuss the advantages and disadvantages of radio as an advertising medium.

Answer:
Radio has five key advantages for advertises. The first is that its audience is targeted. It can be adapted to different parts of the country and can reach people at different times of the day. It is the ideal means for reaching people driving to and from work. The second advantage is flexibility. Of all media, radio has the shortest closing period; copy can be submitted up to airtime. This allows advertisers to adjust to local market conditions, current new events, and even the weather. The third advantage is affordability. Radio may be the least expensive of all media; airtime costs are low, which allows for extensive repetition. Production costs are low, especially if a local station announcer reads the message. Radio's low cost and high reach of target groups make it an excellent supporting medium. Another advantage of radio is the scope it allows for the listener's imagination. Radio uses words, sound effects, music, and tonality to enable listeners to create their own picture of what is happening. The final advantage is radio's high level of acceptance at the local level. Partly because of its passive nature, radio is not perceived as an irritant. People have favorite shows they listen to regularly, and messages delivered in these shows are more likely to be accepted and retained.

Radio also has five key disadvantages. Listeners may be inattentive, perceiving radio as a background and not listening carefully. Radio messages are fleeting and commercials may be missed or forgotten. Second, radio has a lack of visuals. Creating radio ads that encourage the listener to see the product is difficult. Humor, music, and sound effects may help. Third, competing radio stations and heavy repetition has created clutter. Coupled with the fact that radio listeners tend to divide their attention among various activities, this clutter greatly reduces the likelihood that a message will be heard or understood. Fourth, there can be difficulties scheduling and buying radio time. Advertisers seeking to reach a wide audience often need to buy time on several stations, making scheduling and ad evaluation complicated. Last, there's a lack of control. Because most of radio and its growth have come through talk radio, there's always the risk that a radio personality will say something offensive to the listening audience, which may have a negative effect on the sponsor.

Difficulty: 3 Page: 274-276   Key 1: R

CHAPTER 11: THE CREATIVE SIDE OF ADVERTISING

MULTIPLE CHOICE

1. How did Goodby, Silverstein come up with the "Got Milk" campaign?
   a. results of previous campaigns
   b. borrowed the idea from another campaign
   c. consumer research
   d. did not originate the idea, simply continued an old campaign created by another agency
   e. all of the above

   Answer: c Difficulty: 2 Page: 292   Key 1: A

2. A "Big Idea" that is original and dramatizes the selling point is called a/an:
   a. unique selling proposition.
   b. strategy statement.
   c. creative concept.
   d. copy platform.
   e. cliché.

   Answer: c Difficulty: 1 Page: 291   Key 1: R

3. Why not just use the creative conceptstrategy statement for an advertising campaign as well?
   a. The creative concept is the strategy statement.
   b. The client would not accept it.
   c. The strategy statement is not distinctive, attention getting, or memorable.
   d. The copywriters union would object.
   e. The strategy statement does not take the visual component into account.

   Answer: c Difficulty: 2 Page: 291   Key 1: A

4. The essence of the creative idea is that:
   a. it is novel.
   b. it is unexpected.
   c. it is unusual.
   d. no one else has thought of it before.
   e. it is fresh.

   Answer: d Difficulty: 1 Page: 288   Key 1: R

5. Which of the following represents the characteristics of the creative idea?
   a. relevance, originality, impact, and empathy
   b. relevance and impact
   c. relevance, significance, and impact
   d. relevance, originality, and impact
   e. originality, significance, visualization, and empathy

   Answer: d Difficulty: 1 Page: 288-289 Key 1: S

6. _____ is that quality of an advertising message that makes it important to the audience.
   a. Empathy
   b. Originality
   c. Relevance
   d. Impact
   e. Utility

   Answer: c Difficulty: 2 Page: 288   Key 1: R

7. Understanding the feelings, thoughts, and emotions of someone else is called:
   a. impact.
   b. relevance.
   c. emotion.
   d. intuition.
   e. empathy.

   Answer: e Difficulty: 1 Page: 292   Key 1: R

8. A trite expression or an over-used idea is called:
   a. mundane.
   b. creative idea.
   c. ordinary idea.
   d. convergent idea.
   e. cliché.

   Answer: e Difficulty: 1 Page: 289   Key 1: R

9. Which of the following is a characteristic of an idea with impact?
   a. stopping power
   b. focuses the audience's attention on the product
   c. breaks through audience's screen of indifference
   d. helps people see themselves in a new way
   e. all of the above

   Answer: e Difficulty: 2 Page: 289   Key 1: S

10. What must an ad do to be creative?
    a. be original and help solve a marketing problem
    b. be novel and right for the product
    c. artistically provide a solution to a communication problem
    d. be fresh and sell
    e. all of the above

    Answer: e Difficulty: 2 Page: 288-289   Key 1: S

11. What is the primary purpose of impact in creative advertising?
    a. sell the product
    b. break through the target audience's screen of indifference
    c. speak to the right audience with the right message
    d. do something unexpected
    e. make the product important to the target audience

    Answer: b Difficulty: 2 Page: 289   Key 1: R

12. Leo Burnett calls its approach to analyzing ad message design, which
    checks the creative approach to see how well the story line brings the
    product claims to life:
    a. ROI philosophy.
    b. structural analysis.
    c. strategic analysis.
    d. Delphi process.

    Answer: b Difficulty: 1 Page: 292   Key 1: R

13. An exercise in which you describe everything that comes into your mind
    when you think of a word or an image is called:
    a. convergent thinking.
    b. creativity.
    c. free association.
    d. divergent thinking.
    e. brainstorming.

    Answer: c Difficulty: 1 Page: 294   Key 1: R

14. _____ is logical thinking and controls speech and writing. This thinking
    is associated with functions like accounting.
    a. Right-brain thinking
    b. Free association
    c. Rationalization
    d. Divergent thinking
    e. Left-brain thinking

    Answer: e Difficulty: 2 Page: 294   Key 1: R

15. _____ uses logic to arrive at the "right" answer.
    a. Divergent thinking
    b. Rationalization
    c. Free association
    d. Convergent thinking
    e. Right-brain thinking

    Answer: d Difficulty: 1 Page: 289   Key 1: R

16. _____ uses free association to uncover all possible alternatives.
    a. Convergent thinking
    b. Creative thinking
    c. Brainstorming
    d. Divergent thinking
    e. Left-brain thinking

    Answer: d Difficulty: 2 Page: 294   Key 1: R

17. All of the following are characteristics of the creative personality
    EXCEPT:
    a. having a low tolerance for ambiguity.
    b. soaking up experiences like sponges.
    c. being self-sufficient.
    d. being independent.
    e. being self-disciplined.

    Answer: a Difficulty: 2 Page: 298   Key 1: R

18. Which of the following is a characteristic of a person with a creative
    personality?
    a. hard to deal with
    b. withdrawn
    c. does not care much about group standards
    d. good visual imagination
    e. all of the above

    Answer: e Difficulty: 2 Page: 298   Key 1: R

19. _____ is intuitive, nonverbal and emotional thinking. This thinking
    is associated with people such as artists.
    a. Free association
    b. Right-brain thinking
    c. Rationalization
    d. Left-brain thinking
    e. Convergent thinking

    Answer: b Difficulty: 2 Page: 294   Key 1: R

20. In advertising, when does the ability to see images/pictures in the mind come into play?
    a. forming a mental picture of how the finished ad will look
    b. writing copy in print advertising
    c. developing the concept and creating television advertising
    d. helping consumers see the product in their "mind's eye"
    e. all of the above

    Answer: e Difficulty: 3 Page: 295   Key 1: A

21. The ability to see images in the mind, to imagine how an ad or a concept will look when it is finished is called:
    a. vision.
    b. visualization.
    c. imagination.
    d. imaging.
    e. graphic imagery.

    Answer: b Difficulty: 1 Page: 295   Key 1: R

22. Who usually develops the creative concept for an advertising campaign?
    a. copywriter
    b. account executive
    c. client
    d. art director
    e. copywriter/art director team

    Answer: e Difficulty: 3 Page: 295   Key 1: R

23. The person who is primarily responsible for the ad's visual image is called:
    a. copywriter.
    b. account executive.
    c. graphics designer.
    d. art director.
    e. artist.

    Answer: d Difficulty: 2 Page: 296   Key 1: R

24. What is the biggest step in learning to be more creative?
    a. read about creative people
    b. work around creative people
    c. develop an understanding of the creative process
    d. spend a lot of time idle—on the beach, day-dreaming, etc.
    e. all of the above

    Answer: c Difficulty: 1 Page: 299   Key 1: R

25. How does the text say a person can become more creative?
    a. read about creative people
    b. spend time in quiet activities such as day-dreaming or walking on the beach
    c. work hard at accumulating a lot of information on a wide range of topics
    d. work around creative people
    e. all of the above

    Answer: c Difficulty: 2 Page: 299   Key 1: S

26. All of the following are ways to learn to be more creative EXCEPT:
    a. understanding how the creative process works.
    b. developing associative thinking.
    c. learning to work better in groups.
    d. learning to deal with negative thinking.
    e. staying in touch with a variety of media.

    Answer: c Difficulty: 2 Page: 298   Key 1: A

27. Which of the following roles manages the creative process and helps keep the process strategically on target?
    a. copywriter
    b. creative director
    c. art director
    d. account executive
    e. brand manager

    Answer: b Difficulty: 2 Page: 295   Key 1: R

28. Who decides what type of artistic style to use in creating an ad?
    a. creative director
    b. graphic designer
    c. account executive
    d. art director
    e. copywriter

    Answer: d Difficulty: 1 Page: 196   Key 1: R

29. What is a common characteristic of copywriters?
    a. preoccupied with language
    b. read a lot
    c. listen to how people talk
    d. tuned in to current expressions and fads
    e. all of the above

    Answer: e Difficulty: 1 Page: 296-97   Key 1: S

30. The person who writes the text for an advertisement is called a/an:
    a. art director.
    b. account executive.
    c. copywriter.
    d. sales manager.
    e. advertising director.

    Answer: c Difficulty: 1 Page: 296   Key 1: R

31. Which of the following is a characteristic of good advertising copy?
    a. short sentences
    b. very specific
    c. uses as few words as possible
    d. looks easy to understand
    e. all of the above

    Answer: e Difficulty: 3 Page: 297   Key 1: R

32. Adese is advertising copy that is characterized by:
    a. stock phrases.
    b. superlatives.
    c. generalities.
    d. cliches.
    e. all of the above

    Answer: e Difficulty: 1 Page: 297   Key 1: R

33. How do advertising copywriters achieve the proper conversational tone when they write advertising copy?
    a. use "we" copy to personalize it
    b. use the "you" in direct address in the copy
    c. develop a profile of the typical user's personality
    d. write from the company's point of view

    Answer: c Difficulty: 2 Page: 297   Key 1: R

34. Where does the creative process begin?
    a. piling up ideas
    b. finding the right way to get in a creative mood
    c. preparation and analysis
    d. free association
    e. brainstorming

    Answer: c Difficulty: 3 Page: 299   Key 1: R

35. When a creative person takes a break, goes for a walk, and allows the subconscious to take over, this is the _____ stage of the creative process.
a. illumination
b. incubation
c. verification
d. preparation
e. ideation

Answer: b Difficulty: 1 Page: 300   Key 1: A

36. After a long night of work, a creative person yells "Eureka! I've got it!" This artist has arrived at which stage of the creative process?
a. verification
b. illumination
c. incubation
d. preparation
e. association

Answer: b Difficulty: 2 Page: 300   Key 1: A

37. The four steps in the creative process as named in 1926 by an English sociologist are:
a. orientation, preparation, analysis, and ideation.
b. preparation, analysis, ideation, and incubation.
c. analysis, ideation, incubation, and synthesis.
d. ideation, incubation, synthesis, and evaluation.
e. preparation, incubation, illumination, and verification.

Answer: e Difficulty: 3 Page: 299   Key 1: R

38. _____ is the stage in the creative process when we come up with an original or creative idea.
a. Ideation
b. Incubation
c. Illumination
d. Preparation

Answer: a Difficulty: 1 Page: 299   Key 1: R

39. _____ is a creative thinking technique using free association in a group environment to stimulate inspiration.
a. Convergent thinking
b. The Delphi process
c. Creative process
d. Synectics
e. Brainstorming

Answer: e Difficulty: 2 Page: 301   Key 1: R

40. A creative team is in the process of coming up with a number of ideas. In order for the brainstorming to be successful, they should:
    a. generate a few verbally great ideas
    b. defer judgment on the effectiveness of the ideas
    c. generate as many good ideas as possible
    d. use a formal arrangement of the place and process
    e. use analogies to generate ideas

    Answer: b Difficulty: 1 Page: 301   Key 1: A

41. What dimension of the creative side of an advertisement determines what the message says?
    a. execution
    b. creative brief
    c. creative strategy
    d. creative tactic
    e. message strategy

    Answer: c Difficulty: 2 Page: 301   Key 1: R

42. _____ is the dimension of the creative side of an ad that details how the message is said.
    a. Execution
    b. Creative brief
    c. Creative strategy
    d. Creative tactic
    e. Message strategy

    Answer: a Difficulty: 2 Page: 301   Key 1: R

43. _____ is the document or strategic platform that presents and explains the logic behind the advertising message, the creative concept and the execution details that bring the idea to life.
    a. Creative strategy
    b. Advertising strategy
    c. Message tactic
    d. Creative brief
    e. Creative concept

    Answer: d Difficulty: 1 Page: 303   Key 1: R

44. Products used for personal care or sustenance are called:
    a. packaged goods.
    b. service products.
    c. public service goods.
    d. utilitarian goods.
    e. problem solution goods.

    Answer: a Difficulty: 1 Page: 302   Key 1: R

45. _____ is an approach to designing an ad message that will touch the mind and create a response based on logic. The approach is direct and emphasizes tangible product features and benefits.
   a. Hard sell
   b. Soft sell
   c. Rational sell
   d. Product approach
   e. Reasonable sell

   Answer: a Difficulty: 1 Page: 301   Key 1: R

46. A type of ad message that sells moods and dreams more than product features is called:
   a. mood advertising.
   b. soft sell advertising.
   c. image advertising.
   d. public service advertising.
   e. hard sell advertising.

   Answer: b Difficulty: 1 Page: 302   Key 1: R

47. An instruction delivered verbally to present knowledge and facts is called a/an:
   a. drama.
   b. lecture.
   c. speech.
   d. seminar.
   e. address.

   Answer: b Difficulty: 1 Page: 302   Key 1: R

48. A story built around characters in a situation is called a:
   a. drama.
   b. characterization.
   c. plot.
   d. lecture.
   e. tragedy.

   Answer: a Difficulty: 1 Page: 302   Key 1: R

49. Which of the following is an advantage of the lecture advertising message format?
   a. audiences accept messages more readily
   b. can deliver several selling points quickly
   c. emotional impact
   d. involvement of story-telling
   e. all of the above

   Answer: b Difficulty: 2 Page: 302   Key 1: R

50. Which of the following is a disadvantage of the lecture advertising message format?
    a. production cost
    b. efficiency
    c. acceptance of message
    d. directness of message
    e. explicitness of message

    Answer: c Difficulty: 3 Page: 302   Key 1: A

51. What is the source of the power of drama in advertising?
    a. creative originality
    b. audience involvement
    c. seriousness of the story
    d. reality of the characters
    e. all of the above

    Answer: b Difficulty: 3 Page: 303   Key 1: R

52. What is the key to getting the audience involved in an advertising drama?
    a. reality
    b. originality
    c. emotion
    d. logic
    e. creativity

    Answer: a Difficulty: 1 Page: 305   Key 1: R

53. The _____ approach focuses on how to use the product or what it can do for you. The product's strengths take center stage.
    a. Straightforward factual
    b. Comparison
    c. Demonstration
    d. Slice-of-life
    e. Problem-solution

    Answer: c Difficulty: 1 Page: 305   Key 1: R

54. A problem-solution version of the dramatic format of advertising message in which the message begins with some problem and the product is shown as the solution to that problem is:
    a. slice-of-life.
    b. product-as-hero.
    c. demonstration.
    d. problem-avoidance.
    e. lifestyle.

    Answer: b Difficulty: 1 Page: 305   Key 1: R

55. A problem-solution version of the dramatic format of advertising message
in which the problem is avoided because of product use is called:
a. slice-of-life.
b. product-as-hero.
c. problem-avoidance.
d. demonstration.
e. lifestyle.

Answer: c Difficulty: 1 Page: 305   Key 1: R

56. An advertising message format in which the problem-solution message is
built around some common, everyday situation is called:
a. problem-solution.
b. demonstration.
c. comparison.
d. lifestyle.
e. slice-of-life.

Answer: e Difficulty: 1 Page: 305   Key 1: R

57. What is the key problem in using humor in advertising?
a. It may not be funny to everyone.
b. Some part of the audience may be offended.
c. Humor does not work, and does not sell products.
d. Humor may overpower the selling message.
e. all of the above

Answer: d Difficulty: 3 Page: 306   Key 1: R

58. Which of the following advantages do ad visuals present?
a. communicate faster
b. easier to remember
c. work well for undifferentiated products with low-inherent interest
d. getting attention
e. all of the above

Answer: e Difficulty: 2 Page: 295   Key 1: R

59. How does the advertising creative team decide whether to emphasize words
or pictures?
a. Words are always the focus because they carry the selling message.
b. The creative team considers the strategy for the advertisement.
c. Visuals are always the focus because they work more efficiently.
d. The creative team considers the cost of the advertisement.
e. The creative team works from the relative strengths of the creative
team.

Answer: b Difficulty: 3 Page: 291   Key 1: R

60. What are the most important functions of the visual in the advertisement?
    a. technical explanation and benefit illustration
    b. illustrate and explain the benefit
    c. capture attention and add credibility
    d. select the target audience and tell the story
    e. select the target audience and explain the benefit

    Answer: c Difficulty: 3 Page: 296   Key 1: R

61. An ad that combines two unrelated items uses:
    a. juxtaposition
    b. a Big Idea
    c. impact
    d. cleverness
    e. all of the above

    Answer: a Difficulty: 1 Page: 289   Key 1: A

62. Which of the following techniques are used in creating original ideas?
    a. catchy phrasing
    b. analogy
    c. metaphor
    d. combining familiar and strange
    e. all of the above

    Answer: e Difficulty: 1 Page: 289   Key 1: S

63. Free association, divergent thinking, and right-brain thinking are all:
    a. creative ways of thinking.
    b. Big Ideas.
    c. facts.
    d. juxtaposition.
    e. all of the above

    Answer: a Difficulty: 1 Page: 294   Key 1: R

64. To write effective copy, one must:
    a. be succinct.
    b. get personal.
    c. be original.
    d. use variety in print and TV ads.
    e. all of the above

    Answer: e Difficulty: 2 Page: 297   Key 1: R

65. The creative process, or ideation, is portrayed as the following series
    of steps:
    a. preparation, incubation, illumination, and verification
    b. orientation, preparation, analysis, ideation, incubation, synthesis,
       and evaluation
    c. free association, rationalization, conversation, evaluation
    d. all of the above
    e. a and b only

    Answer: e Difficulty: 3 Page: 299   Key 1: S

66. In the creative process, what does the text call the stage where the
    creative person gathers information, investigates, and learns everything
    possible about the problem?
    a. verification
    b. evaluation
    c. immersion
    d. incubation
    e. illumination

    Answer: c Difficulty: 3 Page: 300   Key 1: R

TRUE/FALSE

67. The essence of a creative idea is that no one else has thought of it.
    a. True
    b. False

    Answer: a Difficulty: 1 Page: 288   Key 1: A

68. Effective ads are built on strong creative concepts.
    a. True
    b. False

    Answer: a Difficulty: 1 Page: 288   Key 1: A

69. Advertising is a goal-oriented discipline.
    a. True
    b. False

    Answer: a Difficulty: 1 Page: 291   Key 1: A

70. The creative idea that does not conform to strategy can be considered if
    it makes a big enough impression on the target audience.
    a. True
    b. False

    Answer: b Difficulty: 2 Page: 291   Key 1: A

71. In the Leo Burnett approach to analyzing ad messages, the ideal ad makes it hard to remember whether the impact is derived from the power of the story or the strength of the claim.
    a. True
    b. False

    Answer: a Difficulty: 1 Page: 295   Key 1: R

72. The creative process is a free-wheeling, undisciplined process where the big idea pops into the mind of the truly creative person almost spontaneously.
    a. True
    b. False

    Answer: b Difficulty: 1 Page: 299   Key 1: A

73. Creative ideas come only after hard work.
    a. True
    b. False

    Answer: a Difficulty: 1 Page: 299   Key 1: A

74. Creativity is a special form of problem solving.
    a. True
    b. False

    Answer: a Difficulty: 1 Page: 299   Key 1: A

75. True advertising creativity involves coming up with crazy, off-the-wall ideas.
    a. True
    b. False

    Answer: b Difficulty: 1 Page: 298   Key 1: R

76. Joe has been described as moody and withdrawn as a college student. He has flitted from major to major. He excels for a time, then gets bored and changes majors again. He is skeptical and intuitive. Most people find him hard to get along with—even abrasive. Joe seems to have the personality make-up for advertising creative work.
    a. True
    b. False

    Answer: a Difficulty: 1 Page: 298   Key 1: A

77. The educational process tends to help kids develop creativity.
    a. True
    b. False

    Answer: b Difficulty: 2 Page: 298   Key 1: A

78. Research indicates that creativity is something a person either is born with or not.
   a. True
   b. False

   Answer: b Difficulty: 2 Page: 298   Key 1: R

79. Creative advertising people are weird, off-the-wall, unconventional, and eccentric.
   a. True
   b. False

   Answer: b Difficulty: 1 Page: 298   Key 1: R

80. Good advertising writers must be able to visualize.
   a. True
   b. False

   Answer: a Difficulty: 1 Page: 298   Key 1: R

81. The creative mind can be developed with the proper work and practice.
   a. True
   b. False

   Answer: a Difficulty: 2 Page: 298   Key 1: A

82. The copywriter usually comes up with the creative ideas for advertising.
   a. True
   b. False

   Answer: b Difficulty: 1 Page: 298   Key 1: R

83. Most advertising visuals are photographs.
   a. True
   b. False

   Answer: a Difficulty: 2 Page: 296   Key 1: R

84. The secret to successful brainstorming is to defer judgment of the ideas that are generated.
   a. True
   b. False

   Answer: a Difficulty: 1 Page: 301   Key 1: R

85. In advertising, the term drama can refer to comic sketches and cartoons.
   a. True
   b. False

   Answer: a Difficulty: 2 Page: 302   Key 1: A

86. Stressing the inherent drama in the product only distracts the audience rather than convincing them to buy the product.
    a. True
    b. False

    Answer: b Difficulty: 2 Page: 303   Key 1: A

87. One of the key problems in the use of drama in advertising is the tendency to forget to emphasize the selling premise.
    a. True
    b. False

    Answer: a Difficulty: 2 Page: 303   Key 1: A

88. Demonstrations typically have a straightforward tone.
    a. True
    b. False

    Answer: a Difficulty: 1 Page: 305   Key 1: R

89. It is not enough to be funny in an ad message, even if the humor is original and memorable.
    a. True
    b. False

    Answer: a Difficulty: 2 Page: 306   Key 1: A

90. For a humorous ad to be effective, the selling premise needs to be the focus of the humor.
    a. True
    b. False

    Answer: a Difficulty: 1 Page: 306   Key 1: R

91. A local restaurant "borrowing" an ad that has worked well for a competitor is an example of copycat advertising.
    a. True
    b. False

    Answer: a Difficulty: 1 Page: 289   Key 1: R

92. A commercial with impact has the stopping power that comes from an intriguing idea, something you have often thought of before.
    a. True
    b. False

    Answer: b Difficulty: 1 Page: 289   Key 1: R

93. The ad for British airways that associates an airplane lounge with a green oasis in the middle of a desert is an idea that involves a mind shift.
a. True
b. False

Answer: a Difficulty: 1 Page: 289   Key 1: R

94. To be creative, an advertising concept must be both original and strategic.
a. True
b. False

Answer: a Difficulty: 1 Page: 291   Key 1: R

95. In order to identify with their target audience, creative people working on an ad for a diet plan might go on a diet themselves.
a. True
b. False

Answer: a Difficulty: 1 Page: 292   Key 1: R

96. The two aspects of narrative and product claim should always be well integrated.
a. True
b. False

Answer: a Difficulty: 1 Page: 294   Key 1: R

97. A creative person working on a cookie ad goes through the process of listing facts, new names, similarities, and new definitions. This is a the idea-generating process.
a. True
b. False

Answer: a Difficulty: 1 Page: 294   Key 1: R

98. Using analogies and metaphors is a creative way to see new patterns and relationships.
a. True
b. False

Answer: a Difficulty: 2 Page: 294   Key 1: R

99. All agencies have broadcast producers who develop the creative concept and craft the execution of the advertising idea.
a. True
b. False

Answer: b Difficulty: 3 Page: 295   Key 1: R

100. Usually both members of the creative team generate concept, word, and picture ideas.
   a. True
   b. False

   Answer: a Difficulty: 1 Page: 298   Key 1: R

101. The least frequently used tools in a creative person's tool kit are art and copy.
   a. True
   b. False

   Answer: b Difficulty: 1 Page: 295   Key 1: R

102. To learn how and when to use visuals effectively, advertisers must focus only on three key points: attention, memory, and distinction.
   a. True
   b. False

   Answer: b Difficulty: 3 Page: 296   Key 1: R

103. An ad picturing a slim, healthy-looking, smiling person wearing brand name tennis shoes is an example of instant communication.
   a. True
   b. False

   Answer: a Difficulty: 1 Page: 296   Key 1: A

104. If an ad can communicate a concept with words more easily than with pictures, it may be trying to convey abstract qualities.
   a. True
   b. False

   Answer: a Difficulty: 2 Page: 296   Key 1: A

105. The person who is most responsible for the graphic image of the ad is the underrated gaffer.
   a. True
   b. False

   Answer: b Difficulty: 1 Page: 296   Key 1: R

106. A company marketing recycled goods may consider using the shades green and brown in its ad to convey a sense of the natural.
   a. True
   b. False

   Answer: a Difficulty: 2 Page: 296   Key 1: A

107. In advertising copy, every word counts because space and time are expensive.
    a. True
    b. False

    Answer: a Difficulty: 1 Page: 297   Key 1: R

108. The more elaborate and explanatory the copy is, the easier it is to understand and the greater its impact.
    a. True
    b. False

    Answer: b Difficulty: 2 Page: 297   Key 1: R

109. Execution refers to what an ad says, and creative strategy refers to how it is said.
    a. True
    b. False

    Answer: b Difficulty: 2 Page: 301   Key 1: R

110. A soft sell uses a rational message designed to touch the mind and create a response based on logic.
    a. True
    b. False

    Answer: b Difficulty: 2 Page: 302   Key 1: R

ESSAY

111. Explain the characteristics of the creative idea, the implications of each characteristic for creating ads, and techniques for creating original ideas.

Answer:
Relevance, originality, and impact are three characteristics that help explain what makes ideas creative in advertising. Creative ideas must also support the advertising and marketing strategy. Advertising tries to deliver the right message to the right person at the right time, which is more important than how much the creative people or the clients like the ad. In effective persuasion, ideas have to mean something important to the audience, i.e., the ideas must be relevant. An idea is considered original when it is novel, fresh, unexpected, and unusual. The essence of a creative idea is that no one else has thought of it before. In regard to originality, copycat advertising is a concern. To be creative, ideas must also have impact. Many ads simply wash over the audience but, ideally, a good commercial has stopping power that comes from an intriguing idea, something the audience members never though about before.

To create original ideas, one can use the techniques of unexpected twists, unexpected situations, catchy phrasing, word plays, analogy and metaphor, and juxtaposition of the familiar with the strange. To avoid unoriginal ideas, avoid using common or predictable depictions, avoid copycatting, cliches, and tasteless comments.

Difficulty: 2   Page: 288-289   Key 1: S

112. Discuss the different types of thinking associated with creativity.

Answer:
A lot of what happens when you get an idea comes from just letting the mind wander. The most common structured techniques that creative thinkers use are free association, divergent thinking, analogies and metaphors, and right-brain thinking. Free association creates the juxtaposition of two seemingly unrelated thoughts. In free association, you think of a word and then describe everything that comes into your mind. Divergent thinking differs from rational, linear thinking used to arrive at the "right" conclusion. Divergent thinking, which is the heart of creative thinking, uses association and exploration to search for all possible alternatives. Analogies and metaphors are used to see new patterns or relationships. One researcher, Gordon, discovered that new ideas are often expressed as analogies. He has a program that trains people to problem-solve by applying analogies. Right-brain thinking is intuitive, nonverbal, and emotional (opposite of left-brain). A right-brain dominant person tends to deal in expressive visual images, emotion, intuition, and complex interrelated ideas that must be understood as a whole rather than as pieces.

Creative aerobics is a thought-starter process that works well in advertising because it uses both the head and heart. This four-step idea-generating process includes coming up with 1) a list of facts about the product you're trying to create new concept for, 2) creating new names for the product, 3) finding similarities between dissimilar objects, and 4) creating new definitions for things related to the product.

Difficulty: 1   Page: 294   Key 1: R

113. Describe the creative person using the factors discussed in the text including personality traits and skills associated with the creative person.

Answer:
Research indicates that creative people tend to be independent, self-assertive, self-sufficient, persistent, and self-disciplined, with a high tolerance for ambiguity. They are risk takers with powerful egos and are internally driven. They don't care much about group standards and opinions, and typically have inborn skepticism and strong curiosity. Creative problem solvers are alert, watchful, and observant and reach conclusions through intuition rather than through logic. They tend to have good senses of humor and a mental playfulness that allows them to make novel associations.

Aside from personal characteristics, creative people have the ability to visualize, and are open to new experiences. Writers as well as designers must be able to visualize, and to describe what something looks like, sounds like, smells like, and tastes like. The creative person can visualize a mental picture of the finished ad while it is still in the talking, or idea, state. Openness to new experience is another identifying characteristic of creative people. For creative directors, they must not only be creative themselves, but also be able to recognize and inspire creative work in their copywriters and art directors. Over the course of a lifetime, openness to experience may bring more adventures from which ideas can be drawn.

Difficulty: 2 Page: 298-299   Key 1: S

114. What makes a creative message effective? Discuss the 12 recurring qualities found in some of the most sales-effective advertising.

Answer:
Brand rewards/benefits are highly visible through demonstration, dramatization, lifestyle, feelings, or analogy. 2) The brand is the major player in the experience. 3) The link between the brand and the execution is clear (the scenario revolves around and highlights the brand). 4) The execution has a focus (there's a limit to how many images and vignettes the consumer can process). 5) Feelings (emotional connectives) are anchored to the needs and aspirations of the targeted consumer. 6) Striking, dramatic imagery is characteristic of many successful executions, enhancing their ability to break out of clutter. 7) An original, creative signature or mystique exists in many of the best commercials to bond the consumer to the brand and give it a unique personality. 8) In food and beverage advertising, high taste appeal is almost always essential. 9)The best creative ideas for mature brands often use fresh new ways of revitalizing the message. 10) Music (memorable, bonded tunes and lyrics) is often a key to successful executions for many brands. 11) When humor is used, it is relevant, with a clear product purpose. 12) When celebrities are used, they are well matched to brands and have credibility as user/endorsers, and their delivery is believably enthusiastic.

Difficulty: 2 Page: 307   Key 1: R

115. Discuss the advantages and disadvantages of the lecture approach to copy writing as compared to the drama approach.

Answer:
In addition to communicating the product category, advertisements are designed to touch the head or the heart (hard sell or soft sell). Most advertising messages use a combination of two basic literary techniques to reach the head or the heart: lectures and dramas. A lecture is a serious, structured instruction given verbally by a teacher. Lectures are a form of direct address. The speaker presents evidence (broadly speaking) and uses such techniques as argument to persuade the audience. Assuming they aren't dull, the advantages of lectures are many. They cost less to produce, and are more compact and efficient. A lecture can deliver a dozen selling points in seconds, and get right to the point and make the point explicitly, whereas drama relies on the viewer to make inferences.

A drama is a story or play built around characters in some situation. In a drama the characters speak to each other, not to the audience. Like fairy tales, movies, novels, parables, and myths, advertising dramas are essentially stories about how the world works. Viewers learn from these commercial dramas by inferring lessons from them and by applying those lessons to their everyday lives. When a drama rings true, viewers join in, draws conclusions from it, and apply those conclusions to their own lives.

Difficulty: 2 Page: 302-303 Key 1: S

CHAPTER 12: CREATING PRINT ADVERTISING

MULTIPLE CHOICE

1. What is the foundation of modern advertising message strategy and design?
   a. Aristotle's rhetoric
   b. early television commercial formats
   c. early print formats
   d. early journalism story formats

   Answer: c Difficulty: 1 Page: 314   Key 1: R

2. The earliest mass-produced commercial messages appeared in:
   a. TV programs.
   b. radio programs.
   c. magazines.
   d. newspapers.
   e. books.

   Answer: d Difficulty: 1 Page: 314   Key 1: R

3. The key elements of print advertising are:
   a. originality and creativity.
   b. visual and graphic design.
   c. copy and creative strategy.
   d. type and graphic design.
   e. copy and art.

   Answer: e Difficulty: 3 Page: 314   Key 1: S

4. All of the following are considered written elements in print advertising EXCEPT:
   a. signatures.
   b. headlines.
   c. taglines.
   d. captions.
   e. body copy.

   Answer: a Difficulty: 2 Page: 323   Key 1: S

5. What medium is the primary source for local advertising?
   a. Newspapers
   b. Television
   c. Magazines
   d. Radio
   e. Internet

   Answer: a Difficulty: 1 Page: 315   Key 1: R

6. Which of the following type of advertising is NOT considered intrusive?
   a. television
   b. direct
   c. newspaper
   d. radio
   e. all of the above

   Answer: c Difficulty: 1 Page: 315   Key 1: S

7. All of the following are beneficial characteristics of newspaper advertising EXCEPT:
   a. serious tone can carry over to advertising.
   b. newspaper ads do not have to work as hard to catch attention.
   c. not considered intrusive.
   d. high quality color production.
   e. do not have to compete as entertainment.

   Answer: d Difficulty: 2 Page: 315   Key 1: S

8. Why is newspaper reproduction traditionally of such low quality?
   a. demand for speed
   b. use of inexpensive paper
   c. low cost printing techniques
   d. use of spongy paper
   e. all of the above

   Answer: e Difficulty: 1 Page: 315

9. A precise matching of color and images within an advertisement is called:
   a. keyline.
   b. in register.
   c. overline.
   d. surprinting.
   e. mechanical.

   Answer: b Difficulty: 2 Page: 315   Key 1: R

10. What is a serious limitation of the use of color in newspaper advertising?
    a. too expensive
    b. cannot guarantee hue
    c. too long lead-time
    d. color may not be in register
    e. all of the above

    Answer: d Difficulty: 1 Page: 315   Key 1: S

11. How is the Big Idea best communicated in print advertising?
    a. words
    b. pictures and words together
    c. headline
    d. picture
    e. color and picture combination

    Answer: b Difficulty: 3 Page: 324   Key 1: S

12. What is a difference between magazines and newspapers in terms of production quality?
    a. paper quality
    b. printing process quality
    c. photographic reproduction
    d. ink used
    e. all of the above

    Answer: e Difficulty: 3 Page: 316   Key 1: S

13. The elements of the print advertisement that the reader sees in his or her original scanning, which are usually set in larger type sizes are called:
    a. headlines.
    b. taglines.
    c. display copy.
    d. body copy.
    e. captions.

    Answer: c Difficulty: 2 Page: 323   Key 1: R

14. What is the most important display element in a print advertisement?
    a. body copy
    b. captions
    c. tagline
    d. visual
    e. headline

    Answer: e Difficulty: 3 Page: 324   Key 1: R

15. Which of the following is NOT a function of the headline?
    a. select the right prospect
    b. introduce the selling premise
    c. speak to the interests of the target audience
    d. lures readers into body copy
    e. get the prospect to read the entire advertisement

    Answer: e Difficulty: 2 Page: 324   Key 1: S

16. Which of the following is a way of stopping and grabbing the attention of the target audience?
    a. promise something
    b. ask a question
    c. involve them in completing the message
    d. make a puzzling statement
    e. all of the above

    Answer: e Difficulty: 3 Page: 325   Key 1: S

17. All of the following are direct headlines EXCEPT:
    a. assertion.
    b. command.
    c. challenge.
    d. how-to statement.
    e. news announcement.

    Answer: c Difficulty: 2 Page: 325   Key 1: S

18. What percentage of readers look at an ad, just read the headline and then move on?
    a. 25%
    b. 50%
    c. 65%
    d. 80%
    e. 100%

    Answer: d Difficulty: 2 Page: 325   Key 1: A

19. What are two general headline categories in print advertising?
    a. general and specific
    b. questions and answer
    c. image and product
    d. direct and indirect
    e. promise and assertion

    Answer: d Difficulty: 2 Page: 325   Key 1: R

20. Straightforward and informative headlines are called:
    a. direct.
    b. answer.
    c. indirect.
    d. promise.
    e. blind.

    Answer: a Difficulty: 1 Page: 325   Key 1: R

21. _____ are not as selective and many do not provide as much information, but they may be better at luring the reader into the message. They are provocative and intriguing, and they compel people to read on to find out the point of the message.
    a. Direct headlines
    b. General headlines
    c. Image headlines
    d. Indirect headlines
    e. Curiosity headlines

    Answer: d Difficulty: 1 Page: 325   Key 1: R

22. All of the following are strengths of the direct headline in print advertising EXCEPT:
    a. state a claim or promise.
    b. select the audience.
    c. identify product category.
    d. link the brand with a benefit.
    e. are provocative and intriguing.

    Answer: e Difficulty: 2 Page: 325   Key 1: S

23. What is the main strength of the indirect headline in print advertising?
    a. select the audience
    b. highly targeted
    c. link the brand with a benefit
    d. lure the reader into the body copy
    e. all of the above

    Answer: d Difficulty: 3 Page: 325   Key 1: S

24. All of the following are functions of the body copy EXCEPT:
    a. select target audience.
    b. give the explanation of the sales message.
    c. state the argument.
    d. develop the sales message.
    e. provide support for the sales message.

    Answer: a Difficulty: 3 Page: 325   Key 1: S

25. A style of copywriting, that tells a story is called:
    a. dialogue.
    b. narrative.
    c. conversational.
    d. blind.
    e. straightforward.

    Answer: b Difficulty: 1 Page: 325   Key 1: R

26. What has research in direct mail shown about the role of the headline in producing consumer response to print advertising? Changing the headline while keeping other elements constant:
    a. has little or no effect.
    b. can only produce small increases in response.
    c. can double or even quadruple response.
    d. actually produces small decreases in response.
    e. none of the above

    Answer: c Difficulty: 1 Page: 324   Key 1: R

27. Sectional headlines used to break up masses of type are called:
    a. overlines.
    b. captions.
    c. subheads.
    d. underlines.
    e. taglines.

    Answer: c Difficulty: 2 Page: 326   Key 1: R

28. Short descriptions of the content of a photograph or an illustration are called:
    a. underlines.
    b. taglines.
    c. subtitles.
    d. captions.
    e. overlines.

    Answer: d Difficulty: 1 Page: 325   Key 1: R

29. A memorable phrase that sums up the concept or key point of the ad is called a/an:
    a. logo.
    b. signature.
    c. tagline.
    d. underline.
    e. cutline.

    Answer: c Difficulty: 1 Page: 324   Key 1: R

30. Which of the following paragraphs in body copy get special attention from copywriters?
    a. lead-in
    b. middle
    c. second
    d. next to last
    e. all of the above

    Answer: a Difficulty: 2 Page: 327   Key 1: S

31. What is the role of layout in developing print advertising?
    a. cost estimation
    b. translate the visual concept so that it can be discussed and revised
    c. guide for the copywriter who will unite copy to fit the space
    d. guide for production of typesetting, art, photos and paste-up
    e. all of the above

    Answer: e Difficulty: 2 Page: 327   Key 1: S

32. What is the most common layout format for print advertising?
    a. copy-dominated advertisement where headline is treated as type art
    b. cartoon style
    c. single dominant visual with headline and copy block
    d. dominant visual with cluster of smaller visuals
    e. panel layout with several visuals

    Answer: c Difficulty: 3 Page: 328   Key 1: S

33. All of the following are steps in the normal development of a print layout EXCEPT the:
    a. mechanical.
    b. thumbnail sketch.
    c. interlock.
    d. rough.
    e. comprehensive.

    Answer: c Difficulty: 2 Page: 329-30   Key 1: S

34. What is the first stage of the normal development of a print ad layout?
    a. comprehensive
    b. thumbnail sketch
    c. mechanical
    d. semicomp
    e. rough sketch

    Answer: b Difficulty: 2 Page: 329   Key 1: R

35. Which of the following stages in the development of a print layout is done in the actual size of the advertisement?
    a. mechanical
    b. rough layout
    c. comprehensive
    d. semicomp
    e. all of the above

    Answer: e Difficulty: 2 Page: 329-330   Key 1: S

36. Most advertising layouts are presented to clients in what form?
    a. final
    b. comprehensive
    c. semicomp
    d. mechanical
    e. thumbnail sketch

    Answer: a Difficulty: 2 Page: 330   Key 1: R

37. A small preliminary sketch of various layout ideas is called:
    a. keyline.
    b. semicomp.
    c. comprehensive.
    d. thumbnail.
    e. rough layout.

    Answer: d Difficulty: 1 Page: 329   Key 1: R

38. A layout drawn to exact size that shows the art and display type while
    body copy is simply represented by lines is called:
    a. mechanical.
    b. semicomp.
    c. keyline.
    d. comprehensive.
    e. thumbnail.

    Answer: b Difficulty: 2 Page: 330   Key 1: R

39. Layouts done to size but not with any great attention to how they look
    are called:
    a. thumbnails.
    b. keylines.
    c. roughs.
    d. semicomps.
    e. mechanicals.

    Answer: c Difficulty: 1 Page: 329   Key 1: R

40. What is the final stage of the production process for print advertising?
    a. the interlock
    b. developing the mechanical
    c. developing the comprehensive
    d. final layout
    e. typesetting

    Answer: b Difficulty: 2 Page: 330   Key 1: R

41. A creative team has produced a layout that looks as much like the final printed advertisement as possible. This is called a:
    a. keyline.
    b. comprehensive.
    c. mechanical.
    d. semicomp.
    e. thumbnail.

    Answer: b Difficulty: 2 Page: 330   Key 1: A

42. What stage of the development of print ad layouts is electronic publishing eliminating?
    a. mechanical
    b. rough
    c. thumbnail sketch
    d. comprehensive
    e. semicomp

    Answer: a Difficulty: 2 Page: 330   Key 1: A

43. What is the normal starting point for the eye in looking at a print advertisement?
    a. upper left corner
    b. lower right corner
    c. center
    d. upper right corner
    e. lower left corner

    Answer: a Difficulty: 2 Page: 331   Key 1: R

44. In advertising design, when the art director is concerned about the pattern of the placement of the elements in a layout, what is the design principle involved?
    a. unity
    b. direction
    c. balance
    d. consistency
    e. visual organization

    Answer: e Difficulty: 2 Page: 331   Key 1: A

45. A visual path that flows from the upper left corner to the lower right is called:
    a. focal path.
    b. normal pattern.
    c. American Z.
    d. organization.
    e. Gutenberg diagonal.

    Answer: e Difficulty: 1 Page: 331   Key 1: R

46. When the art director is trying to place the elements of the advertisement in such as way as to control the path that the reader's eye will follow, what design principle is involved?
   a. organization
   b. pattern
   c. balance
   d. direction
   e. proportion

   Answer: d Difficulty: 2 Page: 331   Key 1: R

47. Which of the following is a factor in developing unity in a layout?
   a. have headline lead into text
   b. keep caption and pictures together
   c. stick to the dominant artistic style
   d. use one typeface
   e. all of the above

   Answer: e Difficulty: 2 Page: 331   Key 1: S

48. A creative team is in the process of taking the disparate elements of their ad and fusing them into one coherent image. This design principle is called:
   a. balance.
   b. unity.
   c. proportion.
   d. organization.
   e. simplicity.

   Answer: b Difficulty: 1 Page: 331   Key 1: A

49. What are the two ways white space is used in layouts?
   a. links elements or highlights elements
   b. frames elements or separates elements
   c. directs the eye or highlights elements
   d. frames elements or links elements
   e. fuses elements or makes elements coherent

   Answer: b Difficulty: 2 Page: 332   Key 1: S

50. Which of the following is important in creating contrast?
   a. size
   b. color
   c. shape
   d. all of the above

   Answer: d Difficulty: 1 Page: 330   Key 1: S

51. What element of the layout usually dominates in proportion to other elements?
    a. art
    b. body copy
    c. headline
    d. slogan
    e. subhead

    Answer: a Difficulty: 3 Page: 333   Key 1: R

52. Ads that are in a state of visual equilibrium, or _____, seem to be evenly weighted on all sides.
    a. unity
    b. balance
    c. contrast
    d. conflict
    e. consistency

    Answer: b Difficulty: 2 Page: 332   Key 1: R

53. _____ is symmetrical, left to right.
    a. White space
    b. Contrast
    c. Informal balance
    d. Unity
    e. Formal balance

    Answer: e Difficulty: 3 Page: 332   Key 1: R

54. _____ is asymmetrical and creates a more visually exciting or dynamic layout.
    a. Unity
    b. Formal balance
    c. Proportion
    d. Informal balance
    e. Consistency

    Answer: d Difficulty: 2 Page: 332   Key 1: R

55. Which of the following is the purpose of color in advertisements?
    a. establish mood
    b. build brand identity
    c. attract attention
    d. provide realism
    e. all of the above

    Answer: e Difficulty: 2 Page: 333   Key 1: S

56. A second color used in an ad to highlight important elements is called:
    a. spot color.
    b. color separation.
    c. process color.
    d. line color.
    e. bleed.

    Answer: a Difficulty: 2 Page: 333   Key 1: R

57. What are the two types of balance?
    a. artistic and journalistic
    b. proportional and disproportional
    c. formal and informal
    d. aesthetic and mathematical
    e. unity and contrast

    Answer: c Difficulty: 1 Page: 332   Key 1: S

58. All of the following create legibility problems EXCEPT:
    a. flush left.
    b. all caps copy.
    c. reverse type.
    d. all of the above

    Answer: a Difficulty: 2 Page: 336   Key 1: S

59. A style of typesetting in which letters appear to be white against a darker background is called:
    a. overprinting.
    b. reverse type.
    c. bold type.
    d. halftone.
    e. surprinting.

    Answer: b Difficulty: 2 Page: 336   Key 1: R

60. Art in which all elements are solid with no intermediate shades or tones is called:
    a. photograph.
    b. line art.
    c. sketch.
    d. halftone.
    e. illustration.

    Answer: b Difficulty: 1 Page: 336   Key 1: R

61. What are two general types of print images?
    a. photograph and illustration.
    b. line art and continuous tone art.
    c. halftone and illustration.
    d. color and black and white.
    e. grayline and halftone.

    Answer: b Difficulty: 1 Page: 336   Key 1: S

62. What determines the quality of the image produced by a halftone?
    a. ink used
    b. printing process
    c. fineness of screen
    d. paper
    e. photograph process

    Answer: c Difficulty: 3 Page: 336   Key 1: A

63. An image made up of a pattern of dots so that it gives the illustration
    of a continuous range of shades from light to dark is called:
    a. line art.
    b. paste.
    c. continuous tone.
    d. halftone.
    e. grayline.

    Answer: d Difficulty: 1 Page: 336   Key 1: R

64. Images that show a full range of gray tones between black and white are
    called:
    a. halftones.
    b. line art.
    c. continuous tone.
    d. process color.
    e. grayline.

    Answer: c Difficulty: 3 Page: 336   Key 1: R

65. Which of the following will produce the highest quality halftone?
    a. 65 lines per inch
    b. 90 lines per inch
    c. 100 lines per inch
    d. 120 lines per inch
    e. 200 lines per inch

    Answer: e Difficulty: 3 Page: 337   Key 1: R

66. An artist working with the four-color process decides to add black. Why?
    a. adds depth to shadows and dark tones in an image
    b. combines with yellow to create green
    c. combines with red to create purple
    d. combines with blue to create green
    e. all of the above

    Answer: a Difficulty: 2 Page: 339   Key 1: A

TRUE/FALSE

67. Most readers of newspapers see newspaper advertising as a form of news rather than intrusive messages.
    a. True
    b. False

    Answer: a Difficulty: 1 Page: 315   Key 1: A

68. Newspapers are the primary source of local advertising.
    a. True
    b. False

    Answer: a Difficulty: 2 Page: 315   Key 1: R

69. A business should choose a photograph rather than an illustration for its newspaper ad because photographs reproduce better than illustrations in newspapers.
    a. True
    b. False

    Answer: b Difficulty: 2 Page: 315   Key 1: A

70. A problem with color printing in newspapers is that it may or may not be in register.
    a. True
    b. False

    Answer: a Difficulty: 1 Page: 315   Key 1: R

71. Color reproduction is better in newspapers than in magazines.
    a. True
    b. False

    Answer: b Difficulty: 1 Page: 315   Key 1: R

CHAPTER 12:   CREATING PRINT ADVERTISING

72. The most important display element in a print advertisement is the body copy.
a. True
b. False

Answer: b Difficulty: 2 Page: 324   Key 1: A

73. The Big Idea is best communicated in print advertising through the words in the advertising.
a. True
b. False

Answer: b Difficulty: 2 Page: 324   Key 1: R

74. In print advertising, tell as much of the story in the headlines as possible because only 20 percent of the readers go on to read the body copy.
a. True
b. False

Answer: a Difficulty: 1 Page: 325   Key 1: R

75. One way a headline can stop and grab readers is to involve them in completing the message.
a. True
b. False

Answer: a Difficulty: 2 Page: 325   Key 1: A

76. Ideally a good headline will stop only readers who are prospects.
a. True
b. False

Answer: a Difficulty: 1 Page: 325   Key 1: R

77. The persuasive heart of print advertising is the body copy.
a. True
b. False

Answer: a Difficulty: 1 Page: 326   Key 1: R

78. The most common layout format for print advertising is a dominant visual with a cluster of smaller visuals.
a. True
b. False

Answer: b Difficulty: 2 Page: 318   Key 1: R

79. A print advertisement usually starts in the upper half of the layout.
    a. True
    b. False

    Answer: a Difficulty: 1 Page: 331   Key 1: R

80. Normally, the dominant element in an ad is a visual.
    a. True
    b. False

    Answer: a Difficulty: 1 Page: 331   Key 1: R

81. The fewer the elements, the stronger the impact.
    a. True
    b. False

    Answer: a Difficulty: 1 Page: 331   Key 1: R

82. Equal proportions are visually uninteresting.
    a. True
    b. False

    Answer: a Difficulty: 1 Page: 332   Key 1: A

83. Copy and art should be proportionately the same.
    a. True
    b. False

    Answer: b Difficulty: 1 Page: 331   Key 1: R

84. In designing ads, more is less, so when in doubt eliminate the element
    in question.
    a. True
    b. False

    Answer: a Difficulty: 1 Page: 333   Key 1: A

85. Contrary to popular belief, research shows that advertisements without
    color get more attention than advertisements with color.
    a. True
    b. False

    Answer: b Difficulty: 1 Page: 333   Key 1: R

86. Make as much of the ad as bold as possible in order to grab the reader's
    attention.
    a. True
    b. False

    Answer: b Difficulty: 2 Page: 332   Key 1: A

87. Setting type in all caps improves the legibility of the copy.
    a. True
    b. False

    Answer: b Difficulty: 1 Page: 336   Key 1: R

88. In the four-color process, black adds depth to shadows and dark tones in an image.
    a. True
    b. False

    Answer: a Difficulty: 1 Page: 339   Key 1: R

89. The most common printing process used for newspapers and magazines is letterpress printing.
    a. True
    b. False

    Answer: b Difficulty: 3 Page: 339   Key 1: R

90. In print advertising, the computer has taken over the entire process and the ad goes directly from the computer to the printed publication.
    a. True
    b. False

    Answer: b Difficulty: 1 Page: 340   Key 1: A

91. Magazine advertising is often more creative than newspaper advertising.
    a. True
    b. False

    Answer: a Difficulty: 1 Page: 316   Key 1: R

92. Newspaper ads are turning to more creative, attention-getting devices such pop-up visuals, scent strips, and computer chips that play melodies.
    a. True
    b. False

    Answer: b Difficulty: 2 Page: 316   Key 1: R

93. A person creating a yellow page ad should be concerned with image, simplicity, and art, among other things.
    a. True
    b. False

    Answer: a Difficulty: 2 Page: 317   Key 1: A

94. Size, maps, neighborhoods, and index and headings are all relevant issues when creating yellow page ads.
   a. True
   b. False

   Answer: a Difficulty: 2 Page: 317   Key 1: R

95. Out-of-home advertising includes posters, kiosks, billboards, kinetic boards, inflatables, and painted walls.
   a. True
   b. False

   Answer: a Difficulty: 1 Page: 318   Key 1: R

96. Messages posted in public spots first began to fulfill a human need for public communication around the 1800s.
   a. True
   b. False

   Answer: b Difficulty: 2 Page: 318   Key 1: R

97. Posters became a serious art form in the mid-1880s.
   a. True
   b. False

   Answer: a Difficulty: 2 Page: 318   Key 1: R

98. Some kiosks are located in public places where people walk by; others are located in places where people wait.
   a. True
   b. False

   Answer: a Difficulty: 2 Page: 318   Key 1: R

99. One of the most famous billboard campaigns was created for a little company called Burma Shave.
   a. True
   b. False

   Answer: a Difficulty: 1 Page: 320   Key 1: R

100. The Burma Shave poems worked well for 40 years, and became even more popular with the national interstate system.
   a. True
   b. False

   Answer: b Difficulty: 2 Page: 320   Key 1: R

101. Because of the need for instantaneous communication, graphics remain central to the design of poster and outdoor advertising.
    a. True
    b. False

    Answer: a Difficulty: 1 Page: 320   Key 1: R

102. Critical design considerations for high visibility, as recommended by the IOA, include graphics, color, size, and typography.
    a. True
    b. False

    Answer: a Difficulty: 2 Page: 321   Key 1: R

103. Figure/ground is concerned with concealing the relationship between foreground and background.
    a. True
    b. False

    Answer: b Difficulty: 3 Page: 321   Key 1: R

104. Creating a compelling visual in outdoor advertising by using illuminated billboards is also known as spectaculars.
    a. True
    b. False

    Answer: a Difficulty: 2 Page: 322   Key 1: R

105. Disk-like wheels and glittery things that flicker in the wind can be added to outdoor boards to create the appearance of color change.
    a. True
    b. False

    Answer: a Difficulty: 2 Page: 322   Key 1: R

106. Car cards are horizontal and can have longer and more complex messages than exterior panels.
    a. True
    b. False

    Answer: a Difficulty: 3 Page: 322   Key 1: R

107. Headlines and subheads are sometimes called collateral materials because they are used in support of an advertising campaign.
    a. True
    b. False

    Answer: b Difficulty: 2 Page: 323   Key 1: S

108. Subheads and taglines are usually set in smaller type sizes to force viewers to read more closely and carefully.
a. True
b. False

Answer: b Difficulty: 2 Page: 323   Key 1: R

109. Headlines are tested carefully to make sure they can be understood at a glance and that they communicate the right message.
a. True
b. False

Answer: a Difficulty: 1 Page: 324   Key 1: R

110. A layout is a map, the art director's equivalent of a blueprint.
a. True
b. False

Answer: a Difficulty: 1 Page: 327   Key 1: R

ESSAY

111. Compare and contrast the key features of newspaper and magazine advertisements.

Answer:
Though there are other sources of news, newspapers are the primary source of local advertising. Newspaper advertising is one of the few types of advertising that is not considered intrusive. People consult the paper for news of sales as well as politics. Newspaper ads don't have to work as hard as other kinds of ads to catch the audience's attention. And, because the editorial environment of a paper is generally serious and doesn't have to compete as entertainment, most newspaper ad copy is straightforward and informative. Daily papers are printed at high speed on inexpensive, rough, spongy paper called newsprint, which isn't great for reproducing fine details, especially color photos and delicate typefaces. Also, color may not be perfectly in register. Most newspapers subscribe to an artwork service that supplies art for local advertising, or they use clip art, which satisfies the needs of most local advertisers.

In magazines, advertising that ties in closely with the magazine's special interest may be valued as much as the articles. Readers of professional publications may cut out and file ads away as part of their professional reference libraries. For this reason, magazine ads are often more informative and carry longer copy than newspapers ads do. To catch the attention of the reader who may be more absorbed with an article on the opposite page, magazine ads are often more creative than newspaper ads, using beautiful photography and graphics with strong impact. The copy is carefully crafted for both aesthetic and functional impact. Magazine ads are also turning to more creative, attention-getting devices such as pop-up visuals, scent strips, and computer chips that play melodies when the pages are opened. Magazines also provide useful quality image reproduction.

Difficulty: 2 Page: 315-316   Key 1: S

112. Discuss writing headlines for print advertising including their functions and types. Identify other types of display copy that could be used in a print advertisement and explain the relationship between the headline and other display copy.

Answer:

The headline is the most important display element that, ideally, conveys the point of the ad at a glance. It should speak to the interest group, involve the reader, and lead readers into the body copy. Direct headlines are straightforward and informative; indirect headlines are less selective and provide less information, but may be better at drawing the reader into the message. The four types of direct action headlines are assertion (a claim or promise), command (polite order), how-to statements (how to use the product or solve a problem), and news announcements(new product introductions and changes). The two types of indirect action headlines are puzzles (used for provocative power) and associations (use image and lifestyle cues and ambiguity).

Next to headlines, captions have the second highest readership. Captions have pulling power, and serve an information function. Copywriters use subheads along with headlines to help lure the reader into the body copy. Taglines, which are short, catchy phrases, are memorable and are used at the end of an ad to wrap up an idea. Slogans, which are repeated from ad to ad as part of a campaign, also may be used as taglines. Literary techniques such as startling phrases, rhyme, rhythm, alliteration, and parallel construction are used to make subheads, slogans and taglines more attractive and memorable.

Difficulty: 2 Page: 324-327   Key 1: S

113. Discuss the principles of advertising design including organization, direction, unity, contrast, balance, proportion, and simplicity.

   Answer:

   The challenge of arranging all elements of a layout is both functional and aesthetic; the message should be easy to perceive as well as attractive and pleasing to the eye. There are several design principles to follow to achieve these.

   One principle is to impose order. Organized visual images are easier to recognize, perceive, and remember than are random visual images. Order refers to visual organization, or a pattern imposed on the placement of the elements. Another principle is to guide the eye. Establish a sense of direction to create a visual path the eye uses when it scans the element. In Western countries, most readers scan from top to bottom and left to right, a process called the Gutenberg diagonal. A third principle is to create unity: all the elements fuse into one coherent image and the pieces become a whole. The ad's appearance should match its message and speak to the target audience. The typeface should suit the ad's image, and using one typeface is better for unity than using several different ones. A fourth principle is to use contrast and make one element stand out from another to indicate importance. A color ad will stand out in a black and white newspaper, and a black and white ad can create dramatic, high-contrast images in magazines. Another principle is to balance the visual weights. Formal balance is symmetrical and conservative; it suggests stability. Informal balance is asymmetrical and creates a more visually exciting or dynamic layout. Another principle is to use pleasing proportions, the basic idea being that equal proportions are visually uninteresting because they are monotonous, and two visuals of the same size fight for attention. Copy and art should be proportionately different; art usually dominates, covering two-thirds to three-fifths of the page area. Finally, it's important to simplify as much as possible. Less is more. If a layout is crowded, the impact is fragmented; the fewer the elements, the stronger the impact.

   Difficulty: 2 Page: 330-333   Key 1: R

114. Identify the normal steps in developing the layout for a print ad.

Answer:

The steps in the normal development of a print ad may vary from agency to agency or from client to client, but the general steps are sketches, rough layouts, semicomps, comprehensives, and mechanicals.

The first stage is the creation of thumbnail sketches, which are quick, miniature preliminary sketches. These are for the art director's use in developing the concept and positioning the elements. Rough layouts, the second stage, are ads done to size but without great attention to how they look. It's sometimes called a visualization, and helps in making decisions on size and placement. The third stage, semicomps (comp is short for comprehensive), involves a layout drawn to size. All elements are exactly sized and positioned. It's done by hand or computer, and polished for presentation. Art is sketched, color is added, and type is usually set to fit the type specifications. The semicomp is used for most routine presentations. Comprehensives are the fourth layout stage, and are generally presented on special occasions to impress new clients or large clients. The art is at a finished level, and the idea is to make the comp look as much like the finished piece as possible. The fifth layout stage is the mechanical stage, which involves reproduction-quality printouts from the computer that have color separations to guide color reproduction. With computer composition and layout, everything is done on the screen and the computer prints out an electronically assembled digitized image or sometimes a page negative that is another step closer to printing plates. These are strictly for production use.

Difficulty: 1 Page: 329-330 Key 1: R

115. Identify the four shades of ink used to reproduce full-color images, and describe how they are used to reproduce full-color images.

Answer:

A major problem for printers is the reproduction of a full range of color. It would be impossible to set up a printing press with a separate ink roller for every hue and value in a color photo. The solution to this problem is to use a limited number of base colors and mix them to create the rest of the spectrum. Full-color images are reproduced using four distinctive shades of ink called process colors. They are magenta, cyan, yellow, and black. Printing inks are transparent, so when one ink overlaps another, a third color is created. Red and blue create purple; yellow and blue create green; yellow and red create orange. Black is used for type and, in four-color printing, adds depth to the shadows and dark tones in an image.

The process used to reduce the original color image to four halftone negatives is called color separation. The separation is done photographically from the original full-color images. A separate color filter is used to screen out everything but the desired hue for each of the four process colors. Lasers are now used to scan images and make separations.

Difficulty: 1 Page: 337-339 Key 1: R

CHAPTER 13: CREATING BROADCAST ADVERTISING

MULTIPLE CHOICE

1. All of the following are true about TV advertising EXCEPT:
   a. people pay more attention to radio and other media.
   b. viewers consider TV advertising an unwelcome intrusion.
   c. viewers tend to leave the room during commercial breaks.
   d. viewers tend to switch channels to avoid commercials.
   e. all of the above

   Answer: a Difficulty: 2 Page: 349   Key 1: R

2. A message that forces itself on the audience in order to catch the audience's attention is called:
   a. reinforcement.
   b. impact.
   c. intrusive.
   d. coercion.
   e. forceful.

   Answer: c Difficulty: 3 Page: 349   Key 1: A

3. All of the following are common message strategies for television commercials EXCEPT:
   a. storytelling.
   b. dialogue.
   c. use of emotion.
   d. combining action and motion.
   e. demonstration.

   Answer: b Difficulty: 1 Page: 351   Key 1: S

4. Most ad programming on television is:
   a. demonstration.
   b. animation.
   c. infomercials.
   d. storytelling.
   e. humorous.

   Answer: d Difficulty: 1 Page: 356   Key 1: S

5. All of the following are strengths of television advertising EXCEPT:
   a. moving visuals.
   b. production costs.
   c. emotion.
   d. demonstration.
   e. interaction of sight and sound.

   Answer: b Difficulty: 2 Page: 351   Key 1: S

6. Television uses motion and action to create:
   a. average commercials.
   b. calm.
   c. physical sensation.
   d. mental conditioning.
   e. impact.

   Answer: e Difficulty: 2 Page: 351   Key 1: S

7. What is the most important difference between television and other media?
   a. drama
   b. emotion
   c. moving images
   d. actors
   e. sound

   Answer: c Difficulty: 2 Page: 351   Key 1: A

8. Which one of the following media has the ability to touch emotions and feelings more than any other advertising medium?
   a. television
   b. radio
   c. magazines
   d. newspapers
   e. billboards

   Answer: a Difficulty: 1 Page: 351   Key 1: A

9. Why is the infomercial considered ideal for demonstration?
   a. cost
   b. production control
   c. distribution
   d. flexibility
   e. length

   Answer: e Difficulty: 2 Page: 352   Key 1: R

10. What is the key to effective TV advertising?
    a. demonstration of selling point
    b. presenting detailed information
    c. humor
    d. combination of sight and sound
    e. all of the above

    Answer: d Difficulty: 3 Page: 350   Key 1: A

11. What medium is best for demonstration?
    a. radio
    b. magazines
    c. direct mail
    d. television
    e. newspapers

    Answer: d Difficulty: 1 Page: 351   Key 1: A

12. Demonstrations are persuasive on television because:
    a. the volume is increased during the transmission.
    b. we do not usually believe what we see.
    c. we believe what we see.
    d. they are much less costly than other techniques.
    e. none of the above

    Answer: c Difficulty: 2 Page: 351   Key 1: A

13. What dominates perception of the message in TV advertising?
    a. sound effects
    b. visual
    c. music
    d. actors
    e. words

    Answer: b Difficulty: 2 Page: 351   Key 1: S

14. What is the most complex type of advertising to make?
    a. magazines
    b. radio
    c. newspapers
    d. television
    e. billboard

    Answer: d Difficulty: 3 Page: 350   Key 1: A

15. Why is it so vital for a TV commercial to fuse the audio and visual
    elements of the message?
    a. People have trouble listening and watching when the audio and video
       are not the same.
    b. The humor of the commercial is lost when the audio and visual are
       different.
    c. The message loses credibility.
    d. The audio produces an internally visualized setting into which the
       actual video must fit.
    e. Fusion of the audio and visual is not important.

    Answer: a Difficulty: 2 Page: 350   Key 1: R

16. An off-camera announcer talking about the on-camera scene in a commercial is called:
    a. off-camera.
    b. narration.
    c. voice-over.
    d. overline.
    e. mixing.

    Answer: c Difficulty: 2 Page: 350   Key 1: R

17. People who appear in television commercials are called:
    a. talent.
    b. cast.
    c. actors.
    d. characters.
    e. setting.

    Answer: a Difficulty: 3 Page: 359   Key 1: R

18. What is the most important prop in a television commercial?
    a. audience's minds
    b. set
    c. voice
    d. product
    e. lighting

    Answer: d Difficulty: 1 Page: 359   Key 1: A

19. Sixty second television commercials may cost as much as:
    a. $50,000.
    b. $100,000.
    c. $250,000.
    d. half a million dollars.
    e. a million dollars.

    Answer: d Difficulty: 2 Page: 362   Key 1: R

20. _____ describes how languid or upbeat the action is in a television commercial.
    a. Pacing
    b. Gait
    c. Dramatic timing
    d. Mood
    e. Tone

    Answer: a Difficulty: 2 Page: 359   Key 1: S

21. How are most television commercials shot today?
    a. computer video
    b. film
    c. videotape
    d. animation
    e. claymation

    Answer: b Difficulty: 3 Page: 363   Key 1: R

22. What is the advantage of videotape?
    a. records sound and images instantly
    b. can be replayed immediately
    c. cheap
    d. can be changed immediately
    e. all of the above

    Answer: e Difficulty: 1 Page: 363   Key 1: S

23. The chief drawback to animation in television commercials is:
    a. lack of effectiveness.
    b. not taken seriously.
    c. competes with selling point for memorability.
    d. cost.
    e. all of the above

    Answer: d Difficulty: 1 Page: 363   Key 1: S

24. How many frames-per-second are used for film?
    a. 16
    b. 24
    c. 30
    d. 60
    e. 100

    Answer: b Difficulty: 3 Page: 563   Key 1: R

25. Filming inanimate objects one frame at a time, creating the illusion of movement is called:
    a. stop motion.
    b. animation.
    c. claymation.
    d. animatic.
    e. interlock.

    Answer: a Difficulty: 1 Page: 363   Key 1: A

26. A technique that uses figures sculpted from clay and filmed one frame at a time is called:
    a. animation.
    b. stop motion.
    c. claymation.
    d. photoboard.
    e. animatic.

    Answer: c Difficulty: 2 Page: 363   Key 1: R

27. What is the most common length for a broadcast television commercial?
    a. 10 seconds
    b. 20 seconds
    c. 30 seconds
    d. 45 seconds
    e. 60 seconds

    Answer: c Difficulty: 3 Page: 352   Key 1: R

28. A single frame of a TV commercial that summarizes the heart of the message is called a/an:
    a. tagline.
    b. crawl.
    c. key frame.
    d. cut.
    e. embedding.

    Answer: c Difficulty: 2 Page: 358   Key 1: A

29. Why has the 60-second television commercial become so rare?
    a. lack of effectiveness
    b. production costs
    c. air time costs
    d. desire for more repetition in media plans
    e. talent costs

    Answer: c Difficulty: 3 Page: 358   Key 1: R

30. A 15-second cake mix ad sharing a 30-second spot with a 15-second frosting ad is:
    a. piggybacking.
    b. splitting.
    c. pairing.
    d. blocking.
    e. linking.

    Answer: a Difficulty: 2 Page: 358   Key 1: A

31. What is the most common length for an infomercial?
    a. 30 seconds
    b. 60 seconds
    c. 30 minutes
    d. 60 minutes
    e. none of the above

    Answer: c Difficulty: 3 Page: 352   Key 1: S

32. The dancing raisins of the California Raisin Board campaign are an example of:
    a. animation.
    b. interlocking.
    c. stop motion.
    d. animatic.
    e. claymation.

    Answer: e Difficulty: 1 Page: 363   Key 1: A

33. How many frames will the storyboard for a 30-second TV commercial normally have?
    a. one to two
    b. three to five
    c. six to eight
    d. nine to ten
    e. more than ten

    Answer: d Difficulty: 3 Page: 362   Key 1: R

34. A series of frames sketched to illustrate how the story line will develop in a TV commercial is:
    a. rough cut.
    b. interlock.
    c. animatic.
    d. storyboard.
    e. photoboard.

    Answer: d Difficulty: 2 Page: 362   Key 1: R

35. How is the script for television advertising formatted?
    a. one column with the video first on the top and then audio below
    b. two columns with the video on the right and audio on the left
    c. two columns with the video on the left and audio on the right
    d. three columns with the video description in the first column, video instructions in the second column, and audio in the third column
    e. three columns with the audio in the first column, video description in the second column, and video instructions in the third column

    Answer: c Difficulty: 3 Page: 361   Key 1: R

36. A preliminary version of a TV commercial with the storyboard frames recorded on videotape along with a rough sound track is called:
   a. interlock.
   b. animatic.
   c. rough cut.
   d. answer print.
   e. photoboard.

   Answer: b Difficulty: 2 Page: 362   Key 1: R

37. A type of rough TV commercial similar to an animatic except that the frames are photos of the action, is a/an:
   a. rough cut.
   b. interlock.
   c. animatic.
   d. answer print.
   e. photoboard.

   Answer: e Difficulty: 3 Page: 362   Key 1: A

38. What form of a TV commercial would creative people usually use for client presentations?
   a. storyboard
   b. animatic
   c. photoboard
   d. interlock
   e. rough cut

   Answer: b Difficulty: 3 Page: 362   Key 1: A

39. What does the art director do to develop a TV commercial?
   a. establishes the look of the commercial
   b. supervises and coordinates creation of the commercial
   c. is in charge of actual filming of the commercial
   d. manages the flow of the action of the commercial
   e. writes the script for the commercial

   Answer: a Difficulty: 3 Page: 354   Key 1: R

40. The person who supervises and coordinates all of the elements that go into the creation of a television commercial is called the:
   a. director.
   b. producer.
   c. executive producer.
   d. art director.
   e. advertising manager.

   Answer: b Difficulty: 3 Page: 354   Key 1: R

41. The person in charge of the actual filming or taping of the TV commercial is called the:
    a. producer.
    b. art director.
    c. director.
    d. copywriter.
    e. advertising manager.

    Answer: c Difficulty: 3 Page: 354   Key 1: A

42. A person who orchestrates the music for the various instruments, voices, and scenes for a TV commercial is called the:
    a. editor.
    b. composer.
    c. arranger.
    d. director.
    e. writer.

    Answer: c Difficulty: 2 Page: 354   Key 1: A

43. The person who assembles the best shots to create scenes and who synchronizes the audio track with images for a TV commercial is called:
    a. director.
    b. producer.
    c. art director.
    d. editor.

    Answer: d Difficulty: 3 Page: 354   Key 1: R

44. The person who records the commercial at the time of the shooting and sets up the recording equipment including microphones is called a:
    a. synchronizer.
    b. mixer.
    c. sound man.
    d. dubber.
    e. gaffer.

    Answer: b Difficulty: 2 Page: 363   Key 1: R

45. The processed film with the scenes shot on a particular day for a TV commercial is called:
    a. rushes.
    b. interlock.
    c. roughs.
    d. dailies.
    e. answer prints.

    Answer: d Difficulty: 3 Page: 363   Key 1: R

46. The matching of the audio to the video in a TV commercial is called:
    a. mixing.
    b. synchronizing.
    c. dubbing.
    d. rushes.
    e. editing.

    Answer: b Difficulty: 1 Page: 365   Key 1: R

47. Rough versions of the TV commercial assembled from unedited footage are called:
    a. rushes.
    b. rough cuts.
    c. interlocks.
    d. answer prints.
    e. release prints.

    Answer: a Difficulty: 1 Page: 364   Key 1: R

48. A preliminary edited version of the TV commercial is called:
    a. rushes.
    b. interlock.
    c. storyboard.
    d. photoboard.
    e. rough cut.

    Answer: e Difficulty: 1 Page: 365   Key 1: R

49. A version of the TV commercial with the audio and video timed together, although the two are still recorded separately, is called:
    a. rough cut.
    b. release prints.
    c. answer print.
    d. interlock.
    e. rushes.

    Answer: d Difficulty: 1 Page: 365   Key 1: R

50. The final version of the TV commercial with the audio and video recorded together is called:
    a. rushes.
    b. interlock.
    c. answer print.
    d. release print.
    e. rough cut.

    Answer: c Difficulty: 1 Page: 365   Key 1: R

51. The successful television commercial should:
    a. involve the viewer.
    b. have one visual that sums up the entire selling message.
    c. always try to show the product up close at the end of the commercial.
    d. capture the viewer's interest within the first 5 seconds.
    e. all of the above

    Answer: e Difficulty: 2 Page: 349   Key 1: S

52. What is meant by the idea that radio is the theater of the mind?
    a. listeners are active participants in constructing the radio message
    b. visual elements of the radio messages have to be created in the
       audiences' minds
    c. radio messages are created in the mind of the listener
    d. creative success of the radio message depends on the imagination of
       the audience
    e. all of the above

    Answer: e Difficulty: 1 Page: 346   Key 1: S

53. A person who is listening and using his/her imagination to visualize a
    story is probably responding to which media?
    a. radio
    b. television
    c. newspaper
    d. magazine
    e. outdoor

    Answer: a Difficulty: 2 Page: 346   Key 1: A

54. Which of the following is NOT a strength of radio advertising?
    a. human voice
    b. intimacy
    c. image advertising
    d. reminder messages
    e. all of the above

    Answer: c Difficulty: 2 Page: 346   Key 1: S

55. Which of the following is a problem for radio advertising?
    a. intrusiveness
    b. instantaneous quality of the message
    c. distracted listeners
    d. complicated messages
    e. all of the above

    Answer: e Difficulty: 2 Page: 347   Key 1: S

56. All of the following are characteristic of effective radio copywriting EXCEPT:
    a. writing conversationally.
    b. using short sentences.
    c. using distinctive patterns of the target audience.
    d. using slang.
    e. using sentence fragments.

    Answer: d Difficulty: 3 Page: 356   Key 1: S

57. What is the most important element in developing radio advertising messages?
    a. music
    b. human voice
    c. script
    d. copy
    e. sound effects

    Answer: b Difficulty: 1 Page: 347   Key 1: R

58. What primary tools are used to develop radio advertising messages?
    a. conversation, narrative, and sound
    b. music and copy
    c. sound effects, voice, and music
    d. jingles, narrative, and dialogue
    e. copy, music, and jingles

    Answer: c Difficulty: 2 Page: 347   Key 1: R

59. What element of radio advertising has been found to be more effective than celebrity endorsements or product demos?
    a. music
    b. sound effects
    c. human voice
    d. dialogue
    e. all of the above

    Answer: a Difficulty: 1 Page: 348   Key 1: R

60. How is music important to radio commercials?
    a. attention
    b. memorability
    c. intrusiveness
    d. awareness
    e. all of the above

    Answer: b Difficulty: 3 Page: 348   Key 1: R

61. All of the following are common radio commercial lengths EXCEPT:
    a. 10 seconds.
    b. 20 seconds.
    c. 30 seconds.
    d. 60 seconds.
    e. 120 seconds.

    Answer: e Difficulty: 3 Page: 359   Key 1: R

62. What is the maximum number of words in a 30-second all-copy commercial?
    a. 50
    b. 90
    c. 150
    d. 180
    e. 200

    Answer: b Difficulty: 3 Page: 360   Key 1: R

63. How is the copy for radio advertising formatted?
    a. 1 column with the sound source first on top and the actual content of the message below
    b. 2 columns with the sound source on the right and the actual content on the left
    c. 2 columns with the sound source on the left and the actual content on the right
    d. 3 columns with the sound source first, instructions in the middle, and actual content third
    e. 3 columns with the actual content first, sound source second, and instructions third

    Answer: c Difficulty: 2 Page: 361   Key 1: A

64. How is anything that is not spoken in a radio commercial typed?
    a. all lowercase characters
    b. all capital characters
    c. capital and lowercase characters
    d. underlined
    e. bold-faced

    Answer: b Difficulty: 1 Page: 361   Key 1: R

65. Commercials lasting 30 or 60 minutes that provide extensive product information are called:
    a. publicity ads.
    b. sales promotions.
    c. infomercials.
    d. data ads.
    e. late night television programming.

    Answer: c Difficulty: 1 Page: 352   Key 1: R

66. The effort to "zap proof" television commercials has led to:
    a. more informative commercials.
    b. more intriguing and intrusive commercials.
    c. more sales-oriented commercials.
    d. shorter commercials.
    e. longer commercials.

    Answer: b Difficulty: 2 Page: 350   Key 1: R

TRUE/FALSE

67. Advertising is considered an unwelcome interruption on television.
    a. True
    b. False

    Answer: a Difficulty: 1 Page: 349   Key 1: R

68. Most people give more attention to radio than they do television.
    a. True
    b. False

    Answer: b Difficulty: 1 Page: 350   Key 1: A

69. To be effective, television ads must be intrusive and intriguing.
    a. True
    b. False

    Answer: a Difficulty: 1 Page: 349   Key 1: R

70. The audio dominates the perception of the message in a television commercial.
    a. True
    b. False

    Answer: b Difficulty: 1 Page: 350   Key 1: R

71. One strength of television is its ability to reinforce verbal messages with visuals or visual messages with verbal.
    a. True
    b. False

    Answer: a Difficulty: 2 Page: 350   Key 1: R

72. Creating an effective TV commercial is much like making a play, television show, or movie.
    a. True
    b. False

    Answer: a Difficulty: 2 Page: 350   Key 1: R

73. Radio advertising is the most complex of all advertising forms.
    a. True
    b. False

    Answer: b Difficulty: 1 Page: 350   Key 1: R

74. The most important prop in a television commercial is the product.
    a. True
    b. False

    Answer: a Difficulty: 1 Page: 359   Key 1: R

75. Hundreds of people and as much as $500,000 may be needed to make a sixty-second national TV spot.
    a. True
    b. False

    Answer: a Difficulty: 1 Page: 250   Key 1: R

76. Very few television commercials are shot live today.
    a. True
    b. False

    Answer: a Difficulty: 1 Page: 363   Key 1: R

77. Even "live" TV commercials are not really live because of use of tape-delay in transmission.
    a. True
    b. False

    Answer: a Difficulty: 1 Page: 363   Key 1: R

78. When preparing a TV script, the audio is typically placed on the right.
    a. True
    b. False

    Answer: a Difficulty: 2 Page: 361   Key 1: A

79. An effective TV commercial should have one key visual that sums up the entire selling message.
    a. True
    b. False

    Answer: a Difficulty: 2 Page: 350   Key 1: A

80. Of all advertising media, radio relies most heavily on the copywriter.
    a. True
    b. False

    Answer: a Difficulty: 3 Page: 347   Key 1: R

81. Radio is the most personal of all media.
    a. True
    b. False

    Answer: a Difficulty: 1 Page: 347   Key 1: R

82. Radio copy could correctly include sentence fragments.
    a. True
    b. False

    Answer: a Difficulty: 2 Page: 356   Key 1: A

83. Complex sentences are seldom used in radio or in common speech.
    a. True
    b. False

    Answer: a Difficulty: 2 Page: 356   Key 1: A

84. The most important element in developing radio advertising messages is music.
    a. True
    b. False

    Answer: b Difficulty: 1 Page: 347   Key 1: R

85. In the radio ad copy format, the message content of the ad is typed on the left side of the page.
    a. True
    b. False

    Answer: b Difficulty: 3 Page: 361   Key 1: R

86. The person in ultimate control of making a radio commercial is the director.
    a. True
    b. False

    Answer: b Difficulty: 2 Page: 354   Key 1: R

87. Zap proofing television commercials means designing them to be informative and useful.
    a. True
    b. False

    Answer: b Difficulty: 2 Page: 349   Key 1: R

88. In radio, music genres are oriented toward the tastes of particular groups of people.
    a. True
    b. False

    Answer: a Difficulty: 1 Page: 347   Key 1: R

89. In radio, an average of three mentions in a 30-second commercial and five mentions in a 60-second commercial is always too frequent.
    a. True
    b. False

    Answer: b Difficulty: 2 Page: 347   Key 1: R

90. Research has indicated that it's more persuasive to use music rather than celebrity endorsements for ad.
    a. True
    b. False

    Answer: a Difficulty: 2 Page: 348   Key 1: A

91. A custom-made jingle can cost $10,000 or more.
    a. True
    b. False

    Answer: a Difficulty: 1 Page: 348   Key 1: R

92. Sound effects can be taken from records, but more often they are original.
    a. True
    b. False

    Answer: b Difficulty: 2 Page: 349   Key 1: R

93. Good television advertising uses the effect of action and motion to attract attention and sustain interest.
    a. True
    b. False

    Answer: a Difficulty: 1 Page: 351   Key 1: R

94. Television has the ability to touch emotions, and fear, in particular, works well on television.
    a. True
    b. False

    Answer: b Difficulty: 3 Page: 351   Key 1: R

95. Because the advertising strategy was not successfully planned for a cross-cultural market, the Snickers brand name has become a swear word in Russia.
    a. True
    b. False

    Answer: a Difficulty: 1 Page: 352   Key 1: S

96. Cultural pride is strong and advertisers need to fit their commercials into the market's cultural milieu.
    a. True
    b. False

    Answer: a Difficulty: 1 Page: 352   Key 1: R

97. Infomercials of 5, 10, and even 60 minutes in length are being used for messages that need more length for demonstration and explanation.
    a. True
    b. False

    Answer: b Difficulty: 3 Page: 352   Key 1: R

98. Trailers are advertisements similar to TV commercials but generally longer and better produced.
    a. True
    b. False

    Answer: a Difficulty: 1 Page: 353   Key 1: R

99. Some people resent movie trailers as a form of advertising because they are waiting for a film to begin and can't concentrate on the trailer.
    a. True
    b. False

    Answer: b Difficulty: 3 Page: 353   Key 1: R

100. The television show Seinfeld is particularly known for its high product placement.
    a. True
    b. False

    Answer: a Difficulty: 1 Page: 353   Key 1: R

101. Infomercials are the inclusion of branded products, services, or brand identifiers within the content of other pop culture programming.
    a. True
    b. False

    Answer: b Difficulty: 1 Page: 353   Key 1: R

102. A locally produced TV or radio commercial rarely uses the station's personnel for most of the production roles.
    a. True
    b. False

    Answer: b Difficulty: 3 Page: 354   Key 1: R

103. A producer handles the bidding and all production arrangements and arranges for casting talent.
    a. True
    b. False

    Answer: a Difficulty: 2 Page: 354   Key 1: R

104. Writing successful copy for radio includes identifying sound effects, keeping it simple, and being wary of comedy.
    a. True
    b. False

    Answer: a Difficulty: 2 Page: 355   Key 1: R

105. When writing radio copy, one thing to do is to tailor your commercial to the time, place, and specific audience. For example, if your commercial is running at 8 AM in Denver, you might tailor it to commuter traffic.
    a. True
    b. False

    Answer: a Difficulty: 1 Page: 355   Key 1: A

106. One of Jewler's tips for successful TV commercials is to always try to show a close-up of your product first thing.
    a. True
    b. False

    Answer: b Difficulty: 3 Page: 357   Key 1: R

107. A run-on is computer-generated letters that appear to be moving across the bottom of the screen.
    a. True
    b. False

    Answer: b Difficulty: 2 Page: 359   Key 1: R

108. Stock footage is a previously recorded image, either video, still slides, or moving film, used for scenes that aren't accessible to normal shooting.
    a. True
    b. False

    Answer: a Difficulty: 1 Page: 359   Key 1: R

109. Most television commercial film is shot as a negative, processed, then transferred to videotape.
    a. True
    b. False

Answer: a Difficulty: 2 Page: 360   Key 1: R

110. In a production shoot, the grip is the person who moves things around.
    a. True
    b. False

Answer: a Difficulty: 1 Page: 364   Key 1: R

ESSAY

111. Discuss the four steps of the TV commercial production process.

    Answer:
    Steps of the production process can be grouped into four categories: message design, preproduction, production (the shoot), and postproduction. The first step, message design, involves gaining client approval on the advertising strategy, choosing the message format, creating a key frame, writing the script, storyboarding the action and scenes, and getting client approval of the script and storyboard.

    The second step, preproduction, involves finding the right director and production or animation house, working out details in the preproduction meeting, locating or building the set, casting the talent, locating props, costumes and photographic stills, and getting bids for all the production operations.

    Production, or the shoot, is managed by the director. Other technicians include the gaffer (chief electrician), the grip (set mover), and the script clerk who checks dialogue and other script details. The action, music, voices, and sound effects are all recorded, and on-screen and computer graphics are created during this stage.

    In postproduction, the film is edited, which involves rough cut, interlock, answer print, release print versions. During this stage, audio track is mixed; video and audio are synchronized; the client is given a presentation tape for approval, and videotapes are duplicated for distribution.
    Difficulty: 2 Page: 364-366   Key 1: R

112. Discuss the roles of the producer, director, and editor in the production of a TV or radio commercial.

Answer:
The producer, who is often an agency staff member, takes charge of the production, handles the bidding on all production arrangements, finds the specialists, arranges for casting talent, and makes sure the budget and the bids come in. Although a locally produced TV or radio commercial uses the station's personnel for most of the production roles, the director and editor are usually outside people. The director is the person who has responsibility for the actual filming or taping, including scene length, who does what, how lines are spoken, and the characters played. In TV, the director determines how the camera records the flow of action. The editor puts everything together toward the end of the filming or taping process. The editor evaluates how to assemble scenes and which audio elements work best with the dialogue.

Difficulty: 1 Page: 354   Key 1: R

113. Discuss the problems and opportunities of copywriting for radio and TV.

Answer:
Radio urges the copywriter to reach into the depth of imagination and cunning to create an idea that rouses the inattentive listener. To meet the challenge of writing successful copy for radio, a writer should consider the following guidelines: identify sound effects, use music as a sound effect, build the commercial around a sound, fight for the longer 60-second spots, consider using a distinctive voice or a powerful message instead of sound effects, if using comedy begin with an outrageous premise, keep it simple, tailor comments to time, place, and specific audiences, and present the commercial to the client on tape, if possible. The key to successful radio advertising is to evoke visual images based on what the listener hears. Writers need to capitalize on radio's intimacy and the listener's imagination. The message should be anchored through repetition, entertainment value, and relevance. Message should be conversational and use vernacular. Word choice should reflect the speech of the target audience.

Television is different from radio in many ways, the most important being that it is a medium of moving images. These images must be fused with the words to present a creative concept as well as a story. In television, the verbal message can be enforced with visuals, or vice versa. The point of audiovisual fusion is that words and pictures work together, lest the commercial show one thing and say another. Storytelling is important; most of television programming is narrative. Commercial stories must be imaginative to hold their own against the programming that surrounds them. Stories can be used to entertain and to make a point; they can be funny, warm, silly, or heart-rending, as in real life. Emotion is best developed and expressed in a narrative form. Slice-of-life advertising is simply instruction in a soap opera format.

Difficulty: 3 Page: 355-356   Key 1: R

114. Discuss the filming and recording techniques used in producing a television commercial.

Answer:
There are a number of ways to produce a message for a television commercial. It can be filmed live or prerecorded using film or videotape. It can also be shot frame by frame using animation techniques. The history of live filming is filled with traumatic stories, which is why most advertisers prefer to prerecord a commercial. Even a live activity, such as a sports event, has a built-in delay of several seconds so that some errors can be corrected. Very few commercials are actually shown live in real time.

Most TV commercials are shot on 16-mm or 35-mm film. The film is shot as a negative and processed, after which the image is transferred to videotape. Film consists of a series of frames, and each frame is a still shot. Film is shot at 24 frames per second. The term "cut," which comes from the process of editing film by cutting between frames for desired order and effect, describes an abrupt transition from one view of a scene to another. Until the 1980s, videotape was thought inferior to film, and was mainly used by the television news industry for instant recording. Videotape's image has changed as its quality has improved.

The technique of animation records images on film one frame at a time. Cartoon figures, for example, are resketched with slight changes and then shot again with each change. Animation is traditionally shot at 12 or 16 drawings per second. Because of the hand work, animation is labor intensive and expensive. The introduction of computers has accelerated the process, requiring only the beginning and ending frames from illustrators and plotting out the frames in between. A particular type of animation is stop motion, a technique used to film inanimate objects like the Pillsbury Doughboy, a puppet. The puppet is moved a bit at a time, and filmed frame by frame. This technique is also used in claymation, which involve characters made from clay that are photographed one frame at a time.

Difficulty: 2 Page: 362-363 Key 1: R

115. Explain the current ten rules for Web site design, as shown in Chapter 13.

Answer:
The first rule of Web site design, as listed on the eMarketer's site, is to manage your image. Projecting and protecting your brand identity are no less important online than in any other medium. Second, use simple navigation. To stay in business, customers must be able to easily find what they want. Third, Don't waste time. Make sure customers can quickly find the information they're looking for. Fourth, Keep your product fresh. Fifth, give it away. If your site doesn't offer real value, there's no reason for people to visit. Sixth, make sure there's information at the end of someone's search. When someone takes the time to link through your site, reward them with plenty of content. Seventh, get interactive. Mass media are passive; make sure you're up to date with new and interactive media. Eighth, follow the rule of ten. A short list of elements is best. Ninth, promote your site. If you want customers on your site, get smart about promotion. And tenth, the rules will change. Move often and as intelligently as possible, and keep up with fast-changing online business trends.

Difficulty: 1 Page: 367   Key 1: R

CHAPTER 14: CREATING DIRECT-RESPONSE ADVERTISING

MULTIPLE CHOICE

1. The Hilton Honors program is an example of:
   a. direct marketing.
   b. interactive marketing.
   c. effective use of television advertising in marketing.
   d. marketing strategy emerging from creative intuition.
   e. personal marketing.

   Answer: e Difficulty: 2 Page: 379   Key 1: A

2. What is allowing advertisers to develop one-on-one communication with those most likely to be in the market for certain products?
   a. cable TV companies moving into the telephone business
   b. more effective marketing research
   c. computer databases
   d. growth of the Internet
   e. use of 1-800 telephone numbers

   Answer: c Difficulty: 2 Page: 379   Key 1: R

3. Lists of consumers with information that helps target and segment people who are highly likely to be in the market for a certain product are called:
   a. target lists.
   b. direct marketing files.
   c. databases.
   d. mailing lists.

   Answer: c Difficulty: 1 Page: 380   Key 1: R

4. What does tight targeting allow direct marketers to do more than in any other advertising form?
   a. personalize the message
   b. gain more attention
   c. increase credibility
   d. get less resistance from the audience
   e. all of the above

   Answer: a Difficulty: 2 Page: 380   Key 1: R

5. Traditional advertising targets groups of people; database advertising targets:
   a. groups.
   b. masses.
   c. individuals.
   d. database groups.

   Answer: d Difficulty: 2 Page: 380   Key 1: R

6. What is the nature of the revolution that is occurring in marketing communication?
   a. changing from target marketing to mass marketing
   b. one-on-one dialog with consumers
   c. less emphasis on increasing sales
   d. becoming less interactive
   e. all of the above

   Answer: b Difficulty: 2 Page: 380   Key 1: R

7. What benefit does the use of computer databases have for marketers' advertising?
   a. develop one-on-one communication with consumers
   b. use tight target marketing strategy
   c. zero in on primary targets
   d. understand consumers more thoroughly
   e. all of the above

   Answer: e Difficulty: 2 Page: 380   Key 1: R

8. A type of marketing that uses media to contact a prospect directly and elicit a response without the intervention of a retailer or personal sales is called:
   a. marketing promotion.
   b. target marketing.
   c. data-base marketing.
   d. direct marketing.
   e. brand marketing.

   Answer: d Difficulty: 1 Page: 380   Key 1: R

9. You are interested in reaching college professors with an advertising message about a new word-processing program. You decide to buy a mailing list and send each professor a brochure. You are taking advantage of direct mails:
   a. low cost per exposure.
   b. intensive geographic coverage.
   c. "tight" targeting.
   d. flexibility.
   e. mass reach.

   Answer: c Difficulty: 3 Page: 380   Key 1: A

10. Which of the following is a characteristic of direct marketing?
   a. includes a mechanism for the consumer to respond
   b. requires a data base of consumer information
   c. exchange between buyer and seller is not bound to a retail store
   d. provides for measurement of the response
   e. all of the above

   Answer: e Difficulty: 2 Page: 381   Key 1: R

11. In direct marketing, the customer and the marketer engage in:
    a. mass communication.
    b. one-on-one communication.
    c. two-way communication.
    d. group communication.
    e. interpersonal communication.

    Answer: c Difficulty: 2 Page: 381   Key 1: R

12. What are the advantages offered to the consumer by direct marketing?
    a. cost, efficiency, convenience
    b. efficiency, convenience, compression of decision-making time
    c. convenience, flexibility, cost
    d. efficiency, flexibility, convenience
    e. compression of decision-making time, cost, convenience

    Answer: b Difficulty: 2 Page: 382   Key 1: R

13. What is the primary strategy advantage of direct marketing?
    a. measurable response
    b. interactivity
    c. use of database
    d. exchange not bound by retail store
    e. U.S. Postal Service

    Answer: a Difficulty: 2 Page: 382   Key 1: R

14. All of the following are types of direct marketing EXCEPT:
    a. telemarketing.
    b. municipal marketing.
    c. electronic-response marketing.
    d. direct mail.
    e. all of the above

    Answer: b Difficulty: 2 Page: 382   Key 1: R

15. Which of the following statements is correct about direct-response advertising?
    a. It is one of the slowest-growing segments of the advertising industry.
    b. It is the only growing segment of the advertising industry.
    c. It is not related in any way to the advertising industry.
    d. It is one of the fastest-growing segments of the advertising industry.
    e. It is not going to be legal after 2001.

    Answer: d Difficulty: 1 Page: 382   Key 1: R

16. Which of the following is a reason for the growth of direct-response advertising?
   a. the number of women in the work force
   b. the credit card
   c. the number of single-parent households
   d. the general popularity of direct-response advertising
   e. all of the above

   Answer: e Difficulty: 2 Page: 382   Key 1: R

17. What technical advance has had the biggest impact on direct marketing?
   a. the computer
   b. the credit card
   c. the use of "900" telephone numbers
   d. the ZIP codes
   e. the toll-free 800 numbers

   Answer: a Difficulty: 3 Page: 382   Key 1: R

18. Which area of marketing communication was first to adopt the idea of integrated marketing?
   a. advertising
   b. public relations
   c. direct marketing
   d. personal selling
   e. sales promotion

   Answer: c Difficulty: 2 Page: 377   Key 1: R

19. What does integrated direct marketing involve?
   a. using direct marketing together with other forms of marketing communication
   b. synchronizing all the elements of message, medium, and target of direct marketing
   c. synchronizing direct marketing with all areas of the marketing mix
   d. using multiple media to allow consumers to respond in the way most suitable to them
   e. all of the above

   Answer: e Difficulty: 2 Page: 392   Key 1: R

20. What in the direct-marketing piece constitutes all the variables that together are intended to satisfy the needs of the consumer?
   a. message
   b. customer service
   c. promise
   d. package
   e. offer

   Answer: e Difficulty: 2 Page: 377   Key 1: R

21. What is the key to the success of direct marketing?
    a. reaching the right person at the right time
    b. interactivity
    c. offer
    d. medium
    e. customer service

    Answer: a Difficulty: 2 Page: 377   Key 1: R

22. Which of the following is a problem with direct marketing?
    a. tendency of direct marketers to sacrifice long-term considerations
       for short-term gain
    b. inefficient in delivering messages to primary prospects
    c. people do not respond to direct marketing programs
    d. does not mesh well with other areas of marketing communication
    e. all of the above

    Answer: a Difficulty: 2 Page: 377   Key 1: R

23. What is the goal of customer service in direct marketing?
    a. act as the sales agent for direct marketing
    b. overcome resistance to buying through direct response media
    c. reinforce the offer
    d. make the process more efficient
    e. provide a means for measuring consumer response

    Answer: b Difficulty: 2 Page: 377   Key 1: R

24. What is the growth area in direct response advertising?
    a. direct mail
    b. electronic response
    c. telemarketing
    d. World Wide Web
    e. radio

    Answer: c Difficulty: 2 Page: 377   Key 1: R

25. A type of marketing communication that accomplishes the action-oriented
    objective (such as an inquiry, visiting a showroom, answering a
    questionnaire, or purchasing a product) as a result of the advertising
    message and without the intervention of a sales representative or
    retailer is:
    a. advertising.
    b. sales promotion.
    c. data-base advertising.
    d. brand advertising.
    e. direct-response advertising.

    Answer: e Difficulty: 1 Page: 378   Key 1: R

26. Why is direct-response advertising different from other types of advertising?
    a. seeks action-oriented objective such as an inquiry
    b. generally targeted to groups of prospects
    c. effectively develops brand image
    d. targeted audience tends to be larger
    e. all of the above

    Answer: a Difficulty: 2 Page: 378   Key 1: R

27. What is an important characteristic of direct-response advertising?
    a. interactivity
    b. measurability
    c. action objectives
    d. less waste circulation
    e. all of the above

    Answer: e Difficulty: 3 Page: 378   Key 1: R

28. All of the following are problems of direct-response advertising EXCEPT:
    a. irritating to consumers.
    b. invasion of privacy in data collection.
    c. inefficient message delivery.
    d. high cost.
    e. intrusion of telephone messages.

    Answer: c Difficulty: 2 Page: 378   Key 1: R

29. The Texas Tourism Agency runs ads in a number of magazines inviting people to vacation in Texas. As part of the ads, there is a coupon that allows the reader to request free information about Texas vacation destinations. The Tourism Agency is using:
    a. mail-order advertising.
    b. consumer advertising.
    c. direct-response advertising.
    d. direct mail advertising.
    e. direct advertising.

    Answer: c Difficulty: 2 Page: 378   Key 1: A

30. Which of the following is a way the computer impacts direct marketing?
    a. consumers reaching marketers through personal computers
    b. allows marketers to tailor messages precisely to individuals
    c. marketers manage a list of names
    d. grocery carts that show advertised specials
    e. all of the above

    Answer: e Difficulty: 2 Page: 380   Key 1: R

31. Who is the primary target in what the text calls "data-base marketing"?
    a. upscale groups of people
    b. groups of people
    c. market segment
    d. same target markets as traditional advertising
    e. the individual

    Answer: e Difficulty: 2 Page: 379   Key 1: R

32. A form of marketing that uses computerized lists to reach consumers and to collect information about consumers is called:
    a. relationship marketing.
    b. maxi-marketing.
    c. data-base marketing.
    d. direct-response marketing.
    e. all of the above

    Answer: e Difficulty: 2 Page: 379   Key 1: R

33. What have past criticisms of direct-response advertising focused on?
    a. flexibility and cost
    b. reach and frequency
    c. efficiency and cost
    d. effectiveness and efficiency
    e. reach and flexibility

    Answer: c Difficulty: 2 Page: 379   Key 1: R

34. Why is the problem of high cost not as much of a problem as it was historically in direct-response advertising?
    a. less waste coverage
    b. upscale targets make cost less important
    c. cost per impression is decreasing
    d. computers are being used to reduce cost
    e. personal contact of direct-response advertising makes it worth the cost

    Answer: a Difficulty: 2 Page: 379   Key 1: R

35. A new development in marketing in which computerized data bases are used to help marketers develop a deeper and longer-lasting relationship with their customers is called:
    a. data-base marketing.
    b. relationship marketing.
    c. maxi-marketing.
    d. all of the above

    Answer: d Difficulty: 3 Page: 380   Key 1: R

36. What is the principle behind integration in direct marketing?
    a. multiple media multiply response
    b. integration lets everyone in marketing know the marketing strategy
    c. helps direct marketing focus more on the long-term
    d. not all people respond the same way
    e. reduces marketing costs

    Answer: d Difficulty: 2 Page: 380   Key 1: R

37. _____ means the consumer can respond back to the message. The telephone
    is the prime example of a media vehicle that both delivers and receives
    messages.
    a. Feedback
    b. Interactive
    c. Direct-response
    d. Data base
    e. Indirect-response

    Answer: b Difficulty: 2 Page: 393   Key 1: R

38. All of the following are problems with direct marketing EXCEPT:
    a. tendency of direct marketers to sacrifice long-term goals for
       short-term goals.
    b. produces only small sales gains compared to the cost.
    c. very high cost per thousand.
    d. not integrated with other marketing communication activities.
    e. all of the above

    Answer: b Difficulty: 2 Page: 380   Key 1: R

39. Why has direct response advertising been seen as less efficient than
    mass-media advertising?
    a. cost of reaching people individually is very high
    b. while it reaches a lot of people, it also irritates them
    c. the message is too complicated
    d. more waste than mass-media advertising
    e. all of the above

    Answer: a Difficulty: 2 Page: 380   Key 1: R

40. What is a serious problem in the development of massive databases?
    a. software viruses
    b. computer hackers
    c. privacy concerns
    d. finding people to manage them
    e. business secrecy

    Answer: c Difficulty: 2 Page: 380   Key 1: R

41. Which of the following represents the three key players involved in direct-response marketing?
    a. consumers, government, advertisers
    b. nonprofit groups, businesses, government
    c. media, advertisers, government
    d. advertisers, agencies, consumers
    e. consumers, media, advertisers

    Answer: d Difficulty: 2 Page: 381   Key 1: R

42. What are the two key issues in consumers' privacy problems with direct marketers?
    a. intrusiveness and computer secrecy
    b. pushy researchers and telemarketing
    c. computer security and personal information in database
    d. direct mail and telemarketing
    e. intrusiveness and personal information in database

    Answer: e Difficulty: 2 Page: 382   Key 1: R

43. What is the key organization in the direct marketing industry's efforts at self-regulation?
    a. Direct Marketing Association
    b. National Advertising Division
    c. Consumer Privacy Work Group
    d. American Civil Liberties Union
    e. Direct Response Association

    Answer: a Difficulty: 2 Page: 382   Key 1: R

44. Why is the Telecommunications Competition and Deregulation Act of 1996 important to direct marketers?
    a. outlaws unsolicited telephone calls by marketers
    b. ensures that consumers can use media without fear of being unduly exploited
    c. sets restrictions on the use of direct mail
    d. creates rules for storing personal information in databases
    e. all of the above

    Answer: b Difficulty: 2 Page: 382   Key 1: R

45. _____ is a special service firm which takes responsibility for making sure consumers receive whatever they request in a timely manner.
    a. Customer service
    b. Compiling service
    c. Fulfillment house
    d. Response house
    e. Distribution house

    Answer: c Difficulty: 2 Page: 382   Key 1: R

46. Why do consumers put up with the intrusiveness of direct response advertising?
    a. cost
    b. powerful messages
    c. habit
    d. convenience
    e. weak minds

Answer: d Difficulty: 2 Page: 382   Key 1: R

47. One of the historical truths about the direct marketing industry was that merchandisers tended to view the relationship with the consumer as:
    a. short-term.
    b. hostile.
    c. long-term.
    d. interactive.
    e. financial.

Answer: a Difficulty: 2 Page: 394   Key 1: R

48. _____ measures how many purchases a marketer can expect from each purchase segment.
    a. Cost-benefit analysis
    b. Market segmentation
    c. Lifetime customer value
    d. Market-share performance
    e. Customer segment analysis

Answer: c Difficulty: 2 Page: 394   Key 1: R

49. All of the following are objectives of a marketing database EXCEPT:
    a. measure advertising results.
    b. facilitate continuing communication.
    c. measure purchasing performance.
    d. measure customer loyalty.
    e. record customer/prospect names.

Answer: d Difficulty: 2 Page: 391   Key 1: R

50. What is the significance of the concept of lifetime customer value to direct marketers?
    a. helps predict future sales
    b. measures consumer loyalty
    c. evaluates effectiveness of direct marketing campaigns
    d. measures the direct marketers' image
    e. ensures customer privacy

Answer: b Difficulty: 2 Page: 394   Key 1: R

51. Which of the following is an element of the direct marketing piece?
    a. customer service
    b. offer
    c. timing
    d. sequencing
    e. all of the above

    Answer: e Difficulty: 2 Page: 382   Key 1: R

52. What is the historical foundation for the direct-response industry?
    a. telemarketing
    b. direct mail
    c. catalogs
    d. door-to-door
    e. specialty advertising

    Answer: b Difficulty: 2 Page: 382   Key 1: R

53. What is the main medium of direct response messages?
    a. telephone
    b. magazines
    c. computer
    d. direct mail
    e. television

    Answer: d Difficulty: 2 Page: 382   Key 1: R

54. What form of direct marketing generally has the highest response rates
    of any other medium used in direct marketing?
    a. telemarketing
    b. direct-response TV
    c. direct mail
    d. direct-response radio
    e. cable TV

    Answer: c Difficulty: 3 Page: 382   Key 1: A

55. On what basis is the critical decision made on whether or not to read
    direct mail pieces?
    a. the envelope
    b. the paper on which the piece is printed
    c. the brochure
    d. the order card
    e. the letter

    Answer: a Difficulty: 2 Page: 382   Key 1: R

56. What technique is used to get people to open the envelope in direct
    mail?
    a. teaser statement
    b. "peek-through" window
    c. statement of sales offer on the envelope
    d. incentive offer to open the envelope
    e. all of the above

    Answer: e Difficulty: 2 Page: 382   Key 1: R

57. Why are most direct mail letters so long-usually 2-4 pages and many even
    longer?
    a. direct mail copywriters are verbose
    b. people seem to prefer long letters
    c. letters must carry the full weight of advertising, marketing and
       sales effort
    d. because they are usually aimed at older people so the type has to be
       larger
    e. all of the above

    Answer: c Difficulty: 2 Page: 382   Key 1: R

58. All of the following are advantages of direct mail EXCEPT:
    a. engaging the reader's attention.
    b. gaining access to the audiences who are unreachable by other media.
    c. offering a variety of formats.
    d. personalizing messages.
    e. low cost-per-thousand.

    Answer: e Difficulty: 2 Page: 383   Key 1: R

59. All of the following are disadvantages of direct mail EXCEPT:
    a. engaging the reader's attention.
    b. quality of mailing lists.
    c. high cost-per-thousand.
    d. junk mail image.
    e. postage costs.

    Answer: a Difficulty: 2 Page: 383   Key 1: R

60. What is the primary drawback to direct mail?
    a. high cost-per-thousand
    b. junk mail image
    c. engaging reader's attention
    d. postage costs
    e. quality of mailing lists

    Answer: b Difficulty: 2 Page: 383   Key 1: R

61. What percentage of mail pieces does the direct marketing industry estimate get read?
    a. 10%
    b. 25%
    c. 50%
    d. 75%
    e. 100%

    Answer: d Difficulty: 2 Page: 383   Key 1: R

62. A statement or question used to spark curiosity in a direct mailing is called a/an:
    a. string along.
    b. order card.
    c. inserts.
    d. razz.
    e. teaser.

    Answer: e Difficulty: 2 Page: 383   Key 1: R

63. Research on direct mail advertising has found that people with any interest in the product:
    a. will read everything in the letter.
    b. still need strong stimulation to read the letter.
    c. will not read a letter if it is long.
    d. need more than a one-page letter to read.
    e. will not purchase by direct mail.

    Answer: a Difficulty: 2 Page: 383   Key 1: A

64. Which of the following is a function of the direct mail message?
    a. make the sale
    b. explain how to order
    c. get the attention of the target
    d. demonstrate the product
    e. all of the above

    Answer: e Difficulty: 2 Page: 383   Key 1: R

65. Direct mail advertising can only be as effective as the:
    a. letter
    b. mailing list
    c. envelope
    d. return card
    e. objective

    Answer: b Difficulty: 2 Page: 383   Key 1: A

66. What is probably the most valuable list available to a store or company?
    a. response list
    b. broker list
    c. house list
    d. prospect list
    e. compiled list

    Answer: c Difficulty: 2 Page: 383   Key 1: R

67. What are the three types of lists available for direct mail advertising?
    a. house lists, response lists and compiled lists
    b. company lists, broker lists and special lists
    c. created lists, existing lists and special lists
    d. manager lists, broker lists and organization lists
    e. response lists, marketing lists and compiled lists

    Answer: a Difficulty: 2 Page: 383   Key 1: R

68. What is the biggest problem with computer-generated mailing lists?
    a. not well targeted
    b. accuracy
    c. cost too much
    d. take too long to generate
    e. misspelled names

    Answer: b Difficulty: 2 Page: 383   Key 1: R

69. What is the growth area in the catalog business?
    a. videocassette catalogs
    b. computer disk catalogs
    c. specialty catalogs
    d. electronic catalogs
    e. on-line computer catalogs

    Answer: d Difficulty: 2 Page: 385   Key 1: R

70. What is the most important part of a catalog message?
    a. copy
    b. headlines
    c. captions
    d. graphics
    e. type size

    Answer: d Difficulty: 2 Page: 385   Key 1: R

71. What is an advantage of the electronic catalog as a direct-response advertising medium?
    a. cost
    b. interactive
    c. flexibility
    d. mass audience
    e. personal

    Answer: b Difficulty: 2 Page: 385   Key 1: R

72. A type of response that can be sought in direct-response advertising in newspapers is:
    a. telephone
    b. order form
    c. mailing address
    d. coupon
    e. all of the above

    Answer: e Difficulty: 2 Page: 388   Key 1: R

73. Which of the following is a problem with print media as direct response advertising media?
    a. permanence
    b. flexibility
    c. less targeted
    d. complex message
    e. coupons

    Answer: c Difficulty: 2 Page: 388   Key 1: R

74. Which of the following is a problem with television as a direct-response advertising medium?
    a. impact
    b. demonstration
    c. broad target audience
    d. cost
    e. all of the above

    Answer: d Difficulty: 2 Page: 388   Key 1: R

75. What is an advantage of television as a direct-response advertising medium?
    a. cost
    b. flexibility
    c. broad target audience
    d. personal
    e. interactive

    Answer: c Difficulty: 2 Page: 388   Key 1: R

76. Why does cable television work better for direct-response advertising than other major media?
    a. audio-visual environment
    b. wired distribution of cable
    c. more favorable cost-per-thousand figures
    d. more tightly targeted to particular interests
    e. all of the above

    Answer: d Difficulty: 2 Page: 388   Key 1: R

77. What is radio's advantage as a medium for direct response advertising?
    a. visualization
    b. cost
    c. flexibility
    d. targeted audience
    e. interactivity

    Answer: d Difficulty: 2 Page: 388   Key 1: R

78. What is the primary advantage of telemarketing as a direct-response approach?
    a. cost
    b. flexibility
    c. visualization
    d. acceptance
    e. personal

    Answer: e Difficulty: 2 Page: 386   Key 1: R

79. More direct-marketing dollars are spent on this medium than any other.
    a. television
    b. telephone
    c. radio
    d. mail
    e. billboards

    Answer: b Difficulty: 2 Page: 386   Key 1: R

80. Which one of the following statements is true? Personal telephone sales calls are:
    a. very expensive but very persuasive.
    b. relatively inexpensive and very persuasive.
    c. very expensive and not very persuasive.
    d. very inexpensive and not very persuasive.
    e. very cheap and totally ineffective.

    Answer: a Difficulty: 2 Page: 386   Key 1: A

81. A very important advantage of telemarketing is:
    a. two-way conversation.
    b. not intrusive.
    c. demonstration.
    d. cost.
    e. all of the above

    Answer: a Difficulty: 2 Page: 386   Key 1: R

82. Telemarketing is how many times more expensive than direct mail?
    a. 2 to 3 times.
    b. 3 to 4 times.
    c. 4 to 5 times.
    d. 5 to 6 times.
    e. 6 to 7 times.

    Answer: c Difficulty: 3 Page: 386   Key 1: R

83. What is the most important characteristic of the telemarketing message?
    a. strong initial benefit
    b. short
    c. compelling
    d. simple
    e. reason-shy statement

    Answer: d Difficulty: 2 Page: 387   Key 1: R

84. All of the following are characteristics of the telemarketing message
    EXCEPT:
    a. short.
    b. simple.
    c. good for demonstration.
    d. compelling.
    e. strong initial benefit.

    Answer: c Difficulty: 1 Page: 387   Key 1: R

85. What is the newest form of direct media?
    a. telemarketing
    b. interactive online
    c. radio
    d. cable television
    e. CD-ROM

    Answer: b Difficulty: 2 Page: 387   Key 1: R

86. What are the two types of online channels?
    a. web pages and bulletin boards
    b. cyberspace and Internet
    c. Internet and Commercial Online
    d. home shopping service and Web shopping malls
    e. commercial online and home shopping service

    Answer: c Difficulty: 2 Page: 389   Key 1: R

87. All of the following are ways direct marketers can use the Internet EXCEPT:
    a. e-mail.
    b. bulletin boards.
    c. place direct response advertising online.
    d. create electronic storefront.
    e. online magazines.

    Answer: e Difficulty: 2 Page: 389   Key 1: R

88. Which of the following is a way companies and individuals can place advertising on commercial online services?
    a. classified advertising
    b. commercial newsgroups
    c. online billboards
    d. all of the above
    e. none of the above

    Answer: d Difficulty: 2 Page: 389   Key 1: R

89. All of the following are true about expectations for the future of direct marketing EXCEPT:
    a. low cost-per-thousand.
    b. increased level of customer service.
    c. exploding technology applications.
    d. increased Internet retail applications.
    e. spread of new home shopping systems.

    Answer: a Difficulty: 2 Page: 389   Key 1: R

TRUE/FALSE

90. Marketing communication has changed so that communication is increasingly a one-way monologue with consumers talking to advertisers.
    a. True
    b. False

    Answer: b Difficulty: 1 Page: 380   Key 1: A

91. Traditional advertising targets the individual; direct response advertising targets groups.
    a. True
    b. False

    Answer: b Difficulty: 2 Page: 380   Key 1: A

92. Direct marketing is tightly targeted to people who have been identified as prospects.
    a. True
    b. False

    Answer: a Difficulty: 2 Page: 380   Key 1: R

93. Direct marketing is used almost exclusively by consumer products companies.
    a. True
    b. False

    Answer: b Difficulty: 2 Page: 381   Key 1: A

94. The advantages of direct marketing to consumers are convenience, efficiency, and the compression of decision-making time.
    a. True
    b. False

    Answer: a Difficulty: 2 Page: 381   Key 1: R

95. The computer is the technological advance that has had the greatest impact on direct marketing.
    a. True
    b. False

    Answer: a Difficulty: 2 Page: 377   Key 1: R

96. Direct marketing was the first area of marketing communication to adopt the philosophy of integrated marketing.
    a. True
    b. False

    Answer: a Difficulty: 2 Page: 377   Key 1: R

97. Direct-response advertising target audiences tend to be smaller than for other advertising forms.
    a. True
    b. False

    Answer: a Difficulty: 2 Page: 379   Key 1: A

98. Direct-response advertising has a relative high cost per thousand.
    a. True
    b. False

    Answer: a Difficulty: 2 Page: 379   Key 1: R

99. Traditional advertising agencies have readily integrated direct
    marketing into their operations.
    a. True
    b. False

    Answer: b Difficulty: 2 Page: 381   Key 1: R

100. Direct marketers try to enter into a long-term relationship with their
     customers.
     a. True
     b. False

    Answer: a Difficulty: 2 Page: 382   Key 1: R

101. Direct-response is a multimedia field. All conventional advertising mass
     media can be used.
     a. True
     b. False

    Answer: a Difficulty: 1 Page: 394   Key 1: A

102. The main medium for direct-response messages is the telephone.
     a. True
     b. False

    Answer: b Difficulty: 3 Page: 394   Key 1: R

103. A 1991 study found 90 percent of the public consider direct mail an
     invasion of privacy.
     a. True
     b. False

    Answer: a Difficulty: 3 Page: 382   Key 1: A

104. Most direct mail letters are one page long.
     a. True
     b. False

    Answer: b Difficulty: 2 Page: 382   Key 1: R

105. In direct mail, the critical decision, whether to read or toss, is made on the basis of the letter.
    a. True
    b. False

    Answer: b Difficulty: 2 Page: 382   Key 1: R

106. Direct-response letters have to do the work of hundreds of people.
    a. True
    b. False

    Answer: a Difficulty: 2 Page: 382   Key 1: R

107. Direct mail advertising can only be as effective as the envelope.
    a. True
    b. False

    Answer: b Difficulty: 2 Page: 382   Key 1: A

108. The biggest problem with computer-generated mailing lists is their cost.
    a. True
    b. False

    Answer: b Difficulty: 3 Page: 383   Key 1: R

109. People pay for catalogs the way they pay for magazines.
    a. True
    b. False

    Answer: a Difficulty: 2 Page: 385   Key 1: R

110. Direct-response advertising experts view radio as a growth area in the 1990s.
    a. True
    b. False

    Answer: b Difficulty: 2 Page: 388   Key 1: R

111. Telemarketing costs about the same as direct mail.
    a. True
    b. False

    Answer: b Difficulty: 3 Page: 386   Key 1: A

112. The most important part of the catalog message is the graphics.
    a. True
    b. False

    Answer: a Difficulty: 2 Page: 385   Key 1: R

113. The most important thing about telemarketing solicitations is that the message has to be simple.
a. True
b. False

Answer: a Difficulty: 1 Page: 386 Key 1: R

SHORT ANSWER

114. List the five key components of the definition of direct marketing.

Answer:
Interactivity, response mechanism, exchange not bound by store, measurable response, database
Difficulty: 2 Page: 380-381 Key 1: R

115. List the four objectives of the direct marketing database.

Answer:
Record names, vehicle for storing then measuring ad results, vehicle for storing then measuring purchase results, vehicle for continuing communication
Difficulty: 2 Page: 382 Key 1: R

116. List the five components of the direct marketing piece.

Answer: Offer, medium, message, timing and sequencing, customer service

Difficulty: 2 Page: 382-383 Key 1: R

117. List the usual parts of a direct mail package.

Answer: Outer envelope, letter, brochure, response device, return device

Difficulty: 2 Page: 383-384 Key 1: R

ESSAY

118. Discuss the development of the direct response industry.

Answer: Difficulty: 2 Page: 382-384 Key 1: R

119. Discuss the impact of technology on direct-response advertising, including a minimum of the computer and telephone.

Answer: Difficulty: 2 Page: 382-384 Key 1: R

120. Discuss the advantages and disadvantages of direct-response advertising compared to other forms of advertising.

    Answer: Difficulty: 3 Page: 382-394   Key 1: A

121. Explain why it is reasonable to rename direct marketing—"integrated direct marketing."

    Answer: Difficulty: 3 Page: 377-378   Key 1: R

122. Discuss the characteristics of direct-response advertising.

    Answer: Difficulty: 2 Page: 378-380   Key 1: R

123. Discuss the special problems of managing direct marketing.

    Answer: Difficulty: 2 Page: 379-391   Key 1: A

124. Explain how the issue of privacy impacts on the direct marketing industry.

    Answer: Difficulty: 2 Page: 391-394   Key 1: R

125. Discuss the differences in costs of direct mail and telemarketing.

    Answer: Difficulty: 3 Page: 386-391   Key 1: A

126. Discuss the differences in developing messages for direct mail, telemarketing, and catalogs.

    Answer: Difficulty: 3 Page: 386-391   Key 1: A

127. Compare and contrast the advantages and disadvantages of direct mail, catalogs, and telemarketing.

    Answer: Difficulty: 3 Page: 391-394   Key 1: A

CHAPTER 15:   SALES PROMOTION

MULTIPLE CHOICE

1. Marketing activities that add value to the product for a limited period of time to stimulate consumer purchasing and dealer effectiveness are called:
   a. direct-response.
   b. publicity.
   c. advertising.
   d. sales promotion.
   e. product promotion.

   Answer: d Difficulty: 1 Page: 402   Key 1: R

2. What is the main purpose of sales promotion?
   a. stimulate action
   b. enhance brand image
   c. attract attention of target audience
   d. enhance retail outlet image

   Answer: a Difficulty: 1 Page: 402   Key 1: R

3. Which of the following is a form that sales promotion's "extra incentive" takes?
   a. extra amount of the product
   b. prizes
   c. cash
   d. price reduction
   e. all of the above

   Answer: e Difficulty: 2 Page: 403   Key 1: R

4. How does sales promotion try to induce action on the part of the target audience?
   a. information
   b. image
   c. extra incentive
   d. product benefit
   e. entertainment

   Answer: c Difficulty: 1 Page: 403   Key 1: R

5. What are the goals of sales promotion?
   a. increase sales, enhance brand image and entertain target audience
   b. entertain target audience, increase sales force support and enhance image of retail outlet
   c. increase sales, gain reseller support and enhance brand image
   d. entertain target audience, increase sales force support and increase sales
   e. gain reseller support, increase sales force support and increase sales

   Answer: e Difficulty: 2 Page: 404   Key 1: R

6. How do current expenditures on advertising compare to expenditures on sales promotion?
   a. about the same
   b. sales promotion expenditures are slightly smaller
   c. sales promotion expenditures are about half
   d. sales promotion expenditures are slightly larger
   e. sales promotion expenditures are about triple

   Answer: e Difficulty: 2 Page: 404   Key 1: R

7. Which of the following is NOT a reason for the growth of sales promotion expenditures?
   a. accountability
   b. increasing media costs
   c. decreasing power of the local retailer
   d. drive for immediate profits
   e. lack of new-product categories

   Answer: c Difficulty: 2 Page: 404   Key 1: R

8. What is often the most effective strategy in producing immediate increases in market share?
   a. newspaper advertising
   b. sales promotion
   c. television advertising
   d. magazine advertising
   e. radio advertising

   Answer: b Difficulty: 2 Page: 404   Key 1: R

9. Which of the following is an important advantage of sales promotion over advertising?
   a. product introduction
   b. quicker, clearer proof of results
   c. building brand image
   d. entertainment
   e. all of the above

   Answer: b Difficulty: 2 Page: 404   Key 1: R

10. What is the best marketing tool for launching a new product?
    a. public relations
    b. personal selling
    c. sales promotion
    d. advertising
    e. publicity

    Answer: d Difficulty: 2 Page: 403   Key 1: R

11. How does the modern retailer force marketers to provide promotional incentives?
    a. increased concentration of retail buying power among fewer retail accounts
    b. required to have products stocked
    c. required to obtain desirable shelf location
    d. required for special in-store merchandising support
    e. all of the above

    Answer: e Difficulty: 2 Page: 405   Key 1: R

12. Which of the following communication goals is sales promotion NOT good at achieving?
    a. obtaining trial of a new product
    b. increasing consumption of a product
    c. neutralizing competitor promotion
    d. building brand image
    e. establishing a purchasing pattern

    Answer: d Difficulty: 2 Page: 404   Key 1: R

13. On what kinds of appeals does advertising rely?
    a. emotional
    b. rational
    c. price
    d. tangible value
    e. all of the above

    Answer: a Difficulty: 2 Page: 404   Key 1: R

14. The major differences between advertising and sales promotion concern their:
    a. cost and timing.
    b. objectives and cost.
    c. methods of appeal and value added.
    d. timing and methods of appeal.
    e. appeals and objectives.

    Answer: c Difficulty: 2 Page: 404   Key 1: R

15. What is the objective of sales promotion?
    a. stimulate demand
    b. coordinate advertising, public relations, and personal selling activities
    c. improve marketing performance
    d. supplement advertising activities
    e. all of the above

    Answer: e Difficulty: 2 Page: 402   Key 1: R

16. On what kinds of appeals does sales promotion rely?
    a. intangible
    b. emotional
    c. image
    d. rational
    e. brand

    Answer: d Difficulty: 2 Page: 403   Key 1: R

17. When United Airlines, American Airlines, and other large airlines introduced frequent-flyer programs, they were trying to accomplish which one of the following specific objectives of sales promotion?
    a. to get greater cooperation from retailers
    b. to get customers to try a new product
    c. to encourage present customers to use the product in greater quantities
    d. to increase the amount of impulse buying
    e. none of the above

    Answer: c Difficulty: 2 Page: 406   Key 1: A

18. When companies such as Del Monte, Ralph Lauren, and VLI's Today Sponge, distribute more than 500,000 free samples in Daytona Beach, Florida each spring break, they are tying to accomplish which one of the following specific objectives of sales promotion?
    a. to encourage increased spending during the holiday season
    b. to get customers to try a new product
    c. to encourage present customers to use the product in greater quantities
    d. to increase the amount of impulse buying

    Answer: b Difficulty: 3 Page: 409   Key 1: A

19. Convincing members of the distribution network to carry and market a
    certain product is called:
    a. pull promotional strategy.
    b. trade promotional strategy.
    c. consumer promotional strategy.
    d. push promotional strategy.
    e. distribution promotional strategy.

    Answer: d Difficulty: 2 Page: 410   Key 1: R

20. What are the tools used to execute a pull strategy?
    a. consumer advertising and consumer sales promotion
    b. trade advertising and trade sales promotion
    c. public relations and consumer advertising
    d. coupons and sampling
    e. consumer sales promotion and trade sales promotion

    Answer: a Difficulty: 2 Page: 410   Key 1: R

21. What are the tools used to execute a push strategy?
    a. consumer advertising and consumer sales promotion
    b. public relations and consumer advertising
    c. trade advertising and trade sales promotion
    d. point-of-purchase display and advertising allowances
    e. consumer sales promotion and trade sales promotion

    Answer: c Difficulty: 2 Page: 410   Key 1: R

22. Which of the following statements about advertising and sales promotion
    is TRUE?
    a. Both tend to add an intangible value to the product.
    b. Both are interested in creating immediate action.
    c. Both try to change target audience perceptions about the product.
    d. Both contribute greatly to profitability.
    e. all of the above

    Answer: c Difficulty: 3 Page: 410   Key 1: A

23. This promotional strategy convinces consumers of the value of a product,
    and they will go to their supermarkets and demand that the product be
    stocked.
    a. pull
    b. trade
    c. consumer
    d. push
    e. distribution

    Answer: a Difficulty: 2 Page: 410   Key 1: R

24. How do sales promotion experts respond to advertisers' criticism that sales promotion undermines brand building?
    a. it is not so
    b. brand loyalty has not changed much
    c. refer to brands that have used price promotion heavily and maintained brand loyalty
    d. admit continuous emphasis on price promotion does not work
    e. all of the above

    Answer: e Difficulty: 2 Page: 410   Key 1: R

25. When is consumer sales promotion most effective?
    a. for new products
    b. when the product is pre-sold by advertising
    c. with a motivated sales force
    d. when retailers cooperate
    e. with price reductions

    Answer: b Difficulty: 2 Page: 405   Key 1: R

26. What are the three primary types of sales promotion?
    a. consumer, distribution, and media
    b. trade, sales force, and consumer
    c. trade, reseller, and consumer
    d. consumer, manufacturer, and retailer
    e. price reductions, coupons, and contests

    Answer: b Difficulty: 2 Page: 405   Key 1: R

27. What are the two types of sales-force sales promotion activities?
    a. enhance sales-force morale and training programs
    b. increase sales-force product knowledge and enhance sales-force morale
    c. programs to help salespeople do their jobs better and motivational incentives to work harder
    d. improve presentation techniques and improve sales manuals
    e. contests and motivational incentives for salespeople to work harder

    Answer: c Difficulty: 2 Page: 405   Key 1: R

28. What sales promotion device dominates programs to motivate salespeople to work harder?
    a. training programs
    b. push money
    c. contests
    d. buying allowance
    e. videos

    Answer: c Difficulty: 2 Page: 407   Key 1: R

29. What is the purpose of consumer sales promotion?
    a. get retailers to stock the product
    b. manipulate inventory held by resellers
    c. build brand image
    d. pre-sell consumers
    e. all of the above

    Answer: d Difficulty: 2 Page: 405   Key 1: R

30. When are price deals effective?
    a. brand image is weak
    b. consumers are not brand loyal
    c. for mature products
    d. on weekends
    e. when coordinated with coupon programs

    Answer: b Difficulty: 3 Page: 406   Key 1: R

31. What are the principal types of consumer price deals?
    a. cents-off deals and price-pack deals
    b. refunds and cents-off deals
    c. refunds and premiums
    d. price-push deals and rebates
    e. rebates and refunds

    Answer: a Difficulty: 2 Page: 406   Key 1: R

32. What are the primary strengths of consumer sales promotions?
    a. cost and effective targeting
    b. positive image and flexibility
    c. accountability and positive image
    d. variety and flexibility
    e. positive image and cost

    Answer: d Difficulty: 2 Page: 405   Key 1: R

33. Which of the following is an "extra incentive" for consumers provided by sales?
    a. price reduction
    b. additional amounts of the product
    c. cash and premiums
    d. game and contest prizes
    e. all of the above

    Answer: e Difficulty: 1 Page: 407   Key 1: R

34. Getting more of the product free when a standard size is purchased at the regular price is called:
    a. banded packs.
    b. premiums.
    c. bonus packs.
    d. in-pack premiums.
    e. promotion packs.

    Answer: c Difficulty: 2 Page: 407   Key 1: R

35. Legal certificates offered by manufacturers and retailers that grant specific savings on selected products when presented for redemption at the point of purchase are called:
    a. rebates.
    b. coupons.
    c. premiums.
    d. refunds.
    e. price deals.

    Answer: b Difficulty: 2 Page: 407   Key 1: R

36. What is the primary advantage of the coupon?
    a. allows advertiser to lower prices without cooperation of retailer
    b. very inexpensive to distribute
    c. redemption rates are high
    d. can be targeted very well
    e. provide a means of avoiding advertising clutter

    Answer: a Difficulty: 3 Page: 407   Key 1: R

37. All of the following are disadvantages of coupons EXCEPT:
    a. counterfeit coupons.
    b. redemption rate is low.
    c. production costs are high.
    d. there is serious coupon clutter.
    e. distribution is very expensive.

    Answer: c Difficulty: 2 Page: 407   Key 1: R

38. When a soap manufacturer offers four bars wrapped together at a reduced price, this is called:
    a. pre-pack deal.
    b. cents off deal.
    c. bonus pack.
    d. coupon pack.
    e. banded pack.

    Answer: e Difficulty: 2 Page: 407   Key 1: R

39. Which of the following could prove to be the end of couponing?
    a. Proctor and Gamble's market test of eliminating coupons
    b. steadily declining distribution of coupons
    c. coupon fraud
    d. rapidly rising overall costs of couponing
    e. steadily declining coupon redemption rates

    Answer: a Difficulty: 2 Page: 407   Key 1: R

40. All of the following are results that can be achieved by a contest or sweepstake EXCEPT:
    a. create interest in low-interest products.
    b. build brand image.
    c. help obtain on-floor displays.
    d. revive lagging sales.
    e. give vitality to advertising.

    Answer: b Difficulty: 2 Page: 407   Key 1: R

41. Sales-promotion activities that require participants to submit their names to be included in a drawing or other type of chance selection are called:
    a. game.
    b. sweepstakes.
    c. raffle.
    d. challenge.
    e. contest.

    Answer: b Difficulty: 2 Page: 407   Key 1: R

42. A type of sweepstake that requires the player to return to play several times is called:
    a. game.
    b. contest.
    c. challenge.
    d. continuity deal.
    e. lottery.

    Answer: a Difficulty: 2 Page: 407   Key 1: R

43. What was the result of Proctor and Gamble's market test of eliminating coupons?
    a. Proctor and Gamble's products have continued to sell well.
    b. Other marketers have copied Proctor and Gamble.
    c. Some marketers have used the opportunity to try other coupon techniques.
    d. Supermarkets have supported Proctor and Gamble's test.
    e. all of the above

    Answer: e Difficulty: 2 Page: 407   Key 1: R

44. What has Proctor and Gamble done that will play a key role in the future of sales promotion?
   a. activating computer system to handle couponing
   b. transforming sales promotion budget to direct response market
   c. integrating advertising and sales promotion budgets
   d. marketing test of moving total marketing communication budget to sales promotion
   e. marketing test of eliminating coupons

   Answer: e Difficulty: 2 Page: 407   Key 1: R

45. The key to the success of a refund is:
   a. to make it for a very large amount of money.
   b. to include a coupon with it.
   c. to make the refund as simple and unrestrictive as possible.
   d. to distribute it through television.
   e. to make the offer in conjunction with a contest.

   Answer: c Difficulty: 2 Page: 408   Key 1: R

46. What are the two general types of premiums?
   a. store and container
   b. tangible and intangible
   c. refund and rebates
   d. direct and mail
   e. price cuts and coupons

   Answer: d Difficulty: 2 Page: 408   Key 1: R

47. An offer by the marketer to return a certain amount of money to the consumer who purchases the product is called:
   a. premium.
   b. price cut.
   c. coupon.
   d. price deal.
   e. refund.

   Answer: e Difficulty: 2 Page: 408   Key 1: R

48. A sales promotion activity in which a tangible reward is received for performing a particular act, such as purchasing a product or visiting the point of purchase is called:
   a. coupon.
   b. incentive.
   c. refund.
   d. rebate.
   e. premium.

   Answer: e Difficulty: 2 Page: 408   Key 1: R

49. All of the following are direct premiums EXCEPT:
    a. container.
    b. bonus pack.
    c. on-packs.
    d. in-packs.
    e. store.

    Answer: b Difficulty: 2 Page: 409   Key 1: R

50. A sales promotion activity in which the incentive is awarded immediately at the time of purchase is called:
    a. immediate premium.
    b. direct premium.
    c. sales premium.
    d. mail premium.

    Answer: b Difficulty: 2 Page: 409   Key 1: R

51. A sales promotion activity in which some proof of purchase and payment must be mailed in before receiving the premium is called a/an:
    a. indirect premium.
    b. free-in-the-mail premium.
    c. continuity plan.
    d. self-liquidator.

    Answer: d Difficulty: 2 Page: 409   Key 1: R

52. A sales promotion activity in which the customer is required to save coupons or special labels attached to the product that can be redeemed for merchandise is called:
    a. indirect premium.
    b. self-liquidator.
    c. free-in-the-mail.
    d. coupon plan.
    e. proof-of-purchase premium.

    Answer: d Difficulty: 2 Page: 409   Key 1: R

53. A sales promotion activity in which the customer mails in a purchase request and proof-of-purchase to the advertiser in order to receive a reward is called a/an:
    a. direct premium.
    b. coupon plan.
    c. self-liquidating premium.
    d. indirect premium.
    e. free-in-the-mail premium.

    Answer: e Difficulty: 2 Page: 409   Key 1: R

54. Which of the following statements about specialty advertising is TRUE?
    a. It is expensive.
    b. Cost per prospect is low.
    c. The most important advantage is its low waste circulation.
    d. Recipients have a positive attitude toward it.
    e. It is very inflexible.

    Answer: d Difficulty: 2 Page: 409   Key 1: R

55. What is the ideal specialty advertising item?
    a. something large and off-shaped
    b. something kept out in the open where many people can see it
    c. something valuable so it is retained
    d. something inexpensive that does not activate a defense mechanism
    e. something entertaining

    Answer: b Difficulty: 2 Page: 409   Key 1: R

56. What is the most important advantage of specialty advertising?
    a. inexpensive
    b. ability to pre-select the audience
    c. long life
    d. flexibility
    e. positive attitude of recipients toward useful items

    Answer: c Difficulty: 2 Page: 409   Key 1: R

57. A sales promotion program that requires the consumer to continue purchasing the product or service in order to receive a reward is called a/an:
    a. continuity program.
    b. coupon plan.
    c. repeat purchase program.
    d. game.
    e. contest.

    Answer: a Difficulty: 2 Page: 409   Key 1: R

58. A sales promotion offer that allows the customer to use or experience the product or service free of charge or for a very small fee is called a/an:
    a. trial offer.
    b. coupon.
    c. cash back.
    d. refund.
    e. sampling.

    Answer: e Difficulty: 1 Page: 409   Key 1: R

59. When is sampling most effective?
   a. when used with a high-cost product
   b. when used with a consumer product
   c. when reinforced on the spot with product coupons
   d. when done in a retail store where product can be demonstrated
   e. when provided to customers who are brand loyal to a competitor product

   Answer: c Difficulty: 2 Page: 409   Key 1: R

60. The trend in marketing sponsorship is:
   a. sponsorship of international events.
   b. sponsorship of national events.
   c. sponsorship of local programs.
   d. all of the above
   e. none of the above

   Answer: c Difficulty: 2 Page: 415   Key 1: R

61. All of the following are examples of interactive sales promotion EXCEPT:
   a. Internet-based promotions.
   b. telemarketing 800-number programs.
   c. pre-paid phonecards.
   d. audiotext-based programs.
   e. telemarketing 900-number programs.

   Answer: d Difficulty: 2 Page: 410   Key 1: R

62. Which of the following is not one of the goals of reseller sales promotions?
   a. expand product distribution to new areas
   b. create excitement about the product among those who sell it
   c. enhance brand image among resellers
   d. stimulate in-store merchandising support
   e. manipulate inventory levels of wholesalers and retailers

   Answer: c Difficulty: 2 Page: 410   Key 1: R

63. What is the ultimate measure of the success of reseller sales promotions?
   a. quality of in-store merchandising support
   b. reseller attitude toward the promotion
   c. reduction in inventory levels
   d. excitement among reseller sales staff
   e. sales increase among ultimate users

   Answer: e Difficulty: 3 Page: 410   Key 1: R

64. A sales promotion display designed by the manufacturer and distributed to retailers in order to promote a particular brand or line of products is called a/an:
    a. push display.
    b. point-of-purchase display.
    c. dealer display.
    d. trade display.
    e. store display.

    Answer: b Difficulty: 2 Page: 410   Key 1: R

65. All of the following are types of trade sales promotion EXCEPT:
    a. sampling.
    b. advertising allowances.
    c. push money.
    d. trade shows.
    e. point-of-purchase displays.

    Answer: a Difficulty: 2 Page: 410   Key 1: R

66. According to the Point-of-Purchase Advertising Institute, what percentage of purchase decisions is made in the store rather than before entering the store?
    a. 25%
    b. 33%
    c. 50%
    d. 66%
    e. 75%

    Answer: d Difficulty: 2 Page: 411   Key 1: R

67. Which of the following is important to successful dealer contests?
    a. not done too frequently
    b. just the right prize
    c. spectacular contests
    d. very impressive prizes
    e. all of the above

    Answer: e Difficulty: 2 Page: 412   Key 1: R

68. All of the following are results of trade shows EXCEPT:
    a. to allow manufacturers to gather information on competitors.
    b. to create excitement in the sales force.
    c. to allow product demonstrations.
    d. to write orders.
    e. to answer questions.

    Answer: b Difficulty: 2 Page: 413   Key 1: R

69. A sales promotion event that allows the producer to demonstrate the product, provide information, answer questions, compare competing brands, and write orders is called a/an:
    a. dealer show.
    b. sales exhibition.
    c. exposition.
    d. trade show.
    e. push show.

    Answer: d Difficulty: 2 Page: 413   Key 1: R

70. A sales promotion activity in which money is offered directly to the reseller by the marketer for doing such things as providing premium shelf space, special displays, etc., is called a/an:
    a. push money.
    b. trade incentive.
    c. bonus.
    d. dealer loader.

    Answer: b Difficulty: 3 Page: 413   Key 1: R

71. A sales promotion activity in which a monetary bonus is paid to a salesperson based on units sold over a period of time is called:
    a. trade incentive.
    b. push money.
    c. trade deal.
    d. bonus money.

    Answer: c Difficulty: 2 Page: 413   Key 1: R

72. When Dole offers to provide an expensive cruise, which the retailer can give away in its own contest, in order to get increased shelf space, this is called:
    a. push money.
    b. buying allowance.
    c. trade incentive.
    d. dealer loader.
    e. trade premium.

    Answer: c Difficulty: 2 Page: 413   Key 1: R

73. A sales promotion activity in which a premium is given to a dealer by a manufacturer for buying a certain quantity of product is called a/an:
    a. trade premium.
    b. buying allowance.
    c. push money.
    d. dealer loader.
    e. trade incentive.

    Answer: d Difficulty: 2 Page: 414   Key 1: R

74. A sales promotion arrangement in which the retailer agrees to give the manufacturer's product a special promotional effort in return for product discounts, goods, or cash is called a/an:
    a. trade incentive.
    b. trade deal.
    c. continuity plan.
    d. self-liquidation deal.
    e. dealer loader.

    Answer: b Difficulty: 2 Page: 414   Key 1: R

75. What is the most important reseller sales promotion technique?
    a. push money
    b. trade deal
    c. trade shows
    d. dealer loader
    e. trade incentive

    Answer: b Difficulty: 3 Page: 414   Key 1: R

76. What are the two types of trade deals?
    a. buying allowances and advertising allowances
    b. trade premiums and trade incentives
    c. dealer loader and push money
    d. contests and sweepstakes
    e. trade shows and trade exhibits

    Answer: a Difficulty: 2 Page: 414   Key 1: R

77. A sales promotion trade deal in which a manufacturer pays a middleman a set amount of money for purchasing a certain amount of the product during a specified time period is called a/an:
    a. display allowance.
    b. cooperative advertising.
    c. buying allowance.
    d. buying loader.
    e. display loader.

    Answer: c Difficulty: 2 Page: 414   Key 1: R

78. A sales promotion trade deal that involves a direct payment of cash or goods to the retailer if the retailer agrees to set up the display as specified is called a/an:
    a. display allowance.
    b. cooperative advertising.
    c. buying allowance.
    d. buying loader.
    e. display loader.

    Answer: a Difficulty: 2 Page: 414   Key 1: R

79. Experts predict all of the following future trends for sales promotion EXCEPT:
    a. greater use of hi-tech point-of-purchase displays.
    b. continuing concern over price versus value added.
    c. more targeted promotions.
    d. increased use of direct mail.
    e. will continue to diminish the importance of advertising.

    Answer: e Difficulty: 2 Page: 414   Key 1: R

TRUE/FALSE

80. Pressure from top management to get immediate profits has increased the use of advertising.
    a. True
    b. False

    Answer: b Difficulty: 2 Page: 404   Key 1: A

81. Sales promotion has grown because it is relatively easy to determine whether a given sales promotion strategy accomplished its stated objectives.
    a. True
    b. False

    Answer: a Difficulty: 1 Page: 404   Key 1: A

82. About three times as many dollars are now spent on sales promotion as on advertising.
    a. True
    b. False

    Answer: a Difficulty: 2 Page: 404   Key 1: R

83. Advertising is the most effective strategy for increasing market share.
    a. True
    b. False

    Answer: b Difficulty: 2 Page: 405   Key 1: R

84. Sales promotion costs have increased less than advertising costs.
    a. True
    b. False

    Answer: a Difficulty: 2 Page: 405   Key 1: R

85. Consumers have come to expect constant short-term price reductions such as coupons.
    a. True
    b. False

    Answer: a Difficulty: 2 Page: 405   Key 1: R

86. From the consumer's perspective, sales promotion increases the risk associated with purchase.
    a. True
    b. False

    Answer: b Difficulty: 1 Page: 405   Key 1: R

87. Dominant retailers force marketers to provide promotional incentives in order to secure desirable shelf locations.
    a. True
    b. False

    Answer: a Difficulty: 2 Page: 405   Key 1: R

88. Sales promotion is the best tool for launching new products.
    a. True
    b. False

    Answer: b Difficulty: 2 Page: 405   Key 1: R

89. Sales promotion offers an extra incentive for consumers to take action.
    a. True
    b. False

    Answer: a Difficulty: 1 Page: 404   Key 1: R

90. The more specific objectives of sales promotion are quite similar to those of advertising.
    a. True
    b. False

    Answer: a Difficulty: 2 Page: 409   Key 1: R

91. A push promotional strategy creates demand for the product to be stocked. The demand pushes it through the channel of distribution.
    a. True
    b. False

    Answer: b Difficulty: 2 Page: 410   Key 1: R

92. Advertising adds tangible value to the product while sales promotion adds intangible value.
    a. True
    b. False

    Answer: b Difficulty: 2 Page: 410   Key 1: A

93. Advertising contributes moderately to profitability.
    a. True
    b. False

    Answer: a Difficulty: 2 Page: 410   Key 1: A

94. One area in which advertising and promotion work well together is the introduction of new products and services.
    a. True
    b. False

    Answer: a Difficulty: 2 Page: 410   Key 1: R

95. Sales promotion works most efficiently when it is part of a well-integrated advertising/promotion plan.
    a. True
    b. False

    Answer: a Difficulty: 1 Page: 410   Key 1: A

96. Research has found that loyalty to top brands has been steady since 1987.
    a. True
    b. False

    Answer: a Difficulty: 2 Page: 410   Key 1: R

97. Consumer sales promotion is most effective if the product or service is pre-sold by advertising.
    a. True
    b. False

    Answer: b Difficulty: 3 Page: 410   Key 1: A

98. Advertisers claim that sales promotion negates efforts to build brand image by diverting emphasis from brand to price.
    a. True
    b. False

    Answer: a Difficulty: 1 Page: 410   Key 1: R

99. The primary advantage of the coupon is that high redemption rates make it very effective.
    a. True
    b. False

    Answer: b Difficulty: 3 Page: 407   Key 1: R

100. Distribution of coupons has been steadily declining.
     a. True
     b. False

     Answer: a Difficulty: 2 Page: 407   Key 1: R

101. The key to the success of a refund is to make it as complicated and restrictive as possible so that no person attempts to obtain one.
     a. True
     b. False

     Answer: b Difficulty: 2 Page: 409   Key 1: A

102. The ideal specialty advertising item is something very valuable so that it will be retained.
     a. True
     b. False

     Answer: b Difficulty: 2 Page: 409   Key 1: R

103. Sampling is most effective when reinforced on the spot with coupons.
     a. True
     b. False

     Answer: b Difficulty: 2 Page: 409   Key 1: R

104. Research by Target Marketing found that nine out of ten consumers prefer a cent-off coupon to a free sample.
     a. True
     b. False

     Answer: b Difficulty: 2 Page: 409   Key 1: R

105. Research by Target Marketing found that nine out of ten consumers said that not even a positive experience with a sample would cause them to switch brands.
     a. True
     b. False

     Answer: b Difficulty: 2 Page: 409   Key 1: R

106. Point-of-purchase is the only advertising that occurs when all the elements of the sale (the consumer, the money, and the product) come together at the same time.
a. True
b. False

Answer: a Difficulty: 2 Page: 411   Key 1: A

107. Sales promotion budgets are shifting dollars from trade promotion to consumer promotion.
a. True
b. False

Answer: b Difficulty: 2 Page: 411   Key 1: R

108. A trade show is a very inexpensive way to reach resellers.
a. True
b. False

Answer: b Difficulty: 2 Page: 412   Key 1: R

SHORT ANSWER

109. List the three goals sales promotion.

Answer:
Increase immediate sales, increase salesforce support, gain support of resellers
Difficulty: 1 Page: 403   Key 1: R

110. List the reasons for the growth of sales promotion.

Answer:
Short-term solutions, need for accountability, economic factors, lack of new product categories, pricing cycle, increasing power of retailer
Difficulty: 1 Page: 404-405 Key 1: R

111. List the three objectives of sales promotion.

Answer:
Stimulate user/consumer demand, improve marketing performance of resellers, supplement and coordinate advertising, personal selling, and public relations
Difficulty: 1 Page: 409   Key 1: R

112. List the differences between advertising and sales promotion.

Answer:
Sales promotion focuses more on immediate results, relies on rational appeals, adds tangible value, and contributes greatly to profitability. Advertising focuses on long-term image, relies on emotional appeals, adds intangible value, and contributes only moderately to profitability.
Difficulty: 1 Page: 409   Key 1: R

113. List the similarities between advertising and sales promotion.

Answer:
Both share the same role of increasing number of customers and of use of product; both try to change audience perceptions about product; and both try to get people to do something.
Difficulty: 1 Page: 409   Key 1: R

114. List the three primary types of sales promotion.

Answer: Consumer, reseller/trade, salesforce

Difficulty: 1 Page: 410   Key 1: R

115. List the different forms of consumer sales promotion.

Answer:
Price deals, coupons, contests and sweepstakes, refunds and rebates, premium offers, specialty advertising, continuity programs, consumer sampling, sponsorships, tie-in promotions, interactive promotions
Difficulty: 1 Page: 407-411   Key 1: R

116. List the different forms of trade/reseller sales promotion.

Answer:
Point-of-purchase displays, dealer contests and sweepstakes, trade shows and exhibits, trade incentives, trade deals
Difficulty: 1 Page: 411-414   Key 1: R

ESSAY

117. Discuss why companies are spending more and more money on sales promotion.

    Answer: Difficulty: 2 Page: 402-404   Key 1: R

118. Compare and contrast the advantages and disadvantages of advertising and sales promotion.

    Answer: Difficulty: 3 Page: 402-405   Key 1: A

119. Discuss what sales promotion can and cannot do in terms of marketing communication goals.

    Answer: Difficulty: 3 Page: 404-409   Key 1: A

120. Compare and contrast the roles of sales promotion and advertising in marketing.

    Answer: Difficulty: 3 Page: 404-405   Key 1: A

121. Compare and contrast sales promotion and advertising.

    Answer: Difficulty: 2 Page: 405-409   Key 1: R

122. Discuss the types of sales promotion activities used for consumers. Give examples.

    Answer: Difficulty: 2 Page: 405-411   Key 1: R

123. Discuss the types of sales promotion activities used for resellers. Give examples.

    Answer: Difficulty: 2 Page: 411-414   Key 1: R

124. Discuss the implications for sales promotion of Proctor and Gamble's market test of eliminating coupons.

    Answer: Difficulty: 2 Page: 407   Key 1: R

CHAPTER 16:   PUBLIC RELATIONS

MULTIPLE CHOICE

1. All of the following are steps which can be taken when a company finds out somebody in the media is planning a bad story about the company EXCEPT:
   a. hire an independent expert to conduct an independent investigation.
   b. fire the people involved in the problem uncovered by the story.
   c. attack the medium for running the story.
   d. admit to the problem.
   e. explain what the company is doing to solve the problem.

   Answer: c Difficulty: 2 Page: 432   Key 1: R

2. What is the greatest asset any organization can have?
   a. productive work force
   b. motivated sales force
   c. positive brand image
   d. goodwill of the public

   Answer: d Difficulty: 2 Page: 429   Key 1: R

3. What part of the organization is setting the rules for management of Internet communication?
   a. marketing
   b. management information services
   c. public relations
   d. advertising
   e. board of directors

   Answer: b Difficulty: 2 Page: 430   Key 1: R

4. A culture war in organizations over informational control of Internet activities is about to be, or is being, waged between what two parts of the organization?
   a. legal and accounting
   b. marketing and legal
   c. management information services and communication departments
   d. public relations and marketing
   e. legal and management information services

   Answer: c Difficulty: 2 Page: 430   Key 1: R

5. A management function that enables organizations to achieve effective relationships with their various audiences through an understanding of audience opinions, attitudes, and values is:
   a. publicity.
   b. marketing.
   c. public affairs.
   d. corporation commission.
   e. public relations.

   Answer: e Difficulty: 1 Page: 430   Key 1: R

6. Public relations is:
   a. an activity that tries to secure beneficial publicity for organizations.
   b. the set of relationships that exists between an organization with its various audiences.
   c. a management function that helps an organization achieve effective relationships with its various audiences.
   d. an activity that seeks to control the public image of an organization.
   e. all of the above

   Answer: e Difficulty: 2 Page: 430   Key 1: R

7. All of the following statements about public relations are true EXCEPT:
   a. is not advertising.
   b. has no universally accepted definition.
   c. counsels management at all levels in the organization with regard to policy decisions.
   d. is not a management function.
   e. has traditionally been thought of as a communication tool.

   Answer: d Difficulty: 2 Page: 430   Key 1: A

8. Based on 1992 fee income, what is the largest public relations firm in the United States?
   a. Chiat/Day/Mojo Public Relations
   b. Ketchem Public Relations
   c. Shandwick
   d. Hill & Knowlton
   e. Burson-Marsteller

   Answer: c Difficulty: 3 Page: 431   Key 1: R

9. What constitutes the marketing communication strategy of an organization?
   a. advertising
   b. public relations
   c. sales promotion
   d. all of the above
   e. none of the above

   Answer: d Difficulty: 2 Page: 431   Key 1: A

10. An advertisement announcing the opening of a new manufacturing plant is placed in a national trade publication to improve the organization's relationship with distributors and generate support for the organization's products. This is an example of:
    a. sales promotion.
    b. image advertising.
    c. corporate advertising.
    d. advocacy advertising.
    e. public relations advertising.

    Answer: c Difficulty: 2 Page: 431   Key 1: R

11. Why are PR professionals often unwilling to work with people in marketing or selling?
    a. public relations people often have little marketing background
    b. competition among organizational managers
    c. history of hostility between the two areas
    d. public relations people envy marketing people
    e. all of the above

    Answer: a Difficulty: 2 Page: 431   Key 1: R

12. In most companies and other organizations the public relations function is:
    a. not clearly defined.
    b. covered by staff members from various departments as the need occurs.
    c. clearly defined and staffed.
    d. handled by the marketing staff.
    e. the responsibility of the CEO.

    Answer: a Difficulty: 3 Page: 431   Key 1: R

13. What should be the relationship between advertising and public relations?
    a. adversarial
    b. antagonistic
    c. public relations is subordinate to advertising
    d. indifference
    e. complementary

    Answer: e Difficulty: 2 Page: 431   Key 1: R

14. What are the two levels on which public relations works in most companies?
   a. researcher and strategist
   b. communicator and counselor
   c. promoter and salesman
   d. gatekeeper and communicator
   e. manager and counselor

   Answer: b Difficulty: 2 Page: 431   Key 1: R

15. What is the relationship between advertising, sales promotion, and public relations?
   a. no relationship
   b. dependent
   c. interdependent
   d. independent
   e. co-dependent

   Answer: c Difficulty: 2 Page: 431   Key 1: A

16. What is the basic approach of public relations to media?
   a. the same as advertising
   b. purchase time or space
   c. avoid purchase of time or space
   d. barter for time or space
   e. all of the above

   Answer: c Difficulty: 2 Page: 431   Key 1: R

17. Which type of marketing communication is considered "cost-free" because there are no direct media costs?
   a. promotion
   b. publicity
   c. publications
   d. sales promotion
   e. public relations

   Answer: b Difficulty: 2 Page: 432   Key 1: R

18. Which of the following statements about the differences between advertising and PR is TRUE?
   a. Public relations offers more credibility than is usually associated with advertising.
   b. Public relations, whenever possible, avoids purchasing media time or space for messages.
   c. Public relations offers less control in the delivery of messages through the media.
   d. Public relations results are more difficult to measure.
   e. all of the above

   Answer: e Difficulty: 3 Page: 433   Key 1: A

19. Public relations executives try to have their messages placed with writers, producers, editors, talk-show coordinators, and newscasters without cost. The PR executives call these people:
    a. guards.
    b. gatekeepers.
    c. sentinels.
    d. watchmen.

    Answer: b Difficulty: 2 Page: 431   Key 1: R

20. The generation of news about a product, person, or organization that appears in the print or broadcast media and is usually thought of as free is called:
    a. public relations.
    b. sales promotion.
    c. promotion.
    d. publicity.
    e. press agentry.

    Answer: d Difficulty: 2 Page: 432   Key 1: R

21. Allied National Insurance Company runs ad advertisement that supports placing limits on jury awards in personal-injury lawsuits. This is an example of:
    a. corporate advertising.
    b. institutional advertising.
    c. advocacy advertising.
    d. image advertising.
    e. corporate-identity advertising.

    Answer: c Difficulty: 2 Page: 432   Key 1: A

22. All of the following are indications of public relations' lack of control EXCEPT:
    a. difficulty in measuring public relations results.
    b. lack of research expertise of public relations people.
    c. no guarantee that a story will appear.
    d. difficult to measure components of public opinion.
    e. real risk that a story many be rewritten.

    Answer: b Difficulty: 2 Page: 433   Key 1: R

23. A message from an organization that is accepted by a medium and worked into its editorial, news, feature, or program content has the power of media "endorsement." This refers to:
    a. credibility.
    b. authenticity.
    c. reliability.
    d. expertise.

    Answer: a Difficulty: 2 Page: 433   Key 1: R

24. Why is a message published or aired by a medium considered to have more credibility?
    a. consumers assume media to be more trustworthy than an advertisement
    b. amount of information provided by the media
    c. media stories can be more complete
    d. consumers assume media are more objective
    e. all of the above

    Answer: e Difficulty: 2 Page: 433   Key 1: R

25. Those groups or individuals who are involved with an organization, including customers, employees, corporations, and government regulators are called:
    a. markets.
    b. target audiences.
    c. communication targets.
    d. publics.
    e. target markets.

    Answer: d Difficulty: 1 Page: 435   Key 1: R

26. What are the two primary questions the public relations strategist uses to characterize publics?
    a. Who are the publics and where are the publics?
    b. Who are the publics and which publics are most important to the organization?
    c. Which publics are most important to the organization and what do these publics think?
    d. Who are the publics, what do they think and which is most critical to the organization?
    e. all of the above

    Answer: c Difficulty: 2 Page: 435   Key 1: R

27. People's beliefs, based on their conceptions or evaluations of something not fact, are called:
    a. public attitude.
    b. public sentiment.
    c. public opinion.
    d. public stereotype.
    e. public values.

    Answer: c Difficulty: 1 Page: 435   Key 1: R

28. Public relations can be used to:
    a. rally public support for a product.
    b. secure public understanding.
    c. respond to questions from product consumers.
    d. achieve public neutrality.
    e. all of the above

    Answer: e   Difficulty: 1   Page: 435   Key 1: R

29. Although both advertising and public relations try to _____, public
    relations is not _____.
    a. sell products . . . not as effective as advertising
    b. influence relationships with target audiences . . . as cost effective
    c. sell products openly . . . as precise or measurable
    d. influence public attitudes . . . an open attempt to sell
    e. influence public attitudes . . . as cost effective

    Answer: d   Difficulty: 2   Page: 431   Key 1: A

30. What is the difference between the objectives of advertising and public
    relations?
    a. advertising's focus is on brand-related communication goals
    b. public relations' focus is more long-term
    c. public relations' focus is on a company's reputation
    d. advertising's focus is more short-term
    e. all of the above

    Answer: e   Difficulty: 2   Page: 431   Key 1: R

31. _____ are groups of people with a common interest who are affected by or
    can affect the success of an organization.
    a. Publics
    b. Target audiences
    c. Stakeholders
    d. Target markets
    e. Communication targets

    Answer: c   Difficulty: 2   Page: 435   Key 1: R

32. All of the following are stages in Daniel Yankelovich's seven stages of
    the evolution of public opinion EXCEPT:
    a. conviction to act.
    b. dawning awareness.
    c. making a responsible judgment.
    d. wishful thinking.
    e. discovering choices.

    Answer: a   Difficulty: 2   Page: 435   Key 1: R

33. _____ is a public relations function that monitors how public opinion is developing around certain topics of public concern.
    a. Public opinion research
    b. Issues management
    c. Crisis management
    d. Reputation management

    Answer: b Difficulty: 2 Page: 437   Key 1: R

34. What is an organization's reputation built on?
    a. press releases
    b. marketing strategy
    c. policies and actions
    d. corporate advertising
    e. public relations strategy

    Answer: c Difficulty: 2 Page: 438   Key 1: R

35. What are the two categories of communication tools available to the PR practitioner?
    a. sponsored and unsponsored media
    b. mass and personal media
    c. controlled and uncontrolled media
    d. direct and indirect media
    e. special and general media

    Answer: c Difficulty: 1 Page: 441   Key 1: R

36. Media that give the organization total control over how and when the message is delivered are:
    a. mass media.
    b. special media.
    c. direct media.
    d. controlled media.
    e. sponsored media.

    Answer: d Difficulty: 1 Page: 441   Key 1: R

37. A local radio station provides free on-air information about a play being presented at the local university. This is an example of:
    a. house ad.
    b. public service announcement.
    c. public sector ad.
    d. institutional advertising.
    e. personal service ad.

    Answer: b Difficulty: 2 Page: 442   Key 1: R

38. House advertisements, public service announcements, and in-house publications are examples of what category of communication media used in public relations?
    a. controlled
    b. directed
    c. sponsored
    d. indirect
    e. uncontrolled

    Answer: a Difficulty: 2 Page: 442 Key 1: A

39. Who produces virtually all public service announcements that appear on network television?
    a. corporations
    b. federal government
    c. Advertising Council
    d. Public Service Association
    e. American Association of Advertising Agencies

    Answer: c Difficulty: 3 Page: 442 Key 1: R

40. The intense competition for public service announcement time and space has resulted in:
    a. higher quality public service announcements.
    b. a reduction in public service time and space available.
    c. animosity among social action groups.
    d. fewer requests for public service announcements.
    e. higher costs in producing public service announcements.

    Answer: a Difficulty: 2 Page: 442 Key 1: R

41. Advertising used as a part of a company's public relations program:
    a. is designed to enhance a company's citizenship, promote causes, and generate goodwill.
    b. involves only ads that enhance the image of the organization.
    c. is the same as a public service announcement.
    d. creates a push strategy by getting retailers to stock and support the company's products.
    e. dramatizes the rights of the buying public.

    Answer: a Difficulty: 2 Page: 442 Key 1: A

42. Another term used for corporate advertising is:
    a. public relations advertising.
    b. advocacy advertising.
    c. corporate-identity advertising.
    d. image advertising.
    e. institutional advertising.

    Answer: e Difficulty: 3 Page: 442 Key 1: R

43. What problem has emerged from the increase in cause-oriented public service announcements?
    a. increased cost of producing public service advertising
    b. reduced availability of public service time and space
    c. blurring of line between public service and corporation promotion
    d. indirect charging by media for public service announcements
    e. none of the above

    Answer: c Difficulty: 2 Page: 442   Key 1: R

44. What problem arises from the use of paid "public service" ads in "cause-related marketing"?
    a. may hurt chances for groups that don't have access to large sponsoring organizations
    b. blurring of public service advertising and commercial advertising
    c. increased production costs of public service advertising
    d. backlash effect against the social action organizations
    e. all of the above

    Answer: a Difficulty: 2 Page: 442   Key 1: R

45. Advertising carried by a medium owned by the organization that conveys information outside the organization is called:
    a. in-house publication.
    b. corporate advertising.
    c. institutional advertising.
    d. house ad.
    e. advertorials.

    Answer: d Difficulty: 2 Page: 442   Key 1: R

46. Advertising used by firms to enhance or maintain their reputation among specific audiences or to establish a level of awareness of the firm's name and the nature of its business is called:
    a. public relations advertising.
    b. corporate identity advertising.
    c. image advertising.
    d. advocacy advertising.
    e. issue advertising.

    Answer: b Difficulty: 2 Page: 442   Key 1: R

47. Pamphlets, newsletters, information racks and bulletins are examples of what PR technique?
    a. house ads
    b. public relations ads
    c. corporate ads
    d. in-house publications
    e. issue ads

    Answer: d Difficulty: 2 Page: 442   Key 1: R

48. When NBC broadcasts an ad about a new TV program, what type of PR technique is this?
    a. in-house publication
    b. issue ad
    c. house ad
    d. public relations ad
    e. corporate ad

    Answer: c Difficulty: 2 Page: 442   Key 1: R

49. What is a primary purpose of the speakers bureau in public relations?
    a. enhance brand image
    b. maintain visual contact with various publics
    c. fill a need for public speakers for civic groups
    d. sell the company's product
    e. support the sales promotion programs

    Answer: b Difficulty: 2 Page: 443   Key 1: R

50. Large presentations that may have moving parts, sound, videos, and are usually manned by a company representative are called:
    a. speakers bureau.
    b. displays.
    c. exhibits.
    d. staged events.
    e. spectaculars.

    Answer: c Difficulty: 2 Page: 444   Key 1: R

51. Open houses and plant tours are examples of what type of public relations technique?
    a. speakers bureau
    b. displays
    c. special events
    d. exhibits
    e. staged events

    Answer: e Difficulty: 2 Page: 444   Key 1: R

52. What is the nature of the relationship between the PR person and the media representative?
    a. open cooperation
    b. adversarial
    c. antagonistic
    d. hatred
    e. all of the above

    Answer: b Difficulty: 2 Page: 444   Key 1: R

53. What is the primary medium used to deliver PR messages to media editors and reporters?
    a. press conference
    b. news tip sheet
    c. news query
    d. news release
    e. press tour

    Answer: d Difficulty: 2 Page: 444   Key 1: R

54. A public gathering of media people for the purpose of establishing a company's position or making a statement is referred to as a:
    a. press tour.
    b. press association.
    c. press interview.
    d. crisis management.
    e. press conference.

    Answer: e Difficulty: 2 Page: 445   Key 1: R

55. What is one of the riskiest of the public relations activities?
    a. press conference
    b. news release
    c. house publication
    d. public service announcement
    e. advertorial

    Answer: a Difficulty: 3 Page: 445   Key 1: R

56. What is the relationship between public relations and media built on?
    a. reputation for honesty
    b. money
    c. quality information
    d. public's right to know
    e. conflict

    Answer: a Difficulty: 2 Page: 445   Key 1: R

57. What is considered a prerequisite skill for going into public relations?
    a. understanding of marketing strategy
    b. being a good writer
    c. knowledge of computer technology
    d. understanding of research
    e. familiarity with advertising

    Answer: b Difficulty: 2 Page: 445   Key 1: R

58. A _____ is normally in a folder and provides all the important background information to members of the media at a press conference.
    a. background sheet
    b. fact sheet
    c. press kit
    d. news release
    e. news sheet

    Answer: c Difficulty: 2 Page: 445   Key 1: R

59. What is the risk involved in using advance press kits for a press conference?
    a. cost will not be justified by the resulting stories
    b. information provided may not be used
    c. press kits may not all be given out and end up wasted
    d. press conference may become unnecessary
    e. all of the above

    Answer: d Difficulty: 2 Page: 445   Key 1: A

60. Who in the organization has responsibility for handling bad news that results from crises?
    a. chief executive officer
    b. marketing
    c. sales
    d. public relations
    e. personnel

    Answer: d Difficulty: 2 Page: 440   Key 1: A

61. What must the public relations strategist do in handling bad news resulting from crises?
    a. act quickly to address the problem at the heart of the crisis
    b. take steps to ensure that the crisis will not occur again
    c. anticipate the possibility of a crisis
    d. establish a mechanism for dealing with possible crises
    e. all of the above

    Answer: e Difficulty: 3 Page: 440   Key 1: R

62. When a company faces product recalls, hostile takeovers, bankruptcies, a factory accident, or contaminated products, they need effective public relations. This category of public relations would be called:
    a. financial relations.
    b. consumer relations.
    c. corporate communications.
    d. public affairs.
    e. crisis management.

    Answer: e Difficulty: 2 Page: 440   Key 1: R

63. What is the key to handling a crisis?
    a. research
    b. budget
    c. preparation
    d. prevention
    e. advertising

    Answer: c Difficulty: 2 Page: 440   Key 1: R

64. What is a proactive public relations strategy?
    a. reacting to problems effectively
    b. attacking the media for exposing a problem
    c. aggressively dealing with problems
    d. anticipating the possibility of problems
    e. all of the above

    Answer: d Difficulty: 2 Page: 440   Key 1: R

65. What is the biggest change in communications for public relations?
    a. public service announcements
    b. media relations
    c. advertorials
    d. new electronic media
    e. corporate advertising

    Answer: d Difficulty: 2 Page: 445   Key 1: R

66. What is the key limitation of E-mail as a public relations tool?
    a. expensive
    b. slow response
    c. slow
    d. short message
    e. limited reach

    Answer: d Difficulty: 2 Page: 469   Key 1: R

67. What is the hottest new online development?
    a. Web-sites
    b. audiotext
    c. bulletin boards
    d. chat groups
    e. LISTSERVs

    Answer: a Difficulty: 2 Page: 446   Key 1: R

68. What is the key value of the Internet for dealing with publics?
    a. providing hypertext versions of company brochures
    b. distributing news releases to media
    c. full-page advertising
    d. ability to create virtual communities
    e. all of the above

    Answer: d Difficulty: 2 Page: 446   Key 1: R

69. Which of the following is a problem organizations face as a result of the growth of the Internet?
    a. Web-sites which criticize companies
    b. rapid and powerful spread of crisis issues
    c. marketing activities on the Internet
    d. legal liability for Web activities
    e. all of the above

    Answer: e Difficulty: 2 Page: 446   Key 1: R

70. Who usually sponsors noncommercial advertising?
    a. government
    b. nonprofit organizations
    c. corporations
    d. small businesses
    e. all of the above

    Answer: b Difficulty: 2 Page: 449   Key 1: R

71. What are the two factors used by the government to decide whether to grant nonprofit status?
    a. profits and marketing
    b. funding and organization
    c. public goods and quality assurance
    d. charity and education
    e. funding and public goods

    Answer: c Difficulty: 2 Page: 450   Key 1: R

72. Advertising designed to promote a cause rather than to maximize profits is called:
    a. cause advertising.
    b. issue advertising.
    c. noncommercial advertising.
    d. public relations advertising.
    e. advocacy advertising.

    Answer: c Difficulty: 2 Page: 450   Key 1: R

73. Why does the government give "nonprofit" groups special status for business and tax purposes?
    a. They provide "public goods" that would not be provided without a tax subsidy, and they provide services in areas in which consumers cannot readily judge quality.
    b. They provide a public service, and since they do not actually generate a profit, they cannot be held to the same codes as other companies.
    c. They are small and unimportant and are too costly to monitor for tax purposes.
    d. Historically, they haven't been taxed; so, regardless of realities now they won't be taxed.
    e. all of the above

    Answer: a Difficulty: 2 Page: 449   Key 1: A

74. Which of the following is NOT a difference in evaluating the results of PR and advertising?
    a. knowing exact nature of messages that appear in the media
    b. amount of effects produced
    c. changing target audience behavior
    d. hard to access contribution within larger marketing communications mix
    e. connecting changed attitudes to appropriate behaviors

    Answer: d Difficulty: 2 Page: 451   Key 1: R

75. Public relations is being pushed to contribute to which measure of company success?
    a. quarterly earnings
    b. sales
    c. profitability
    d. productivity
    e. all of the above

    Answer: e Difficulty: 2 Page: 451   Key 1: R

76. What are the two categories of public relations evaluation measurement?
    a. open evaluation and closed evaluation
    b. process evaluation and outcome evaluation
    c. strategic evaluation and tactical evaluation
    d. general evaluation and specific evaluation
    e. evaluation message

    Answer: b Difficulty: 2 Page: 451   Key 1: R

77. What is the purpose of process evaluation in public relations?
    a. measure the impact of the program on sales
    b. examine the success of the program in getting the message to the target audiences
    c. evaluate the potential impact of the program on other areas of marketing communication
    d. measure the effect of the public relations message on the target audiences
    e. all of the above

Answer: b Difficulty: 2 Page: 451   Key 1: R

78. What category of public relations evaluation measurement is associated with questions of how many articles were published and has there been a change in audience knowledge?
    a. process evaluation
    b. closed evaluation
    c. outcome evaluation
    d. message evaluation

Answer: a Difficulty: 3 Page: 451   Key 1: R

79. Which of the following is a problem associated with outcome evaluation?
    a. Even if a positive change in attitude can be identified, it is difficult to know the connection between those changes and desired behavior.
    b. The small budget of public relations leads to modest effects that make it even more difficult to isolate and measure results.
    c. It is difficult to assess the public relations contribution within the larger marketing communication mix.
    d. The broad sweep of public relations programs makes measuring success in terms of some specific behavior ambiguous and difficult to determine.
    e. all of the above

Answer: e Difficulty: 3 Page: 451   Key 1: R

80. Measuring the ultimate effect of the public relations effort on the target audience is called:
    a. process evaluation.
    b. open evaluation.
    c. strategic evaluation.
    d. outcome evaluation.

Answer: d Difficulty: 2 Page: 451   Key 1: R

81. Since PR programs have smaller budgets and, presumably, more modest effects, results are:
    a. more difficult to isolate and measure than they are for advertising.
    b. easier to isolate and measure than they are for advertising.
    c. equally as difficult to isolate and measure than they are for advertising.
    d. totally impossible to isolate and measure.

    Answer: a Difficulty: 2 Page: 453   Key 1: A

82. Unless a public relations program is directly aimed at changing a specific audience behavior, such as product purchase, "success" is:
    a. clear and easy to ascertain.
    b. ambiguous and hard to ascertain.
    c. totally impossible to ascertain.
    d. all of the above

    Answer: b Difficulty: 2 Page: 453   Key 1: A

83. What is the traditional measure of public relations success?
    a. attitude change
    b. increased sales
    c. changes in public opinion
    d. news clips generated

    Answer: d Difficulty: 2 Page: 453   Key 1: R

84. _____ is a qualitative research method in which a group of individuals representing a company's target audience is recruited for a guided discussion.
    a. Focus group
    b. Issues management
    c. Public opinion analysis
    d. Opinion survey
    e. Intercept interview

    Answer: a Difficulty: 2 Page: 453   Key 1: R

TRUE/FALSE

85. Public relations, like advertising, is a managed activity.
    a. True
    b. False

    Answer: a Difficulty: 1 Page: 430   Key 1: R

86. Public relations is lobbying and influence peddling.
    a. True
    b. False

    Answer: b Difficulty: 1 Page: 430   Key 1: R

87. There is no universally accepted definition of public relations.
    a. True
    b. False

    Answer: a Difficulty: 2 Page: 430   Key 1: R

88. Although advertising is becoming more common among physicians, dentists, lawyers, architects, and other professionals, public relations remains the primary means of communicating these services.
    a. True
    b. False

    Answer: a Difficulty: 1 Page: 430   Key 1: R

89. Public relations, advertising and sales promotion together constitute the marketing communication strategy of an organization.
    a. True
    b. False

    Answer: a Difficulty: 1 Page: 431   Key 1: R

90. What a company's advertising says, how it says it, and what medium it uses have a direct bearing on the company's public relations strategy.
    a. True
    b. False

    Answer: a Difficulty: 1 Page: 431   Key 1: A

91. Public relations is not part of the marketing mix.
    a. True
    b. False

    Answer: b Difficulty: 1 Page: 431   Key 1: R

92. Public relations is not considered a direct profit generator.
    a. True
    b. False

    Answer: a Difficulty: 2 Page: 432   Key 1: R

93. Public relations has difficulty verifying its accomplishments.
    a. True
    b. False

    Answer: a Difficulty: 2 Page: 432   Key 1: R

94. People working in public relations are often unwilling to work with others outside their field.
a. True
b. False

Answer: a Difficulty: 2 Page: 432   Key 1: R

95. Public relations has often been relegated to a separate department that is brought in occasionally to help publicize a product.
a. True
b. False

Answer: a Difficulty: 1 Page: 432   Key 1: R

96. Public relations inherently has more control of the message content delivered than the media does.
a. True
b. False

Answer: b Difficulty: 1 Page: 433   Key 1: A

97. Public relations practitioners often have more control over their messages than do advertisers.
a. True
b. False

Answer: b Difficulty: 2 Page: 433   Key 1: A

98. Public relations is not a management function.
a. True
b. False

Answer: b Difficulty: 1 Page: 435   Key 1: R

99. Public relations offers a credibility not usually associated with advertising.
a. True
b. False

Answer: a Difficulty: 1 Page: 435   Key 1: A

100. Organizations should not analyze and address public relations opportunities and problems the same way they would any other marketing or business development that affects them.
a. True
b. False

Answer: b Difficulty: 1 Page: 435   Key 1: A

101. Those groups or individuals who are involved with an organization, including customers, employees, and government regulators, are called communication targets.
    a. True
    b. False

    Answer: b Difficulty: 1 Page: 435   Key 1: R

102. Measurement of public opinion has become more and more of an exact science.
    a. True
    b. False

    Answer: b Difficulty: 1 Page: 435   Key 1: A

103. Essentially, all public service announcements appearing on network television have been produced by the Advertising Council.
    a. True
    b. False

    Answer: a Difficulty: 3 Page: 441   Key 1: R

104. Competition for public service announcement time and space is very high.
    a. True
    b. False

    Answer: a Difficulty: 1 Page: 441   Key 1: R

105. Media that give an organization complete control over how and when the message is delivered are called directed media.
    a. True
    b. False

    Answer: b Difficulty: 1 Page: 442   Key 1: R

106. The goal of corporate advertising is to support a social cause.
    a. True
    b. False

    Answer: b Difficulty: 2 Page: 442   Key 1: R

107. The primary purpose of the speakers bureau in public relations programs is to maintain visual contact between the organization and various publics.
    a. True
    b. False

    Answer: a Difficulty: 2 Page: 443   Key 1: R

108. The news release is the primary medium used to get PR messages to
     editors and publishers.
     a. True
     b. False

     Answer: a Difficulty: 1 Page: 444   Key 1: R

109. Advance press kits for press conferences can make the press conference
     seem unnecessary to some media people.
     a. True
     b. False

     Answer: a Difficulty: 2 Page: 445   Key 1: R

110. Classifying an organization as profit or nonprofit is a matter of
     whether or not the organization seeks profit.
     a. True
     b. False

     Answer: b Difficulty: 3 Page: 450   Key 1: A

SHORT ANSWER

111. List the differences between advertising and public relations.

     Answer:
     PR avoids paying for media; advertising always pays. PR has little
     control over the delivery of messages; advertising has total control. PR
     has difficulty measuring results because of the long-time required to
     see results. PR efforts to more credibility than advertising.
     Difficulty: 2 Page: 432-435   Key 1: R

112. List Daniel Yankelovich's seven stages in the evolution of public
     opinion.

     Answer:
     Dawning awareness, greater urgency, discovering the choices, wishful
     thinking, taking a stand intellectually, making a responsible judgment
     morally and emotionally
     Difficulty: 2 Page: 435-436   Key 1: R

113. List five examples of controlled media used in public relations.

     Answer:
     House ads, public service announcements, corporate/institutional
     advertising, in-house publications, speakers, photographs, films,
     displays, exhibits, stages events
     Difficulty: 2 Page: 441-443   Key 1: R

114. List three examples of uncontrolled media used in public relations.

    Answer: Press release, press conference, crisis management

    Difficulty: 2 Page: 440-444 Key 1: R

ESSAY

115. Explain the significance of the fact that public relations is a management function.

    Answer: Difficulty: 3 Page: 430-433 Key 1: A

116. Discuss how public relations is similar to and different from advertising.

    Answer: Difficulty: 2 Page: 432-435 Key 1: R

117. Discuss the problems associated with the measurement of results produced by public relations.

    Answer: Difficulty: 3 Page: 435-442 Key 1: A

118. Discuss the various forms of advertising used for public relations programs.

    Answer: Difficulty: 2 Page: 441-446 Key 1: R

119. Discuss the controlled media that are used in public relations.

    Answer: Difficulty: 2 Page: 441-443 Key 1: R

120. Discuss the uncontrolled media that are used in public relations.

    Answer: Difficulty: 2 Page: 443-446 Key 1: R

121. Discuss process and outcome evaluation in public relations and the strengths and weaknesses of the two approaches.

    Answer: Difficulty: 2 Page: 450-453 Key 1: R

CHAPTER 17: RETAIL AND BUSINESS-TO-BUSINESS ADVERTISING

MULTIPLE CHOICE

1. What is the newest approach to retailing?
   a. catalog shopping
   b. TV shopping
   c. Internet shopping
   d. radio shopping
   e. discount stores

   Answer: c Difficulty: 1 Page: 462   Key 1: R

2. The Internet Shopping Network is a(n) _____ version of the Home Shopping Network.
   a. electronic
   b. interactive
   c. selective
   d. online
   e. inexpensive

   Answer: d Difficulty: 3 Page: 462   Key 1: R

3. Which of the following would typically be used to describe retail and business-to-business ads?
   a. exciting
   b. inspiring
   c. great
   d. all of the above
   e. none of the above

   Answer: e Difficulty: 3 Page: 458   Key 1: R

4. Advertising used by local merchants who sell directly to consumers is called:
   a. retail.
   b. trade.
   c. consumer.
   d. reseller.

   Answer: a Difficulty: 1 Page: 458   Key 1: R

5. Which of the following is considered retail advertising?
   a. advertising for banks
   b. advertising for real estate organizations
   c. advertising for financial services
   d. all of the above

   Answer: b Difficulty: 2 Page: 459   Key 1: R

6. All of the following are functions of retail advertising EXCEPT:
   a. creating a store image of "personality."
   b. enhancing brand image of products.
   c. selling a variety of products.
   d. delivering sales promotion messages.
   e. encouraging store traffic.

   Answer: b Difficulty: 2 Page: 459   Key 1: R

7. What brand is the focus of the retailer?
   a. the cheapest
   b. the one that is selling the best
   c. the store brand
   d. the national brand
   e. all of the above

   Answer: b Difficulty: 2 Page: 460   Key 1: R

8. Which of the following is FALSE concerning the difference between retail advertising and national advertising?
   a. retail advertising has a greater inherent urgency
   b. retail advertising is more targeted at people living in the local community
   c. retail advertising is more concerned with image and attitude change
   d. retail advertising's loyalty is to the brand that sells the most
   e. national advertising delivers a standardized message that often deals in generalities

   Answer: c Difficulty: 3 Page: 460   Key 1: R

9. Which of the following is an objective for building and maintaining retail store traffic?
   a. convince consumers that products and services are high quality
   b. create consumer understanding of products and services offered
   c. build store awareness
   d. convince consumers to shop at a particular store
   e. all of the above

   Answer: e Difficulty: 1 Page: 460   Key 1: R

10. All of the following are objectives of retail advertising EXCEPT:
    a. increase the amount of the average sale
    b. attract new customers
    c. build and maintain store traffic
    d. build brand awareness
    e. help counter season sales lows

    Answer: d Difficulty: 1 Page: 460   Key 1: R

11. All of the following statements are TRUE about the difference between retail and national advertising EXCEPT:
   a. retail advertising is more short-term
   b. retail advertising is more sophisticated
   c. most retailers have little formal training in advertising
   d. retail advertising is usually less creative
   e. retailers cannot justify high production costs that are normal in national advertising

   Answer: b Difficulty: 3 Page: 460   Key 1: R

12. A form of advertising in which the manufacturer reimburses the retailer for part or all of the advertising expenditures is called:
   a. contract advertising.
   b. shared cost advertising.
   c. cooperative advertising.
   d. dealer tag advertising.

   Answer: c Difficulty: 1 Page: 460   Key 1: R

13. In co-op advertising the amount that can change from month to month for each unit bought is:
   a. advertising allowance.
   b. accrual fund.
   c. vendor support program.
   d. purchase allowance.
   e. unit allowance.

   Answer: a Difficulty: 2 Page: 460   Key 1: R

14. When a manufacturer automatically sets aside a certain percentage of a retailer's purchases that the retailer may use for co-op advertising at any time within a specified period, this is called:
   a. advertising allowance.
   b. accrual fund.
   c. advertising quote.
   d. unit allowance.
   e. vendor support program.

   Answer: b Difficulty: 2 Page: 460   Key 1: R

15. Retailers will periodically schedule a special advertising supplement in which suppliers are offered an opportunity to "buy" space. This is called:
   a. advertising allowance.
   b. accrual fund.
   c. supplement program.
   d. vendor support program.
   e. purchase allowance.

   Answer: d Difficulty: 2 Page: 460   Key 1: R

16. The page from a newspaper on which a co-op advertisement appears is called:
    a. tear sheet.
    b. cooperative sheet.
    c. dealer tag sheet.
    d. rip page.
    e. affidavit sheet.

    Answer: a Difficulty: 2 Page: 460   Key 1: R

17. The time left at the end of a broadcast advertisement designed for co-op advertising that permits identification of the local store is called:
    a. tear sheet.
    b. tagline.
    c. dealer tag.
    d. retail time.
    e. trade advertisement.

    Answer: c Difficulty: 2 Page: 461   Key 1: R

18. Retail advertising that presents specific merchandise for sale and urges customers to come to the store immediately to buy is called:
    a. promotional advertising.
    b. sales advertising.
    c. product advertising.
    d. consumer advertising.
    e. local advertising.

    Answer: c Difficulty: 2 Page: 463   Key 1: R

19. What factors are fueling the growth in expenditures in in-store promotions?
    a. increase in new products and growth of sales promotion
    b. increase in new products and splintering of mass market
    c. cost of mass media advertising and growth of sales promotion
    d. splintering of mass market and changes in retailing
    e. changes in retailing and cost of mass media advertising

    Answer: b Difficulty: 2 Page: 464   Key 1: R

20. When the theme of the retail advertisement centers around merchandise that is new, exclusive, and of superior quality and design, it is called:
    a. sales advertising.
    b. promotional advertising.
    c. semi-promotional advertising.
    d. non-promotional advertising.
    e. assortment advertising.

    Answer: d Difficulty: 2 Page: 463   Key 1: R

21. When the sale price dominates the retail advertisement, the type of advertising used is called:
    a. product advertising.
    b. consumer advertising.
    c. price advertising.
    d. promotional advertising.
    e. loss leader advertising.

    Answer: d Difficulty: 2 Page: 464   Key 1: R

22. When in retail advertising sales items are interspersed with regular-priced items, it is called:
    a. sales advertising.
    b. promotional advertising.
    c. semi-promotional advertising.
    d. non-promotional advertising.
    e. assortment advertising.

    Answer: c Difficulty: 2 Page: 464   Key 1: R

23. When the exchange between the manufacturer/retailer and the consumer takes place outside the traditional retail store this is called:
    a. flea market retailing.
    b. garage sale retailing.
    c. non-store retailing.
    d. direct retailing.
    e. non-channel retailing.

    Answer: c Difficulty: 2 Page: 461   Key 1: R

24. What effect does the increase in non-store retailing have on retail advertising?
    a. more like manufacturer advertising with emphasis on image
    b. more emphasis on price
    c. greater interest in mass advertising
    d. caused a shift to increased use of direct advertising
    e. all of the above

    Answer: d Difficulty: 2 Page: 462   Key 1: R

25. Frequent-flyer programs in the airline industry are examples of:
    a. loyalty programs.
    b. nonstore retailing.
    c. accrual contracts.
    d. frequency programs.
    e. cooperative retailing.

    Answer: a Difficulty: 1 Page: 463   Key 1: R

26. Which of the following is FALSE concerning modern changes in retailing?
    a. non-store retailing has grown in popularity
    b. product specialization has increased in retailing
    c. retail activity has shifted from city centers to the suburbs
    d. retailers are placing more emphasis on price in all promotional activities
    e. ownership consolidation in retailing has weakened the bargaining power of retailers

    Answer: e Difficulty: 3 Page: 464   Key 1: R

27. What effect does consolidation of ownership in retailing have on retail advertising?
    a. greater emphasis on price
    b. more emphasis on price and quality comparisons
    c. more like manufacturer advertising
    d. more interest in mass advertising
    e. all of the above

    Answer: d Difficulty: 2 Page: 464   Key 1: R

28. In targeting consumers for retail advertising, what is a retailer's primary concern?
    a. store image
    b. product array
    c. geography
    d. price
    e. store personnel

    Answer: c Difficulty: 2 Page: 465   Key 1: R

29. What is the main objective of retail advertisements?
    a. build store image
    b. promote prices
    c. maintain inventory balance
    d. attract customers
    e. create store awareness

    Answer: d Difficulty: 3 Page: 465   Key 1: R

30. Why are retail markets expected to continue to decrease in size?
    a. growth in online shopping
    b. continued market segmentation
    c. consolidation of retailers
    d. growth of nonstore retailing
    e. decrease in in-store retailing

    Answer: b Difficulty: 2 Page: 465   Key 1: R

31. What effect does product specialization have on retail advertising?
    a. more emphasis on price
    b. more like manufacturers advertising with emphasis on image
    c. must facilitate price and quality comparisons
    d. caused a shift to increase use of direct advertising
    e. all of the above

    Answer: b Difficulty: 2 Page: 465   Key 1: R

32. Retailers are attempting to develop offers that appeal to consumers in different parts of the country as well as in different neighborhoods in the same suburb. This phenomenon geared to increasing diversity in tastes and preferences is called:
    a. target marketing.
    b. retail marketing.
    c. local marketing.
    d. direct marketing.
    e. geomarketing.

    Answer: e Difficulty: 2 Page: 465   Key 1: R

33. Which of the following is a key creative mistake made in retail advertising?
    a. relying on irritating jingles too much
    b. using too much stock artwork
    c. the retailer wanting to be the star of the retail advertising
    d. over-using local celebrities
    e. all of the above

    Answer: c Difficulty: 2 Page: 466   Key 1: R

34. In retail advertising, to what does the "donut" format refer?
    a. production of slick, four-color magazines whose slick editorial content is used to surround retail ads for a shopping center
    b. using same opening and closing for TV ads with the middle changing to spotlight varying merchandise
    c. building retail ads around the retailer who wants to be the star of the advertising
    d. using stock artwork as the centerpiece of retail advertising
    e. advertising format used by Dunkin Donuts

    Answer: b Difficulty: 3 Page: 467   Key 1: R

35. All of the following are groups that are used to create and produce retail advertising EXCEPT:
    a. advertising agencies
    b. graphic design companies
    c. freelancers
    d. local media
    e. in-house staff

    Answer: b Difficulty: 1 Page: 467   Key 1: R

36. What is the most costly way to produce retail advertising?
    a. in-house staff
    b. local media
    c. advertising agencies
    d. freelancers
    e. consultants

    Answer: c Difficulty: 2 Page: 467   Key 1: R

37. What is a problem in using an advertising agency to create retail advertising?
    a. lack of creativity
    b. cannot guarantee a consistent look
    c. lack of skill in print media
    d. cannot respond promptly to frequent changes
    e. all of the above

    Answer: d Difficulty: 2 Page: 467   Key 1: R

38. What is a disadvantage of the in-house staff in creating retail advertising?
    a. cannot guarantee a consistent look
    b. cannot react to changes on short notice
    c. lack of skill in print media
    d. lack of creativity
    e. lack of advertising training

    Answer: d Difficulty: 2 Page: 467   Key 1: R

39. What is an advantage of the in-house staff in creating retail advertising?
    a. react to changes on short notice
    b. developing an image for the retailer
    c. lower cost
    d. greater creativity
    e. all of the above

    Answer: a Difficulty: 2 Page: 467   Key 1: R

40. What is one of the most rapidly changing areas in retail advertising?
    a. buying of local media time and space
    b. creating retail advertising
    c. using newspapers in retail advertising
    d. use of cooperative advertising
    e. targeting of local buyers

    Answer: a Difficulty: 2 Page: 468   Key 1: R

41. What is fueling the increased competition in local media for retail advertising?
    a. local magazines
    b. public television stations
    c. independent TV stations
    d. national cable TV networks
    e. all of the above

    Answer: e Difficulty: 2 Page: 468   Key 1: R

42. What effect on media selling has the increased competition for retail advertising had?
    a. more emphasis on price and circulation
    b. decreased media costs for creating ads
    c. focus on frequency rather than reach
    d. more emphasis on advertising and promotion
    e. all of the above

    Answer: d Difficulty: 2 Page: 468   Key 1: R

43. In media strategy for retail advertising, what is generally emphasized?
    a. continuity
    b. frequency
    c. cost
    d. gross rating points
    e. reach

    Answer: e Difficulty: 2 Page: 468   Key 1: R

44. Which of the following is a key concern in retail media strategy in the purchase of local media?
    a. excessive cost
    b. waste circulation
    c. poor response rates
    d. poor color reproduction
    e. all of the above

    Answer: b Difficulty: 2 Page: 469   Key 1: R

45. What medium has always made up the bulk of the retailer's advertising?
    a. radio
    b. television
    c. newspapers
    d. outdoor
    e. transit

    Answer: c Difficulty: 1 Page: 469   Key 1: R

46. All of the following are advantages of newspapers for retail advertising EXCEPT:
    a. immediacy
    b. prestige
    c. geographic coverage
    d. cost
    e. participative medium often read for advertising

    Answer: b Difficulty: 1 Page: 469   Key 1: R

47. An agreement in which the retailer agrees to use a certain amount of space over the year and pay a certain amount per line, which is lower than the paper's open rate for the same space, is:
    a. co-operative agreement.
    b. advertising allowance contract.
    c. accrual agreement.
    d. space contract.
    e. open rate agreement.

    Answer: d Difficulty: 2 Page: 469   Key 1: R

48. Certain versions of the paper that go to particular counties or cities and greatly reduce the wasted circulation often associated with large newspapers are called:
    a. shoppers.
    b. free inserts.
    c. zone editions.
    d. special advertising sections.
    e. preprint editions.

    Answer: c Difficulty: 2 Page: 469   Key 1: R

49. What is the primary use of broadcast media for local retail advertising?
    a. as the primary retail medium
    b. to replace local magazines as the primary medium
    c. to supplement newspapers
    d. to select special customers
    e. all of the above

    Answer: c Difficulty: 2 Page: 469   Key 1: R

50. Which of the following is an advantage of radio for retail advertising?
a. flexibility in scheduling
b. relatively low cost
c. geographic selectivity
d. creative support
e. all of the above

Answer: e Difficulty: 2 Page: 469   Key 1: R

51. What medium used for retail advertising is the most selective?
a. newspapers
b. shoppers
c. directories
d. direct response
e. radio

Answer: d Difficulty: 3 Page: 470   Key 1: R

52. Which of the following forms of retail advertising research is the most valuable?
a. evaluative research
b. copy testing
c. identifying customers
d. diagnostic research
e. customer recall tests

Answer: c Difficulty: 1 Page: 470   Key 1: R

53. Business-to-business advertising is:
a. advertising directed at businesses that buy products to incorporate in other products.
b. advertising directed at influencing government purchases.
c. advertising directed at people who buy or specify products for business use.
d. advertising used to influence resellers, wholesalers, and retailers.
e. all of the above

Answer: e Difficulty: 2 Page: 471   Key 1: R

54. What is the most common method of communicating with business buyers?
a. business-to-business advertising
b. sales promotion
c. personal selling
d. public relations
e. none of the above

Answer: c Difficulty: 3 Page: 471   Key 1: R

55. What is a major difference between purchase decisions made for businesses and decisions made for consumer purchases?
    a. many people can be involved in the purchase decision
    b. business buyers do not gather information for the decision
    c. business buyers do not proceed through a purchase decision process
    d. business buyers do not consider the alternatives
    e. all of the above

    Answer: a Difficulty: 2 Page: 472   Key 1: A

56. All of the following are markets for business-to-business advertising to reach EXCEPT:
    a. consumer
    b. industrial
    c. trade
    d. professional
    e. agricultural

    Answer: a Difficulty: 2 Page: 472   Key 1: R

57. Advertising directed at businesses that buy products to incorporate into other products or to facilitate the operation of their businesses is called:
    a. manufacturer.
    b. business-to-business.
    c. trade.
    d. industrial.
    e. retail.

    Answer: d Difficulty: 2 Page: 472   Key 1: R

58. When Goodyear places advertisements to persuade General Motors and Chrysler to purchase Goodyear tires, what kind of advertising is involved?
    a. brand
    b. industrial
    c. trade
    d. professional
    e. manufacturer

    Answer: b Difficulty: 2 Page: 472   Key 1: A

59. What information does the trade market seek from the advertising directed to it?
    a. profit margins that can be expected
    b. advertising support
    c. major selling points
    d. promotional support activities
    e. all of the above

    Answer: e Difficulty: 2 Page: 472   Key 1: R

60. Advertising used to influence resellers, wholesalers, and retailers is called:
    a. reseller.
    b. industrial.
    c. retail.
    d. trade.
    e. business.

    Answer: d Difficulty: 2 Page: 472   Key 1: R

61. Advertising directed at people such as lawyers, doctors, and accountants is called:
    a. trade.
    b. legal.
    c. government.
    d. professional.
    e. institutional.

    Answer: d Difficulty: 1 Page: 473   Key 1: R

62. Advertising directed at large and small farmers is called:
    a. rural.
    b. trade.
    c. farm.
    d. industrial.
    e. agricultural.

    Answer: e Difficulty: 1 Page: 473   Key 1: R

63. All of the following are characteristics that differentiate business marketing from consumer marketing EXCEPT:
    a. nature of the purchase decision process.
    b. market concentration.
    c. purchase objectives.
    d. purchase strategy.
    e. decision-makers.

    Answer: a Difficulty: 2 Page: 474   Key 1: R

64. Which of the following is FALSE about the differences between business marketing and consumer marketing?
    a. as many as 15 to 20 people may be involved in a business purchase decision
    b. businesses tend to be guided by a specific strategy
    c. the market for a typical business good is relatively large compared to the typical consumer market
    d. the business purchase decision may be very lengthy
    e. business purchase objectives usually center on rational, pragmatic considerations

    Answer: c Difficulty: 3 Page: 474   Key 1: R

65. All of the following are objectives of business-to-business advertising EXCEPT:
    a. increase customer interest in a supplier's product
    b. decrease overall personal selling costs
    c. increase selling efficiency by reaching hard to identify influentials
    d. creates customer awareness of a supplier's product
    e. supplements personal selling by providing information to distributors and resellers

    Answer: b Difficulty: 2 Page: 476   Key 1: R

66. Which of the following is one of the types of business decision-makers?
    a. innovators
    b. information seekers
    c. hesitants
    d. doubters
    e. all of the above

    Answer: e Difficulty: 2 Page: 475   Key 1: R

67. Which of the following is a difference between business versus consumer advertising?
    a. There will typically be more decision-makers for a business purchase decision.
    b. Business purchases tend to be made by professionals with technical knowledge of the products being purchased.
    c. The business purchase decision typically takes a lot longer than a consumer purchase decision.
    d. The market for a typical business good is relatively small compared to the market for a consumer good.
    e. all of the above

    Answer: e Difficulty: 2 Page: 474   Key 1: R

68. Which of the following is a purchase objective in the business market?
    a. assurance of supply
    b. services
    c. price
    d. quality
    e. all of the above

    Answer: e Difficulty: 2 Page: 475   Key 1: R

69. What is the primary purpose of business advertising?
    a. reduce inventories of distributors
    b. support the selling function
    c. increase store traffic of distributors
    d. create customer awareness

    Answer: b Difficulty: 3 Page: 476   Key 1: R

70. Publications directed to people who hold similar jobs in different
    companies across different industries are called:
    a. vertical.
    b. directory.
    c. professional.
    d. trade.
    e. horizontal.

    Answer: e Difficulty: 2 Page: 477   Key 1: R

71. Publications directed to people who hold different positions in the same
    industries are called:
    a. vertical.
    b. industrial.
    c. trade.
    d. professional.
    e. horizontal.

    Answer: a Difficulty: 2 Page: 477   Key 1: R

72. Advertising that provides detailed technical information is called:
    a. consumer.
    b. technical.
    c. data sheets.
    d. trade.

    Answer: c Difficulty: 2 Page: 477   Key 1: R

73. Which of the following is TRUE about the findings of a study of the
    effectiveness of business advertising by the Advertising Research
    Foundation and the Association of Business Publishers?
    a. increased advertising frequency resulted in increased product sales
    b. business advertising favorably affected purchasers' awareness of
       industrial products
    c. 4 to 6 months were needed to see the results of the advertising
       program
    d. the use of color made a dramatic difference in business advertising
    e. all of the above

    Answer: e Difficulty: 3 Page: 478   Key 1: R

TRUE/FALSE

74. Retail and business-to-business advertising are known for producing
    exciting and inspiring ads.
    a. True
    b. False

    Answer: b Difficulty: 2 Page: 458   Key 1: R

75. Retail advertising is often called local advertising because the target market is frequently local in nature, but not all retail advertising is local.
   a. True
   b. False

   Answer: a Difficulty: 2 Page: 458   Key 1: R

76. Retail advertising has a greater inherent urgency than national advertising.
   a. True
   b. False

   Answer: a Difficulty: 3 Page: 460   Key 1: R

77. Retail advertising is more short-term in approach than national advertising.
   a. True
   b. False

   Answer: a Difficulty: 2 Page: 460   Key 1: R

78. Retailers compensate for their smaller budgets and limited experience by taking advantage of cooperative advertising opportunities provided by manufacturers.
   a. True
   b. False

   Answer: a Difficulty: 2 Page: 460   Key 1: R

79. A rapid growth area in retail promotion communication is in-store promotions.
   a. True
   b. False

   Answer: a Difficulty: 1 Page: 464   Key 1: R

80. Non-store retailing has caused retail advertising to become more like manufacturer advertising with emphasis on image.
   a. True
   b. False

   Answer: b Difficulty: 2 Page: 461   Key 1: R

81. Consolidation of ownership in retailing has resulted in more emphasis on price and quality comparisons in retail advertising.
   a. True
   b. False

   Answer: b Difficulty: 2 Page: 464   Key 1: R

82. When retailers specialize in merchandising certain products, retail advertising becomes more like manufacturer advertising.
    a. True
    b. False

    Answer: a Difficulty: 2 Page: 465   Key 1: R

83. The main objective of retail advertising is to attract customers.
    a. True
    b. False

    Answer: a Difficulty: 1 Page: 465   Key 1: R

84. In targeting consumers for retail advertising, a retailer's first concern is geography.
    a. True
    b. False

    Answer: a Difficulty: 1 Page: 465   Key 1: R

85. The most costly way to produce retail advertising is to use an advertising agency.
    a. True
    b. False

    Answer: a Difficulty: 2 Page: 467   Key 1: R

86. A major concern in retail media strategy in the purchase of media is waste circulation.
    a. True
    b. False

    Answer: a Difficulty: 2 Page: 468   Key 1: A

87. A key advantage to using free-lancers to create retail advertising is lower cost.
    a. True
    b. False

    Answer: a Difficulty: 2 Page: 468   Key 1: R

88. In media strategy for retail advertising, reach is generally emphasized.
    a. True
    b. False

    Answer: b Difficulty: 2 Page: 468   Key 1: R

89. Newspapers have always made up the bulk of the retailer's advertising.
   a. True
   b. False

   Answer: a Difficulty: 1 Page: 469   Key 1: R

90. Radio's relatively low cost is an important advantage over print media for retail advertising.
   a. True
   b. False

   Answer: a Difficulty: 2 Page: 470   Key 1: A

91. The overwhelming majority of retailers advertise in the Yellow Pages.
   a. True
   b. False

   Answer: a Difficulty: 2 Page: 470   Key 1: R

92. The most selective medium used in retail advertising is direct response.
   a. True
   b. False

   Answer: a Difficulty: 1 Page: 470   Key 1: R

93. Business-to-business advertising is the most common method of communicating with business buyers.
   a. True
   b. False

   Answer: b Difficulty: 3 Page: 471   Key 1: R

94. Business-to-business advertising is used to reach the various influencers involved in the business purchase decision and to communicate the different information needs.
   a. True
   b. False

   Answer: b Difficulty: 2 Page: 471   Key 1: R

95. A major difference between purchase decisions made for businesses and decisions for consumer purchases is that many people can be involved in the business purchase decisions.
   a. True
   b. False

   Answer: a Difficulty: 2 Page: 472   Key 1: R

96. A major difference between purchase decisions made for businesses and decisions made for consumer purchases is that business buyers don't gather information for the decision.
a. True
b. False

Answer: b Difficulty: 2 Page: 472   Key 1: R

97. Corporate image advertising is important in influencing purchases in the government market.
a. True
b. False

Answer: a Difficulty: 3 Page: 472   Key 1: R

98. The market for a typical business good is relatively large compared to the market for a typical consumer good.
a. True
b. False

Answer: b Difficulty: 2 Page: 474   Key 1: R

99. In a typical business purchase decision, it is not uncommon for 15 to 20 people to be involved.
a. True
b. False

Answer: a Difficulty: 3 Page: 474   Key 1: R

100. Decision making for business purchases tends to be done using more rational criteria than in consumer decision making.
a. True
b. False

Answer: a Difficulty: 2 Page: 474   Key 1: R

101. Decision making for business purchases tends to be done faster than for consumer purchases.
a. True
b. False

Answer: b Difficulty: 2 Page: 474   Key 1: R

102. As in consumer advertising, the best business-to-business ads are relevant, understandable, and strike an emotion in the prospective client.
a. True
b. False

Answer: a Difficulty: 2 Page: 477   Key 1: R

103. Direct mail emerged as a primary medium for several business-to-business advertisers during the last decade.
    a. True
    b. False

    Answer: a Difficulty: 2 Page: 477   Key 1: R

104. The Advertising Research Foundation and the Association of Business Publishers found that business advertising as currently practiced had little effect on purchasers' awareness of and attitudes toward industrial products.
    a. True
    b. False

    Answer: b Difficulty: 2 Page: 478   Key 1: R

105. Increased advertising frequency in business advertising generates higher profits, according to the Advertising Research Foundation and the Association of Business Publishers.
    a. True
    b. False

    Answer: a Difficulty: 1 Page: 478   Key 1: R

SHORT ANSWER

106. List the types of retail advertising.

    Answer: Product, institutional

    Difficulty: 2 Page: 460   Key 1: R

107. List the key trends in retailing.

    Answer:
    In-store marketing, nonstore marketing, loyalty programs, consolidation, demographic changes, category specialization
    Difficulty: 2 Page: 460-465   Key 1: R

108. List the different groups who are used to create professional retail ads.

    Answer: Advertising agencies, free-lancers, in-house staff, local media

    Difficulty: 2 Page: 467   Key 1: R

109. List the key media alternatives for retail advertising.

Answer:
Newspapers, shoppers and preprints, magazines, broadcast media, directories, direct response
Difficulty: 2 Page: 469-470   Key 1: R

110. List the markets for the business-to-business advertiser to reach.

Answer: Trade, government, professional, agricultural, industrial

Difficulty: 2 Page: 472   Key 1: R

111. List the types of information sought by the trade market from the advertising directed to it.

Answer:
Expected profit margins, advertising support, main selling points, promotional support
Difficulty: 2 Page: 472   Key 1: R

ESSAY

112. Discuss ways to make business-to-business advertising more effective.

Answer: Difficulty: 3 Page: 477-480   Key 1: A

113. Compare and contrast the target audiences and objectives of business-to-business advertising and consumer advertising.

Answer: Difficulty: 2 Page: 471-480   Key 1: A

114. Compare and contrast retail advertising to national brand advertising.

Answer: Difficulty: 3 Page: 459-470   Key 1: A

115. Explain how retailers use co-operative advertising to increase the effectiveness of their advertising expenditures.

Answer: Difficulty: 1 Page: 460-461   Key 1: A

116. Discuss the different types of retail advertising.

Answer: Difficulty: 2 Page: 463-465   Key 1: R

117. Discuss the special retail advertising problems associated with recent trends in retailing.

    Answer: Difficulty: 2 Page: 463-465   Key 1: A

118. Discuss the problems associated with creating retail advertising.

    Answer: Difficulty: 2 Page: 466-468   Key 1: R

119. Discuss the different target markets for business-to-business advertising and the media used to reach them.

    Answer: Difficulty: 2 Page: 472-475   Key 1: R

CHAPTER 18: INTERNATIONAL ADVERTISING

MULTIPLE CHOICE

1. In the early 1990s, the top worldwide marketers began spending what percentage of their advertising budgets outside the United States?
   a. 25%
   b. 33%
   c. 50%
   d. 75%

   Answer: d Difficulty: 3 Page: 483   Key 1: R

2. How many of the top 25 world advertising agencies were headquartered in the U.S. in 1996?
   a. 0
   b. 10
   c. 15
   d. 20
   e. 25

   Answer: b Difficulty: 3 Page: 483   Key 1: R

3. In 1996 what country had the second highest number of Top 25 world advertising agencies headquartered within its borders?
   a. Great Britain
   b. France
   c. Japan
   d. United States

   Answer: c Difficulty: 2 Page: 483   Key 1: R

4. A brand that is marketed in one specific country is called:
   a. national brand.
   b. country brand.
   c. global brand.
   d. international brand.
   e. local brand.

   Answer: e Difficulty: 2 Page: 484   Key 1: R

5. A brand that is available throughout an entire region is called:
   a. regional brand.
   b. area brand.
   c. non-local brand.
   d. international brand.
   e. global brand.

   Answer: a Difficulty: 1 Page: 484   Key 1: R

6. A brand or product that is available in most parts of the world is called:
   a. multinational brand.
   b. global brand.
   c. international brand.
   d. cross-cultural brand.
   e. intercontinental brand.

   Answer: c Difficulty: 1 Page: 484   Key 1: R

7. Advertising designed to promote the same product in different countries and cultures is called:
   a. intercultural advertising.
   b. multinational advertising.
   c. global advertising.
   d. international advertising.
   e. cross-cultural advertising.

   Answer: d Difficulty: 1 Page: 484   Key 1: R

8. Historically, when the emphasis in international trade changed from importing goods to exporting goods, which of the following emerged as an important element in international trade?
   a. shipping
   b. international diplomacy
   c. foreign exchange markets
   d. marketing
   e. military aggression

   Answer: d Difficulty: 2 Page: 484   Key 1: R

9. Historically, when the emphasis in international trace changed from importing goods to exporting goods, what function did advertising perform?
   a. to introduce, explain and sell product benefits in markets outside the home country
   b. to develop brand image in the home-country
   c. to promote an image of the exporting country and the countries to which it was exporting
   d. to encourage traders to bring new products to the export company's attention

   Answer: a Difficulty: 2 Page: 485   Key 1: R

10. International advertising is a recent development in international commerce. It first appeared:
   a. in the late 1800s.
   b. in the early 1900s.
   c. in the 1920s.
   d. in the 1950s.
   e. in the 1980s.

   Answer: a Difficulty: 2 Page: 484   Key 1: R

11. All of the following are factors in causing a company involved in international marketing to shift emphasis from home-country control to local control of the marketing process EXCEPT:
   a. language and cultural problems.
   b. complexity of product size increases.
   c. need for local product adaptation increases.
   d. complexity of pricing increases.
   e. increase in export sales volume.

   Answer: a Difficulty: 2 Page: 485   Key 1: R

12. What is one of the main reasons that companies try to expand into foreign markets?
   a. economic aggression
   b. avoid high labor costs in the home country
   c. seeking to regain sales increases of growth period
   d. avoid taxation in the home country

   Answer: c Difficulty: 2 Page: 485   Key 1: R

13. What are the two methods available when management seeks to recapture the sales gains of the growth period?
   a. introduce new products and improve existing products
   b. improve existing products and decrease the costs of existing products
   c. increase advertising efforts and lower the price of existing products
   d. expand into foreign markets and introduce new products
   e. expand into foreign markets and increase marketing communication efforts

   Answer: d Difficulty: 2 Page: 485   Key 1: R

14. All of the following are reasons that the text gives for companies seeking to expand into international markets EXCEPT:
   a. product saturation of the home-country market.
   b. marketing opportunities in international markets.
   c. avoiding taxation in the home country.
   d. pre-empt competitors from moving into an international market.
   e. acquisitions of foreign companies.

   Answer: c Difficulty: 2 Page: 485   Key 1: R

15. When a company first starts exporting to another country, which is normally responsible for advertising in the local country?
    a. exporting company's advertising department
    b. local country importer/distributor
    c. international advertising agency
    d. exporting company's advertising agency
    e. local branch office of the exporting company

    Answer: b Difficulty: 2 Page: 485   Key 1: R

16. What is the first step in international marketing?
    a. exporting
    b. importing
    c. develop a global product
    d. develop an international product
    e. set-up a distribution/manufacturing facility in a foreign country

    Answer: a Difficulty: 2 Page: 485   Key 1: R

17. If exporters wish to get more control over the product or a larger share of the profits they may:
    a. buy back the rights contracted to the importer.
    b. transfer management to the importing country.
    c. set-up assembly facilities in the importing country.
    d. transfer manufacturing to the importing country.
    e. all of the above

    Answer: e Difficulty: 2 Page: 485   Key 1: R

18. What is the final step in the international expansion of marketing for a firm and its products?
    a. local manufacture of imported products
    b. transfer of management from home-country export manager to on-site management
    c. coordinated global marketing
    d. local manufacture of special products developed in the local market
    e. coordinated regional manufacturing, marketing and advertising

    Answer: c Difficulty: 2 Page: 486   Key 1: R

19. A corporate philosophy that directs products and advertising toward a worldwide, rather than a local or regional market is called:
    a. theory "Z."
    b. global perspective.
    c. multinational scope.
    d. international view.
    e. world perspective.

    Answer: b Difficulty: 2 Page: 486   Key 1: R

20. What is the "global perspective"?
    a. management's view that control of marketing activities should be transferred from the home-country to the local or regional area
    b. corporate philosophy that products and marketing should be tailored to the local markets
    c. management's decision to transfer responsibilities for day-to-day management to an international office
    d. corporate philosophy that directs products and advertising toward a worldwide, rather than a local or regional market
    e. corporate philosophy that international products should be produced as close to the local market as possible

    Answer: d Difficulty: 3 Page: 486   Key 1: R

21. A global perspective is difficult to achieve as long as:
    a. the headquarters is located in the United States.
    b. English is the only language used by the organization.
    c. management is located in one country.
    d. local products form the basis of the company's product line.
    e. all of the above

    Answer: c Difficulty: 2 Page: 486   Key 1: R

22. Which of the following is one of the factors that restrict global advertising?
    a. culture
    b. language
    c. local media
    d. regulation
    e. all of the above

    Answer: e Difficulty: 2 Page: 486   Key 1: R

23. What is required for a company to achieve a global perspective?
    a. set up a world headquarters
    b. hire a global advertising agency
    c. transfer decision-making to a world headquarters
    d. internationalize the company's management group
    e. opt for a global advertising campaign

    Answer: d Difficulty: 3 Page: 486   Key 1: R

24. An international brand is a brand that:
    a. sold in 1 of the market blocs of North America, Europe, Latin America, or Asia-Pacific.
    b. is marketed in one specific country.
    c. is available in at least in two or more of the four major regional blocs.
    d. has the same name, same design, and same strategy everywhere in the world.

    Answer: a Difficulty: 2 Page: 486   Key 1: R

25. A brand that has the same name, same design, and same creative strategy everywhere in the world is called:
    a. international brand.
    b. multinational brand.
    c. world brand.
    d. unitary brand.
    e. global brand.

    Answer: e Difficulty: 2 Page: 487   Key 1: R

26. What brand is almost always used as the example of a global brand?
    a. Marlboro
    b. IBM
    c. Coca-Cola
    d. Toyota

    Answer: c Difficulty: 1 Page: 487   Key 1: R

27. Which of the following is an example of a global brand?
    a. Coca-Cola
    b. IBM
    c. McDonald's
    d. Xerox
    e. all of the above

    Answer: e Difficulty: 2 Page: 487   Key 1: R

28. Who does the text credit with starting the controversy concerning the value of global marketing when it was argued that companies should operate as if there was only one global market?
    a. Philip Kotler
    b. Saatchi & Saatchi
    c. Grey Advertising
    d. Theodore Levitt
    e. Peter Drucker

    Answer: d Difficulty: 3 Page: 487   Key 1: R

29. Which one of the following best describes the reaction of the London-based Saatchi & Saatchi to the June 1983 article in Harvard Business Review professing one global market?
    a. they wrote it so they believed it
    b. strongly disagreed with it
    c. disagreed with it
    d. agreed with it but did not adopt it
    e. adopted it

    Answer: e Difficulty: 2 Page: 487   Key 1: R

30. Which of the following wrote an article in the Harvard Business Review, arguing that companies should operate as if there were only one global market and that differences among nations and cultures were not only diminishing but should be ignored because people throughout the world are motivated by the same basic desires and wants?
    a. Saatchi & Saatchi
    b. Theodore Levitt
    c. Starch Hooper
    d. Takashi Michioka

    Answer: b Difficulty: 2 Page: 487   Key 1: R

31. Which one of the following best describes the impact that most observers believe the trend to global marketing will have on the structure of advertising agencies?
    a. no impact
    b. very little impact
    c. little impact
    d. marked impact

    Answer: d Difficulty: 2 Page: 487   Key 1: A

32. What is the counter-argument to the global approach to marketing?
    a. differences among nations and cultures are increasing
    b. all people throughout the world are not motivated by the same desires and wants
    c. differences among nations and cultures cannot be ignored
    d. the success of international brands is based on variation
    e. businesses are more efficient when they plan for a multinational rather than global market

    Answer: d Difficulty: 3 Page: 487   Key 1: R

33. Which one of the following best describes the reaction of marketing professor Philip Kotler to the June 1983 article in Harvard Business Review professing one global market? He believed:
    a. the overseas success of Coca-Cola, PepsiCo, and McDonald's was misinterpreted.
    b. the success of Coca-Cola, PepsiCo, and McDonald's is based on variation, not offering the same product everywhere.
    c. the concept was incorrect and should be ignored.
    d. all of the above

    Answer: d Difficulty: 2 Page: 487   Key 1: R

34. Which of the following is one of the factors that restrict global advertising?
    a. culture
    b. language
    c. local media
    d. regulation
    e. all of the above

    Answer: e Difficulty: 2 Page: 487   Key 1: R

35. Which of the following is a critical problem for international advertisers?
    a. limits on freedom to advertise
    b. piracy of brands
    c. lack of appreciation for advertising
    d. banning of comparative advertising in some countries
    e. all of the above

    Answer: e Difficulty: 2 Page: 488   Key 1: R

36. What is usually the language of international management?
    a. French
    b. Japanese
    c. English
    d. German
    e. Spanish

    Answer: c Difficulty: 2 Page: 489   Key 1: R

37. To succeed within the company, and sometimes even to be hired into an internationalized company a person needs a working knowledge of which one of the following languages?
    a. French
    b. Spanish
    c. Japanese
    d. English

    Answer: d Difficulty: 1 Page: 489   Key 1: A

38. When an American company is internationalized, the local lawyers, accountants, and bankers find it necessary to speak:
   a. French.
   b. Spanish.
   c. Japanese.
   d. English.

   Answer: d Difficulty: 1 Page: 489   Key 1: A

39. Which one of the following languages normally requires the least space in printed material or airtime?
   a. French
   b. Spanish
   c. Japanese
   d. English

   Answer: d Difficulty: 2 Page: 489   Key 1: R

40. Which one of the following languages contains words estimated in number to be over 900,000?
   a. French
   b. Spanish
   c. Japanese
   d. English

   Answer: d Difficulty: 2 Page: 489   Key 1: R

41. Which one of the following languages adopts words from other languages making it more exact and more economical than other languages?
   a. French
   b. Spanish
   c. Japanese
   d. English

   Answer: c Difficulty: 2 Page: 489   Key 1: R

42. Experience has shown that the only reasonable solution to language problems in international advertising is:
   a. to employ bilingual copywriters who have a full understanding of English.
   b. to use a back translation.
   c. to employ retired schoolteachers to write the ads.
   d. to use multiple back translations.
   e. all of the above.

   Answer: a Difficulty: 2 Page: 489   Key 1: R

43. The model for deciding how to advertise in foreign cultures that is based on the idea that markets share common traits and need to be analyzed to find local opportunities with focuses on market share and size of market is called:
    a. Market Share Model.
    b. Market-Analysis Model.
    c. Local Market Model.
    d. Culture-Oriented Model.
    e. Market-Oriented Model.

    Answer: b Difficulty: 2 Page: 490   Key 1: R

44. The Market-Analysis Model was based on _____ from several countries.
    a. guesstimates and interpolation
    b. presumption and theorization
    c. conjecture and estimates
    d. data and observation

    Answer: d Difficulty: 3 Page: 490   Key 1: R

45. What are the two variables used in the Market-Analysis Model for assessing how to advertise in foreign cultures?
    a. restrictions of the political system and the type of language
    b. share of market of brands within a category and size of the product category
    c. nature of the language and the available media
    d. share of market of brands within a category and nature of the language

    Answer: b Difficulty: 2 Page: 490   Key 1: R

46. From 1976 to 1989, the market share of multinational agencies increased to _____ market share of worldwide advertising billings?
    a. 10%
    b. 20%
    c. 30%
    d. 40%
    e. 50%

    Answer: c Difficulty: 3 Page: 490   Key 1: R

47. The model for deciding how to advertise in foreign cultures that emphasizes the cultural differences among people and nations, that recognizes the sharing of universal needs but that also stresses that these needs are met differently in different cultures is called:
   a. Cultural Differences Model.
   b. Market-Oriented Model.
   c. International Model.
   d. Culture-Oriented Model.
   e. Culture Context Model.

   Answer: d Difficulty: 2 Page: 491   Key 1: R

48. In a high-context culture, words:
   a. can have more than one meaning depending on the preceding or following sentences.
   b. have very clearly defined meanings.
   c. can be understood as independent entities.
   d. all of the above
   e. none of the above.

   Answer: a Difficulty: 2 Page: 491   Key 1: R

49. When the meaning of a message can be understood as an independent entity, this is called:
   a. high-context culture.
   b. low-context culture.
   c. context-sensitive culture.
   d. context-insensitive cultures.
   e. contextual culture.

   Answer: b Difficulty: 2 Page: 491   Key 1: R

50. Countries such as Japan, China, and Arabia would fall under which of the following categories?
   a. high-context culture.
   b. low-context culture.
   c. context-sensitive culture.
   d. context-insensitive cultures.
   e. contextual culture.

   Answer: a Difficulty: 2 Page: 491   Key 1: R

51. As far as language goes, English would be categorized under which of the following headings?
   a. high-context culture.
   b. low-context culture.
   c. context-sensitive culture.
   d. context-insensitive cultures.
   e. contextual culture.

   Answer: b Difficulty: 2 Page: 491   Key 1: R

52. As far as language goes, Japanese would be categorized under which of the following headings?
    a. high-context culture.
    b. low-context culture.
    c. context-sensitive culture.
    d. context-insensitive cultures.
    e. contextual culture.

Answer: a Difficulty: 2 Page: 491   Key 1: R

53. What is the major difference between the approach to advertising in a high-context culture such as Japan and the approach in a low-context culture such as the United States?
    a. High-context culture focuses more on product differences.
    b. High-context culture would not necessarily explain product differences in words.
    c. High-context culture would emphasize the unique differences of the product.
    d. High-context culture focuses more on how dissimilar a product is from its competitors.

Answer: b Difficulty: 3 Page: 491   Key 1: R

54. Final budgets in international companies are negotiated by:
    a. the central office.
    b. local management.
    c. outside consultants.
    d. the foreign government.
    e. local work force.

Answer: b Difficulty: 3 Page: 492   Key 1: R

55. What is the dominant means for developing advertising on the international level?
    a. within the companies
    b. freelancers
    c. local retailers/resellers/wholesalers
    d. advertising agencies
    e. all of the above

Answer: d Difficulty: 3 Page: 492   Key 1: R

56. Which of the following are the two approaches to organizing international ad agencies?
    a. decentralized control and centralized control
    b. central global agency with local satellite agencies and New York based central agency
    c. loose democratic network of local agencies and centralized control
    d. tight central control and centralized resources with moderate control

Answer: d Difficulty: 2 Page: 493   Key 1: R

57. All of the following are techniques used by international agencies to develop advertising for international marketing EXCEPT:
   a. matching the client
   b. centralized resources with moderate control (central strategy, local application)
   c. local control with central support (local strategy, local application)
   d. tight central international control (central strategy, central application)
   e. none of the above

   Answer: c Difficulty: 2 Page: 494   Key 1: R

58. International advertising agencies with few international clients can easily offer which one of the following organization patterns?
   a. matching the client
   b. centralized resources with moderate control
   c. tight central international control
   d. independent centralized autonomy
   e. none of the above

   Answer: a Difficulty: 2 Page: 494   Key 1: R

59. The international ad agency is more likely to have a headquarters group assigned to the client with a tactical team ready to fly anywhere a problem needs to be solved when the client is:
   a. more decentralized.
   b. more centralized.
   c. wealthier.
   d. working on a scanty budget.
   e. none of the above

   Answer: b Difficulty: 2 Page: 494   Key 1: R

60. In international marketing, where does almost every successful global or international brand come from?
   a. research and development
   b. minds of consumers
   c. successful local brand
   d. derivation of another global or international brand
   e. all of the above

   Answer: c Difficulty: 2 Page: 494   Key 1: A

61. According to an old axiom, "All business is:
   a. global."
   b. international."
   c. regional."
   d. local."

   Answer: d Difficulty: 2 Page: 493   Key 1: R

62. Which of the following is a starting point for international advertising campaigns?
    a. a centrally conceived new product or directive
    b. success in one country
    c. a centrally identified need
    d. a centrally conceived strategy
    e. all of the above

    Answer: e Difficulty: 2 Page: 495   Key 1: R

63. Which of the following is one of the approaches for developing a global advertising campaign?
    a. worldwide team originates a centrally conceived campaign for the global market
    b. working from a central strategy, local offices have the autonomy to develop and approve local applications
    c. modify a successful campaign that was originally conceived for national use
    d. campaign is developed by a local "lead agency" which then becomes the central control point for worldwide implementation
    e. all of the above

    Answer: b Difficulty: 2 Page: 495   Key 1: R

64. What do global brands need for efficient advertising execution?
    a. emphasis on music
    b. copywriting by native copywriters in each market
    c. consistency of image
    d. focus on hard sell selling strategy
    e. all of the above

    Answer: c Difficulty: 2 Page: 495   Key 1: R

65. What factors in marketing communication tend to transfer well across cultures?
    a. campaign theme
    b. brand identification
    c. selling message
    d. packaging
    e. all of the above

    Answer: e Difficulty: 2 Page: 495   Key 1: R

66. What is the key decision for the global marketing communication strategy?
    a. whether to translate ad copy or have it written by local copywriters
    b. whether to standardize marketing communication or to adapt it for each market
    c. whether to use a hard sell or a soft sell strategy
    d. whether to hire an international ad agency or do the advertising in-house
    e. all of the above

    Answer: b Difficulty: 2 Page: 495   Key 1: R

67. When an international agency decentralizes the development of ad campaigns and allows a local office to originate a campaign and then serve as the coordinating point to develop all the needed pattern elements and a manual for the international campaign, the local office is called:
    a. central control office.
    b. lead agency.
    c. local control office.
    d. coordinating agency.

    Answer: b Difficulty: 3 Page: 494   Key 1: R

68. The two or three ads that introduce an advertising campaign are called:
    a. pattern ads.
    b. lead ads.
    c. theme ads.
    d. introductory ads.
    e. campaign ads.

    Answer: a Difficulty: 2 Page: 494   Key 1: R

69. What media organization has become the closest thing to a global medium that is available to the international media planner?
    a. International Satellite Network (ISN)
    b. British Broadcasting Company (BBC)
    c. American Broadcasting Company (ABC)
    d. Cable News Network (CNN)
    e. Time Magazine

    Answer: d Difficulty: 2 Page: 496   Key 1: R

70. Media planning for an international campaign follows:
    a. a completely different set of principles than those used to reach a national target audience.
    b. the same principles for reaching a national target audience.
    c. not only the principles for reaching a national target audience but an additional set concerned with the sensitivity of the international audience.
    d. no rules.

    Answer: b Difficulty: 2 Page: 497   Key 1: A

71. Which of the following would the international media planner NOT be able to do if an international campaign was to be locally funded?
    a. set the criteria for selecting media
    b. set media objectives
    c. establish the media definition of the target audience
    d. lay down a media strategy

    Answer: b Difficulty: 3 Page: 498   Key 1: R

72. Which of the following is the method used to buy media to reach an international target audience for a consumer product?
    a. through a multitude of local, national or regional media buying services
    b. through an international agency
    c. through an international media-buying service
    d. through an international consortium of agencies
    e. all of the above

    Answer: e Difficulty: 2 Page: 498   Key 1: R

73. If the target audience for an international advertising campaign is for a consumer product:
    a. global media planning and purchasing are required.
    b. global media planning and local purchasing are required.
    c. local media planning and global purchasing are required.
    d. local media planning and purchase are required.
    e. global media planning is optional but local purchasing is required.

    Answer: d Difficulty: 3 Page: 498   Key 1: R

74. If a campaign is being handled by one of the international advertising agencies, the media orders will be placed in most cases:
    a. locally.
    b. globally.
    c. a minimum of 2 years prior to air date.
    d. via a member of the international advertising agency's headquarters only.

    Answer: a Difficulty: 2 Page: 498   Key 1: R

75. When western culture is imposed on other cultures through advertising, this is called:
a. global marketing.
b. marketing intrusion.
c. cultural invasion.
d. marketing imperialism.

Answer: d Difficulty: 3 Page: 500   Key 1: R

76. What country is the only major country in the world that still distinguishes between business and international business?
a. China
b. Japan
c. United States
d. France

Answer: c Difficulty: 3 Page: 501   Key 1: R

TRUE/FALSE

77. Fewer than 1/2 of the top 25 world advertising agencies are headquartered in the United States.
a. True
b. False

Answer: a Difficulty: 2 Page: 483   Key 1: R

78. Historically, when the focus in international trade changed from importing goods to exporting goods, the function advertising performed was to develop brand image in the home country.
a. True
b. False

Answer: b Difficulty: 2 Page: 484   Key 1: R

79. Japanese companies typically have not given global assignments to large Japanese agencies to extend their services for clients outside the home islands.
a. True
b. False

Answer: a Difficulty: 3 Page: 485   Key 1: R

80. A key decision in the development of a truly global perspective is the creation of a global headquarters with the separation of the North American and global operations.
a. True
b. False

Answer: a Difficulty: 1 Page: 486   Key 1: R

81. The messages created by advertisers for high-context cultures can easily be interpreted by low- context cultures too.
    a. True
    b. False

    Answer: b Difficulty: 2 Page: 486   Key 1: A

82. Virtually every product category can be separated into local, regional, and international brands.
    a. True
    b. False

    Answer: a Difficulty: 2 Page: 486   Key 1: A

83. A global brand is one that is marketed in two or more of the four major regional market blocs.
    a. True
    b. False

    Answer: b Difficulty: 2 Page: 487   Key 1: R

84. A global brand and an international brand are the same thing.
    a. True
    b. False

    Answer: b Difficulty: 1 Page: 487   Key 1: R

85. In the global controversy, Theodore Levitt argued that differences among nations and cultures should be ignored because people throughout the world are driven by similar desires and wants.
    a. True
    b. False

    Answer: a Difficulty: 2 Page: 487   Key 1: R

86. Products or services are global; the ideas that embody those ideas might not be.
    a. True
    b. False

    Answer: b Difficulty: 3 Page: 488   Key 1: A

87. The marketplace is increasingly international in scope, but each market is its own facet of the larger mosaic.
    a. True
    b. False

    Answer: a Difficulty: 1 Page: 488   Key 1: A

88. While the communist bloc moves toward greater economic freedom, the Common Market and North America new restrictions on international economic activity are increasing.
    a. True
    b. False

    Answer: a Difficulty: 2 Page: 488   Key 1: R

89. English is usually the language of international management.
    a. True
    b. False

    Answer: a Difficulty: 3 Page: 489   Key 1: R

90. When ad copy is to be used in another country, the copy developed for the second country should be re-written in the second country's language by a copywriter who is bilingual.
    a. True
    b. False

    Answer: a Difficulty: 3 Page: 489   Key 1: R

91. Of the two largest agencies in international advertising, neither one is American.
    a. True
    b. False

    Answer: b Difficulty: 3 Page: 490   Key 1: R

92. The culture-oriented model recognizes that people worldwide share certain needs, but it stresses the fact that these needs are met differently in different cultures.
    a. True
    b. False

    Answer: a Difficulty: 2 Page: 491   Key 1: R

93. In English words have clear meanings that are not highly dependent on surrounding words.
    a. True
    b. False

    Answer: a Difficulty: 2 Page: 491   Key 1: R

94. Although the function of advertising is the same throughout the world, the expression of its message varies in different cultural settings.
    a. True
    b. False

    Answer: a Difficulty: 1 Page: 491   Key 1: A

95. The old axiom, "All business is local" should be modified in the international marketplace to state that all ideas are local.
   a. True
   b. False

   Answer: b Difficulty: 2 Page: 495   Key 1: R

96. International advertising campaigns always evolve from a success in one country.
   a. True
   b. False

   Answer: b Difficulty: 2 Page: 495   Key 1: A

97. Central approval for an international advertising campaign is necessary not only to launch the campaign but also to keep it on track.
   a. True
   b. False

   Answer: a Difficulty: 2 Page: 495   Key 1: R

98. The more central the management and the more similar the products, the more common their advertising will be around the world.
   a. True
   b. False

   Answer: a Difficulty: 2 Page: 495   Key 1: R

99. The selling concept that propels a brand in its first market will probably not be the selling concept that succeeds in every other market.
   a. True
   b. False

   Answer: b Difficulty: 3 Page: 497   Key 1: R

100. Global media do not currently exist.
   a. True
   b. False

   Answer: a Difficulty: 1 Page: 497   Key 1: R

101. The lack of global media forces advertisers to plan regionally or globally but to execute plans locally or regionally.
   a. True
   b. False

   Answer: a Difficulty: 2 Page: 497   Key 1: R

102. Media planning for an international campaign follows a completely different set of principles than those used to reach a national target audience.
a. True
b. False

Answer: b Difficulty: 2 Page: 496   Key 1: R

103. International advertising campaigns are always centrally funded.
a. True
b. False

Answer: b Difficulty: 2 Page: 498   Key 1: R

104. If an international campaign involves a consumer product, local media planning and purchase are required.
a. True
b. False

Answer: a Difficulty: 2 Page: 498   Key 1: R

105. The United States is the only country in the world that still distinguishes between business and international business.
a. True
b. False

Answer: a Difficulty: 2 Page: 501   Key 1: R

SHORT ANSWER

106. List the four types of brands.

Answer: Local, regional, international, global

Difficulty: 1 Page: 483-487   Key 1: R

107. List the special problem areas encountered by international advertisers.

Answer:
Customs and culture, marketing imperialism, time, inertia, resistance, rejection, politics
Difficulty: 2 Page: 498-501 Key 1: R

108. List the two ways international agencies organize global advertising campaigns.

Answer: Tight central control, centralized resources with moderate control

Difficulty: 2 Page: 493   Key 1: R

ESSAY

109. Discuss the steps in the process of international expansion that lead to international marketing and advertising.

    Answer: Difficulty: 1 Page: 483-486   Key 1: R

110. Compare and contrast local, regional, international, and global brands.

    Answer: Difficulty: 2 Page: 483-501   Key 1: R

111. Discuss how the advertising for a brand might change as the brand evolves from a local to a regional to an international and finally to a global brand.

    Answer: Difficulty: 3 Page: 483-501   Key 1: A

112. Discuss the impact of changes in Eastern Europe on international marketing in the area.

    Answer: Difficulty: 2 Page: 485-486   Key 1: A

113. Discuss the major positions in the debate over the value of the "global perspective" in international marketing.

    Answer: Difficulty: 2 Page: 486-489   Key 1: R

114. Discuss how management practices must change when the company becomes an international concern, i.e., one more country is added to the company's operations.

    Answer: Difficulty: 2 Page: 489-492   Key 1: R

115. Compare and contrast the Market-Analysis Model versus the Culture-Oriented Model for assessing how to advertise in foreign countries.

    Answer: Difficulty: 3 Page: 490-492   Key 1: R

116. Discuss opportunities and problems associated with advertising in a high-context versus a low-context culture.

    Answer: Difficulty: 3 Page: 491-492   Key 1: A

117. Discuss the various organizational approaches used by international advertising agencies to control the development of international advertising campaigns. Give examples.

    Answer: Difficulty: 2 Page: 492-494   Key 1: R

118. Discuss the various approaches used by international advertising agencies to create international advertising campaigns. Give examples.

Answer: Difficulty: 2 Page: 494-498 Key 1: R

119. Discuss the problems and limitations associated with media planning for an international advertising campaign.

Answer: Difficulty: 2 Page: 495-498 Key 1: R

CHAPTER 19:   THE CAMPAIGN PLAN

MULTIPLE CHOICE

1. What is the purpose of the advertising campaign plan?
   a. make an impression on the target audience
   b. inform the audience
   c. solve some critical problem
   d. entertain the audience
   e. be creative

   Answer: c Difficulty: 2 Page: 508   Key 1: R

2. What is a "single-shot" ad?
   a. free-standing ad unrelated to other ads
   b. ad unrelated to ads that preceded or followed it
   c. ad that is not part of a campaign process
   d. ad that lacks a core message that ties it to other ads
   e. all of the above

   Answer: e Difficulty: 2 Page: 508   Key 1: R

3. From what area of planning was the term "campaign" borrowed?
   a. engineering
   b. economics
   c. military
   d. politics

   Answer: d Difficulty: 2 Page: 508   Key 1: R

4. A comprehensive advertising plan for a series of different but related ads that appear in different media across a specified time period is called:
   a. Situation Analysis.
   b. Campaign Analysis.
   c. Plansbook.
   d. Advertising Campaign.
   e. Creative Strategy.

   Answer: d Difficulty: 1 Page: 508   Key 1: R

5. What is the usual time frame for an advertising campaign plan?
   a. 3 months or less
   b. 6 months or less
   c. 1 year or less
   d. 2 years or less
   e. 5 years or less

   Answer: c Difficulty: 2 Page: 508   Key 1: R

6. Which one of the following focuses on identifying the key problems and opportunities, specifying the objectives for the advertising, targeting the appropriate audience, identifying the competitive advantage, and locating the best position?
   a. situation analysis
   b. advertising strategy
   c. positioning strategy
   d. advertising campaign
   e. creative plan

   Answer: d Difficulty: 2 Page: 508   Key 1: R

7. A written summary of an Advertising Campaign plan that is presented to the client is called:
   a. Situation Analysis.
   b. Campaign Plan.
   c. Advertising Campaign Plan.
   d. Campaign Summary.
   e. Plans book.

   Answer: e Difficulty: 2 Page: 509   Key 1: R

8. A section of an Advertising Campaign Plan that summarizes the relevant information available about the company, the product, the competition, the marketplace, and the consumer is called:
   a. Research.
   b. Background Research.
   c. Situation Analysis.
   d. Plans book.
   e. Marketing Summary.

   Answer: c Difficulty: 1 Page: 509   Key 1: R

9. What is a plansbook?
   a. comprehensive plan for a series of ads that appear in the media across a specified period
   b. written summary of the relevant research findings for an advertising plan
   c. document containing the complete advertising campaign plan to be presented to the client
   d. written summary of an Advertising Campaign Plan that is presented to the client
   e. all of the above

   Answer: d Difficulty: 2 Page: 509   Key 1: R

10. All of the following are found in the Situation Analysis of an Advertising Campaign EXCEPT:
    a. Competitive Situation.
    b. Market Research.
    c. Consumer Research.
    d. Product/Company Research.
    e. Strengths, Weaknesses, Opportunities, and Threats Analysis.

    Answer: e Difficulty: 2 Page: 510   Key 1: R

11. What is the role of the Situation Analysis of the Advertising Campaign Plan in dealing with the key problem to be solved by advertising?
    a. summarizes key strategic decisions that will guide campaign in solving the key problem
    b. assembles all the information necessary to understand the problem that must be solved and to make the strategic decisions to solve the problem
    c. describes problems and opportunities that form the basis for the key campaign decisions
    d. summarizes the advertising plan for the client
    e. all of the above

    Answer: b Difficulty: 2 Page: 510   Key 1: A

12. A situation analysis is obtained using which of the following research techniques?
    a. primary research
    b. secondary research
    c. primary and secondary research
    d. evaluative research
    e. diagnostic research

    Answer: c Difficulty: 2 Page: 510   Key 1: R

13. What does the text say the Situation Analysis is sometimes called?
    a. background information
    b. business review
    c. SWOT analysis
    d. plans book

    Answer: b Difficulty: 3 Page: 509   Key 1: R

14. Where in the Advertising Campaign Plan would you find primary and secondary research findings about the company, the product, the competition, the marketplace, and the consumer?
   a. Advertising Objectives
   b. SWOT Analysis
   c. Research
   d. Situation Analysis
   e. Campaign Strategy

   Answer: d Difficulty: 2 Page: 509   Key 1: R

15. Which of the following is found in the Situation Analysis of an Advertising Campaign Plan?
   a. Competitive Situation
   b. Consumer and Market Research
   c. Campaign Strategy
   d. Target Audience
   e. Product/Company Research

   Answer: a Difficulty: 2 Page: 509   Key 1: R

16. In what section of the Situation Analysis would the advertising planner document the size of the industry, industry price trends and industry growth trends?
   a. Consumer and Market Research
   b. Competitive Situation
   c. Industry Trends
   d. Selling Strategy
   e. Product/Company Research

   Answer: e Difficulty: 1 Page: 509   Key 1: R

17. In what section of the Situation Analysis would the advertising planner consider the attitudes, interests, motivations and lifestyles of the ultimate users of the product?
   a. Consumer and Market Research
   b. Industry Analysis
   c. Selling Strategy
   d. Competitive Situation
   e. Product/Company Research

   Answer: a Difficulty: 2 Page: 509   Key 1: R

18. In what section of the Situation Analysis would the advertising planner describe the consumer demographically and psychographically?
    a. Consumer and Market Research
    b. Competitive Situation
    c. Product/Company Research
    d. Market Analysis
    e. Scope of Project

    Answer: a Difficulty: 2 Page: 509   Key 1: R

19. In what section of the Situation Analysis would the advertising planner document the characteristics of the company's products, benefits provided to consumers, problems associated with product use, and the sociological and psychological factors involved in use of the product?
    a. Consumer and Market Research
    b. Competitive Review
    c. Product
    d. Industry Trends
    e. Product/Company Research

    Answer: e Difficulty: 1 Page: 509   Key 1: R

20. What are the key points in deciding if a product has a competitive advantage for a feature?
    a. position and brand recognition
    b. perceived image, brand recognition, and brand preference
    c. important to consumer, product strength, and competitor weakness
    d. product quality, position, and competitive comparison
    e. uniqueness, brand recognition, and position

    Answer: c Difficulty: 3 Page: 509   Key 1: R

21. In performing the Situation Analysis, some planners recast the information gathered in terms of internal and external factors. What do internal factors involve?
    a. traits of the organization, the product/service, and the production/creation process
    b. strengths that lead to opportunities
    c. traits of the organization, the product/services, and the production/creation process
    d. weaknesses that make the brand vulnerable to threats from outside
    e. all of the above

    Answer: b Difficulty: 2 Page: 509   Key 1: R

22. In performing the Situation Analysis, some planners recast the information gathered in terms of internal and external factors. What do external factors involve?
   a. traits of the product/service users as well as social, political, or economic conditions
   b. strengths that lead to opportunities
   c. traits of the organization, the product/services, and the production/creation process
   d. weaknesses that make the brand vulnerable to threats from outside

   Answer: d Difficulty: 2 Page: 509   Key 1: R

23. What section of the Situation Analysis is where the significance of the kinds of research described is analyzed? This section serves as a transition that leads directly into the key strategic decisions that serve as a foundation for the campaign plan.
   a. Consumer and Market Analysis
   b. Strengths, Weaknesses, Opportunities, and Threats Analysis
   c. Problem Analysis
   d. Product/Company Research

   Answer: b Difficulty: 2 Page: 509   Key 1: R

24. Which of the following would you expect to find in the Strengths, Weaknesses, Opportunities, and Threats Analysis section of the Situation Analysis of the Advertising Campaign Plan?
   a. explanation of the position of the product
   b. identification of the key marketing problem
   c. comparison of the product to the competition
   d. detailed description of the target audience
   e. all of the above

   Answer: c Difficulty: 2 Page: 509   Key 1: R

25. What part of the Advertising Campaign Plan serves as a transition that leads directly into the key decisions that form the foundation of the plan?
   a. Campaign Strategy
   b. Advertising Objectives
   c. SWOT Analysis
   d. Creative Strategy

   Answer: c Difficulty: 2 Page: 509   Key 1: R

26. Which of the following is included in the SWOT Analysis of the Situation Analysis?
    a. weaknesses
    b. threats
    c. strengths
    d. opportunities
    e. all of the above

    Answer: e Difficulty: 1 Page: 511   Key 1: R

27. In the SWOT Analysis what is a threat?
    a. downturn in economic conditions
    b. social problems
    c. external factors that impact upon a marketing communication program
    d. competition
    e. all of the above

    Answer: e Difficulty: 2 Page: 511   Key 1: R

28. Which of the following is a problem that could be identified in the SWOT Analysis?
    a. advertising needs after loss of market exclusivity
    b. launching a new product
    c. advertising to help open up new territories
    d. advertising to meet intense competition
    e. all of the above

    Answer: e Difficulty: 2 Page: 511   Key 1: R

29. Where in the Advertising Campaign Plan would you find an explanation of the product's competitive advantage?
    a. Situation Analysis
    b. SWOT Analysis
    c. Campaign Theme
    d. Creative Plan
    e. Campaign Strategy

    Answer: b Difficulty: 2 Page: 511   Key 1: R

30. When a product feature is important to consumers and the product is strong on this feature and the competition is weak, this is called:
    a. positioning.
    b. unique selling proposition.
    c. competitive advantage.
    d. key selling point.
    e. brand preference.

    Answer: c Difficulty: 2 Page: 512   Key 1: R

31. IBM has an edge on competitor products because of its dominant name recognition in the marketplace. If name recognition is an important factor for consumers and the competition is weak on name recognition, IBM's edge in name recognition is called:
    a. position.
    b. unique selling proposition.
    c. brand preference.
    d. competitive advantage.

    Answer: d Difficulty: 3 Page: 512   Key 1: A

32. What does "competitive advantage" mean?
    a. how a product is seen in the marketplace in the mind of the target audience
    b. feature that is important to the consumer, a product strength, and a competition weakness
    c. a unique feature that gives a product a selling advantage over the competition
    d. a strategy that moves a brand from a product-oriented to a consumer-oriented market

    Answer: b Difficulty: 3 Page: 512   Key 1: R

33. Which of the following would you expect to find in Campaign Strategy?
    a. key decisions that will guide the campaign
    b. explanation of the position of the product
    c. advertising objectives
    d. detailed description of the target audience
    e. all of the above

    Answer: e Difficulty: 2 Page: 512   Key 1: R

34. Where in the Advertising Campaign Plan would you find the advertising objectives, the target audience, the competitive advantage and the position?
    a. Situation Analysis
    b. Competitive Situation
    c. Marketing Communication Activities
    d. Campaign Strategy
    e. Creative Plan

    Answer: d Difficulty: 2 Page: 512   Key 1: R

35. All of the following are parts of the Campaign Strategy section of the Advertising Campaign Plan EXCEPT:
    a. creative theme.
    b. money for campaign.
    c. positioning.
    d. objective.
    e. target audience.

    Answer: a Difficulty: 2 Page: 512   Key 1: R

36. Where in the Advertising Campaign Plan would you find the advertising objective?
    a. Situation Analysis
    b. Creative Theme
    c. Marketing Communication Activities
    d. Evaluation
    e. Campaign Strategy

    Answer: e Difficulty: 2 Page: 512   Key 1: A

37. Where in the Advertising Campaign Plan would you find a detailed description of the target audience selected for the campaign?
    a. Situation Analysis
    b. Campaign Strategy
    c. SWOT Analysis
    d. Marketing Communication Activities
    e. Creative Plan

    Answer: b Difficulty: 2 Page: 513   Key 1: A

38. Where in the Advertising Campaign Plan would you find the positioning of the product?
    a. Campaign Strategy
    b. Creative Theme
    c. Marketing Communication Activities
    d. SWOT Analysis

    Answer: a Difficulty: 2 Page: 513   Key 1: A

39. What term is used to refer to how a product is seen in the marketplace by the target audience? This is the product's place in the consumer's mind relative to the competition.
    a. competitive advantage
    b. positioning
    c. unique selling proposition
    d. brand recognition
    e. consumer perception

    Answer: b Difficulty: 2 Page: 513   Key 1: R

40. The Macintosh computer holds a place in the minds of computer buyers as the "user-friendly" computer. What is this called?
    a. position
    b. unique selling proposition
    c. key selling point
    d. competitive advantage
    e. brand preference

    Answer: a Difficulty: 3 Page: 513   Key 1: A

41. What does "position" mean?
    a. how the product is seen in the marketplace in the mind of the target audience
    b. a unique product feature that gives a product a selling advantage over the competition
    c. a product feature that is important to the consumer, is a strength of the product, and is a weakness of the competition
    d. a strategy that moves a brand from a product-oriented to a consumer-oriented market

    Answer: a Difficulty: 3 Page: 513   Key 1: R

42. In the Milk Mustache campaign, the campaign tried to change the perception of milk from something a child drinks to a drink for adults. What strategic consideration is involved?
    a. targeting
    b. competitive advantage
    c. positioning
    d. geographic strategy

    Answer: c Difficulty: 3 Page: 513   Key 1: A

43. Where in the Campaign Plan would you find the amount of money available for the campaign?
    a. Situation Analysis
    b. Creative Theme
    c. Campaign Strategy
    d. Marketing Communication Activities
    e. Creative Plan

    Answer: c Difficulty: 2 Page: 512   Key 1: R

44. Which of the following is included in the Marketing Communications Activities section of the Advertising Campaign?
    a. creative tactics
    b. media objectives
    c. creative theme
    d. creative strategy
    e. all of the above

    Answer: e Difficulty: 2 Page: 516-519 Key 1: R

414

45. All of the following are parts of the Marketing Communications Activities of the Campaign Plan EXCEPT:
    a. Positioning.
    b. Creative Theme.
    c. Media Plan.
    d. Other Marketing Communications Activities.
    e. Creative Strategy and Tactics.

    Answer: a Difficulty: 2 Page: 516-519   Key 1: R

46. Where in the Advertising Campaign Plan would you find the creative theme, the creative strategy and executions for different media, and the media plan?
    a. Creative Plan
    b. Campaign Strategy
    c. SWOT Analysis
    d. Marketing Communications Activities
    e. Situation Analysis

    Answer: d Difficulty: 2 Page: 516   Key 1: R

47. A series of ads built around a central theme is called a/an:
    a. campaign.
    b. copy plan.
    c. creative platform.
    d. plans book.
    e. creative strategy.

    Answer: a Difficulty: 1 Page: 512   Key 1: R

48. What is the purpose of the creative theme in the Advertising Campaign Plan?
    a. create a link from ad to ad
    b. allows continuity while matching messages for different audiences
    c. intensity the impact of the campaign through synergy
    d. create excitement and memorability
    e. all of the above

    Answer: e Difficulty: 1 Page: 516   Key 1: R

49. _____ is used in advertising campaign planning to create a link from ad to ad.
    a. Positioning
    b. Image transfer
    c. Tactics
    d. Targeting
    e. Continuity device

    Answer: e Difficulty: 2 Page: 516   Key 1: R

50. _____ means an advertising message in one medium causes the audience to think about the message when seen or heard in another medium.
   a. Message recall
   b. Image transfer
   c. Positioning
   d. Resonance
   e. Continuity device

   Answer: b Difficulty: 2 Page: 517   Key 1: R

51. When a campaign uses ads placed in cheaper media such as radio to remind the target audience of ads in more expensive media such as television, the planner is taking advantage of:
   a. synergy.
   b. a continuity link.
   c. image transfer.
   d. positioning.
   e. resonance.

   Answer: c Difficulty: 2 Page: 517   Key 1: R

52. _____ describes what must be said to the target audience to solve the problem, usually getting them to buy the product.
   a. Creative tactics
   b. Positioning
   c. Image transfer
   d. Creative strategy
   e. Advertising objective

   Answer: d Difficulty: 2 Page: 517   Key 1: R

53. The means for carrying out the creative strategy are outlined in the:
   a. creative tactics.
   b. advertising objectives.
   c. creative platform.
   d. positioning.
   e. situation analysis.

   Answer: a Difficulty: 2 Page: 517   Key 1: R

54. What is the purpose of an advertising pretesting?
   a. improve the efficiency of advertising
   b. eliminate approaches that do not work
   c. help avoid costly mistakes
   d. predict relative strength of alternative approaches
   e. all of the above

   Answer: e Difficulty: 2 Page: 518   Key 1: R

55. What are the two objectives of media planning?
    a. targeting and continuity
    b. reach and frequency
    c. cost and frequency
    d. media mix and targeting
    e. efficiency and effectiveness

    Answer: b Difficulty: 1 Page: 518　　Key 1: R

56. All of the following are parts of the media plan EXCEPT:
    a. final campaign budget.
    b. media objectives.
    c. geographic strategies.
    d. continuity devices.
    e. media schedules.

    Answer: d Difficulty: 2 Page: 518　　Key 1: R

TRUE/FALSE

57. A comprehensive advertising plan for a series of different but related ads that appear in different media across a specified time period is called a Plansbook.
    a. True
    b. False

    Answer: b Difficulty: 1 Page: 508　　Key 1: R

58. Advertising campaigns are designed to make consumers aware of products by repeating a meaningful theme in different media.
    a. True
    b. False

    Answer: a Difficulty: 2 Page: 508　　Key 1: R

59. All ads seen in the media are part of an advertising campaign.
    a. True
    b. False

    Answer: b Difficulty: 2 Page: 508　　Key 1: R

60. The advertising campaign is designed strategically to solve some critical problem.
    a. True
    b. False

    Answer: a Difficulty: 1 Page: 508　　Key 1: R

61. The usual time frame for an advertising campaign plan is five years.
    a. True
    b. False

    Answer: b Difficulty: 2 Page: 508   Key 1: R

62. An advertising campaign is presented to the client in a formal business presentation and in a written summary called Campaign Documentation.
    a. True
    b. False

    Answer: b Difficulty: 1 Page: 509   Key 1: R

63. The Situation Analysis of the Campaign Plan is sometimes called a Business Review.
    a. True
    b. False

    Answer: a Difficulty: 3 Page: 509   Key 1: R

64. The SWOT Analysis of the Situation Analysis is sometimes called Problems and Opportunities.
    a. True
    b. False

    Answer: a Difficulty: 1 Page: 511   Key 1: R

65. The Advertising Conclusions section of the Situation Analysis serves as a transition that leads directly into the strategic decisions that are the foundation of the Advertising Campaign Plan.
    a. True
    b. False

    Answer: b Difficulty: 2 Page: 511   Key 1: R

66. The problems identified in the SWOT Analysis will be different from year to year and situation to situation.
    a. True
    b. False

    Answer: b Difficulty: 1 Page: 511   Key 1: R

67. Competitive advantage is a unique product feature that gives a product a selling advantage over the competition.
    a. True
    b. False

    Answer: b Difficulty: 2 Page: 512   Key 1: A

68. The advertising objectives are found in the Campaign Strategy section of the Advertising Campaign Plan.
    a. True
    b. False

    Answer: a Difficulty: 2 Page: 512   Key 1: R

69. A detailed description of the target audience is found in the Campaign Strategy of the Advertising Campaign Plan.
    a. True
    b. False

    Answer: a Difficulty: 2 Page: 513   Key 1: R

70. How the product is seen in the minds of the target audience is competitive advantage.
    a. True
    b. False

    Answer: b Difficulty: 2 Page: 512   Key 1: R

71. Users see the Macintosh computer as the "user-friendly" computer; this is a position.
    a. True
    b. False

    Answer: a Difficulty: 3 Page: 513   Key 1: A

72. The creative theme is a continuity device that creates a link from ad to ad in the ad program.
    a. True
    b. False

    Answer: a Difficulty: 1 Page: 516   Key 1: R

73. The media plan is driven by the advertising appropriation.
    a. True
    b. False

    Answer: a Difficulty: 1 Page: 518   Key 1: R

74. A formal evaluation builds a research effort around the campaign's objectives to see if it reached them.
    a. True
    b. False

    Answer: a Difficulty: 2 Page: 521   Key 1: R

SHORT ANSWER

75. List the major sections of the advertising campaign plan.

Answer:
Situation analysis, SWOT analysis, campaign strategy, marketing communications activities, phases of a campaign, evaluation
Difficulty: 2 Page: 509 Key 1: R

76. List the parts of the situation analysis.

Answer:
Consumer and market research, product/company research, competitive situation
Difficulty: 2 Page: 509-510 Key 1: R

77. List the stages of the SWOT analysis.

Answer: Problem analysis, market analysis, competitive analysis

Difficulty: 2 Page: 509-512 Key 1: R

78. List the parts of the campaign strategy.

Answer: Objectives, targeting, positioning, the appropriation

Difficulty: 2 Page: 512 Key 1: R

79. List the parts of the marketing communication activities.

Answer:
Creative theme, creative strategy and tactics, media plan, other communication activities
Difficulty: 2 Page: 516-520 Key 1: R

80. List the parts of the media plan in the Milk Mustache campaign.

Answer:
Media objectives, strategies, selection, geographic strategies, schedules, final campaign budget
Difficulty: 2 Page: 518 Key 1: R

ESSAY

81. Discuss how the Situation Analysis of the Advertising Campaign Plan contributes to identifying and solving the advertising problem of the plan. Use the Orlando plan to illustrate your discussion.

    Answer: Difficulty: 3 Page: 509   Key 1: A

82. Discuss how the Campaign Strategy of the Advertising Campaign Plan uses the information assembled in the Situation Analysis to make strategic decisions to solve the advertising problem of the plan. Use the Orlando plan to illustrate your discussion.

    Answer: Difficulty: 3 Page: 509   Key 1: A